# Outside and In-Between

# Studies in Critical Social Sciences Book Series

Haymarket Books is proud to be working with Brill Academic Publishers (www.brill.nl) to republish the *Studies in Critical Social Sciences* book series in paperback editions. This peer-reviewed book series offers insights into our current reality by exploring the content and consequences of power relationships under capitalism, and by considering the spaces of opposition and resistance to these changes that have been defining our new age. Our full catalog of *SCSS* volumes can be viewed at https://www.haymarketbooks.org/series_collections/4-studies-in-critical-social-sciences.

*Series Editor*
**David Fasenfest** (Wayne State University)

*Editorial Board*
**Eduardo Bonilla-Silva** (Duke University)
**Chris Chase-Dunn** (University of California–Riverside)
**William Carroll** (University of Victoria)
**Raewyn Connell** (University of Sydney)
**Kimberlé W. Crenshaw** (University of California–LA and Columbia University)
**Heidi Gottfried** (Wayne State University)
**Karin Gottschall** (University of Bremen)
**Alfredo Saad Filho** (King's College London)
**Chizuko Ueno** (University of Tokyo)
**Sylvia Walby** (Lancaster University)
**Raju Das** (York University)

# Outside and In-Between

Theorizing Asian-Canadian Exclusion and the Challenges of Identity Formation

Edited by
Rose Ann Torres
Kailan Leung
Vania Soepriatna

Haymarket Books
Chicago, IL

First published in 2021 by Brill Academic Publishers, The Netherlands
© 2021 Koninklijke Brill NV, Leiden, The Netherlands

Published in paperback in 2022 by
Haymarket Books
P.O. Box 180165
Chicago, IL 60618
773-583-7884
www.haymarketbooks.org

ISBN: 978-1-64259-793-6

Distributed to the trade in the US through Consortium Book Sales and Distribution (www.cbsd.com) and internationally through Ingram Publisher Services International (www.ingramcontent.com).

This book was published with the generous support of Lannan Foundation and Wallace Action Fund.

Special discounts are available for bulk purchases by organizations and institutions. Please call 773-583-7884 or email info@haymarketbooks.org for more information.

Cover design by Jamie Kerry and Ragina Johnson.

Printed in the United States.

10 9 8 7 6 5 4 3 2 1

Library of Congress Cataloging-in-Publication data is available.

# Contents

Acknowledgements IX
Notes on Contributors X

Introduction 1
   *Rose Ann Torres, Kailan Leung and Vania Soepriatna*

## PART 1
## *Theorizing Asian Canada*

1 Critical Reflexivity
   *Re-imagining Asian Canada* 9
      *Rose Ann Torres and Dionisio Nyaga*

2 Mixture and Movement
   *Reflections on Identity, Power and Border Crossing through the Process of Currere* 21
      *Kailan Leung*

3 Transnational Labour Migration of Filipino Nurses to Canada
   *An Organized Historical, Institutional and Social Process* 34
      *Valerie G. Damasco*

4 Theorizing Asian Canada 48
   *Rose Ann Torres*

## PART 2
## *Race, Gender, Multiculturalism, Work*

5 South Asian Women Migrants Living in Canada
   *Prospects and Challenges in the Labor Market* 61
      *Sarah Alam*

6 Unmapping Diasporic Pilipina Geographies 72
   *Rose Ann Torres and Dionisio Nyaga*

7 Reciprocity Policies and Institutional Practices as Exclusionary Exceptions
*Filipino Nurses as Recruited and Excluded Subjects* 84
   Valerie G. Damasco

8 OutsourcEd
*International Practicums as Responses to Internationalization in Canadian Teacher Education* 100
   Kailan Leung

9 Why I Don't Talk about Being Filipino (I Think) 111
   Wallis Caldoza (*in thought with Peyton Caldoza*)

## PART 3
*Citizenship, Multiculturalism, Culture, Identity*

10 The Multicultural Façade
*A Colonial Performance of Diversity in Canada and Indonesia* 125
   Vania Soepriatna

11 Impact and Implications of Rap and Hip-Hop Music as a Form of Resistance 140
   Juanna Nguyen

12 "L'Autore Ha Musicato Fin Qui, Poi è Morto": Diversity, Inclusion and Equity in Modern Staging of Classical Orientalist Opera 155
   Alison Lam

13 South Asian Representations in the Media
*Repetition or Progress?* 171
   Syed Fahad Ali

14 The Fallacy of Native-Speakerism in English Language Education 177
   Jasmine Pham

## PART 4
*Community Resistance and Activism*

15  Feminization of Pandemics
    *Experiences of Filipino Women in the Health Care System*   189
       Rose Ann Torres

16  Multiculturalism
    *A Case for Continued Resistance for Space for Race*   205
       Tika Ram Thapa

17  Brokering Belonging, Shattering Silences and Examining Erasures   221
       Grace Garlow

18  Filipina Activism from a Transnational Theoretical Framework   240
       Rose Ann Torres

19  Framework for Developing Resilience among Filipino-Canadian Youth during the Covid-19 Pandemic   251
       Valerie G. Damasco and Rose Ann Torres

    Index   259

# Acknowledgements

We want to thank all our contributors for joining us in this journey. We also want to thank Dr. David Fasenfest for all the great support and guidance for this volume. We want to acknowledge the staff of Brill for all the support they provided for us to finish this volume.

# Notes on Contributors

*Sarah Alam*
is a doctoral student at the Social Justice Education Department of the University of Toronto, at present she serves as a Graduate Assistant at Ontario Institute for Studies in Education and Internal Commissioner at University of Toronto's Graduate Students Union. She is a social activist and has served the U.S. Mission in Pakistan as a Senior Public Diplomacy Specialist for Sindh and Balochistan provinces. She has numerous published articles on social issues to her credit.

*Syed Fahad Ali*
is pursuing a Master's degree at OISE with a focus on Language and Literacies Education. His interests include rethinking and reimaging concepts of literacy, including critical literacy, as well as integrating social justice into classrooms and schools.

*Wallis Caldoza*
is a PhD student in the department of Social Justice Education at OISE at the University of Toronto. Her work focuses on utilizing her quotidian dramaturgical praxis as a disruption to Othering in the academe. Her doctoral research project, supervised by Dr. Rosalind Hampton, examines how Canadian universities take up institutional recognition in the form of "listening" and "acknowledgement" practices that naturalize white hegemony and construct Black and Indigenous scholars and scholarship as devalued "Other".

*Valerie G. Damasco*
is a Lecturer at University of Toronto who teaches undergraduate courses on mental health and education and graduate courses in community development; gender, race, and labour; and research methods. Damasco's research interests include adult learning and equity; access to education; inclusive teaching and learning; how community development practices contribute to social policies in education, healthcare, and employment; and equality and equity in work and labour policies and practices. While Damasco was completing her doctoral research, which focused on the migration of Filipino nurses who arrived in Canada from the Philippines and via the United States during the 1950s and 1960s, she worked in the Filipino community in Toronto assisting various sub-populations (i.e., Filipina women and youth). She worked closely with various echelons of communities in

community-based research, community organizing, and political campaigns to address the oppression, exploitation, and abuse that immigrant women face. Furthermore, she provided outreach to immigrant women and youth in the areas of employment, healthcare, immigration, social and cultural adjustment, housing, and other concerns. During her involvement in the community, she conducted workshops and group discussions on social justice, human rights, and equity.

*Grace Garlow*
is a Taiwanese-Canadian and an Ontario certified teacher working in the Greater Toronto Area with the York Region District School Board. A community activist and proud mother of two miracle multi-racial Indigene babies, she is currently completing an M.Ed. in Educational Leadership and Policy, and continuing her Ph.D. studies in Social Justice Education, both at the Ontario Institute for Studies in Education (University of Toronto). A former fashion and textile designer and patternmaker, Garlow's research interests in education are multidisciplinary and cover race, gender, spirituality, anti-colonial thought and resistance. Her current research explores the indigenization of education in Canadian schools towards building intercultural futurities, affirming multiple ways of 'knowing and being,' and recovering the wisdom of ancestral knowledges and earthly teachings.

*Alison Lam*
is currently a candidate for her Master of Education at the Ontario Institute of Studies in Education, University of Toronto. She has also published papers in French and English and spoken at conferences in Canada, the United States and Europe, including engagements for Cross-Cultural Professionals Association of Canada, Junior Achievement Canada and GenHERation. She has been a judge for ELLE Canada's Impact2 for Women Social Entrepreneurship Competition and Editor-in-Chief of Acclaim magazine. Additionally, she has given lectures at Schulich School of Business, Dalhousie University, St. Mary's University and Mount Saint Vincent University. With an MBA from the Kellogg-Schulich Global Executive MBA Program and an MA from Queen's University in French Literature, Lam brings a unique perspective to her career, projects and endeavours.

*Kailan Leung*
is an international educator, currently teaching and coordinating service-learning initiatives at a K-12 school in Vancouver, BC. He holds a MEd degree from the Ontario Institute for Studies in Education, as well as a BA in English

Literature from McGill University. His interests include cross-cultural identity formation, Third Culture Kids, and international education.

*Juanna Nguyen*

is a Certified Music Therapist as well as a Counselling Psychology student in the Department of Applied Psychology and Human Development at the Ontario Institute for Studies in Education of the University of Toronto. She is expected to graduate with a MEd in Spring of 2021. This is Nguyen's first contribution to a book publication as an author.

*Dionisio Nyaga*

has a Ph.D. from Social Justice Education-SESE/University of Toronto and a master and bachelor's degrees from Ryerson University-Department of Social Work. He is currently teaching both undergraduate and graduate courses. His Doctoral research focused on uncoupling Black masculinity through the narratives of Kenyan men in Toronto. His areas of teaching, research and practice interests are in Critical Anti-oppression, community development and engagement, Anti Blackness, masculinity studies, diaspora and transnational studies, cultural studies, men and masculinities, social justice, Indigenous and spirituality studies.

*Jasmine Pham*

is an English language educator currently providing academic coaching to students with cognitive disabilities, as well as writing scripts for an ESL podcast under Xenda Education. She is set to complete her MEd degree from the Ontario Institute for Studies in Education in 2021 and holds a BEd in Secondary Education from the University of Alberta. Her research interests include English language education, teacher development, native-speakerism, and international education policies.

*Vania Soepriatna*

is an Indonesian international student in Canada. She is currently pursuing an Education Doctorate in Social Justice Education and Comparative, International, and Developmental Education at Ontario Institute for Studies in Education. Her research so far has focused on diasporic identities within the international student body in higher education institutions.

*Tika Ram Thapa*

is a graduate student at Ontario Institute for Studies in Education, University of Toronto, Canada. He has worked with K-12 children and adult learners both as a specialist educator and a training and development professional. Thapa's life and international experience influence much of his work.

*Rose Ann Torres*
is an Assistant Professor of Sociology in the Department of Social Science at the University of New Brunswick Saint John. Torres has published books and many articles on Asian, African, Indigenous, and Women and Gender studies.

# Introduction

*Rose Ann Torres, Kailan Leung and Vania Soepriatna*

This collection of critical theorizing reflects the lived experiences of racialized Asian Canadian contributors. Grounded in theory and history, these essays illuminate pathways to better understand Asian-ness in contemporary Canada. These academics provide fresh perspectives on Asian Canadian exclusion, examine new spaces for critical resistance, and navigate the challenges of identity formation across racial, cultural, and national boundaries.

Asian Canadians—whether immigrant, international students, naturalized, native-born, or other—are hampered in their exploration and articulation of self by the dearth of critical writing both for them, and by them. Despite the influx of Asian students and their inflated tuition rates to Canadian postsecondary institutions, they are strikingly underrepresented in the literature of the academy. Critical theory focusing on Asian identity, anti-Asian racism, and the Asian-Canadian experience is limited, or presented as an artifact of the past.

Across the globe—but particularly in the English-speaking West—the internationalization of higher education continues its upward trend. 2017 data from the Canadian Bureau for International Education positioned Canada as the fourth-leading destination for international students seeking post-secondary education. The fact that the vast majority of international students at Canadian colleges and universities come from Asia has been well documented in domestic media, but the lived experiences and perspectives of these transnational individuals have not. This edited collection provides much-needed theorizing of Asian Canadian lived experiences, focusing on such themes as: multiculturalism, diversity, race, culture, agency, education, community activism, citizenship, identity, model minority myths, gender, colonization, neoliberalism, and others.

## 1    Part 1: Theorizing Asian Canada

Rose Ann Torres and Dionisio Nyaga on "Critical Reflexivity: Re-imagining Asian Canada" trouble such imperial and corporate spirituality and reimagines Asian spiritualities as power points of imagination and social justice. Torres and Nyaga refocus on the Asian fantasies brought about by their spiritualities in ways that disturb Canadian imaginaries. Torres and Nyaga argue that this point can only be relevant if we present their ways of spiritualities as a point of interrogating the racial erasure of Asian Canadian.

Kailan Leung on "Mixture and Movement: Reflections on Identity, Power and Border Crossing through the Process of *Currere*" draws on lived experiences to explore themes of multiraciality and transnationality in a Canadian context. Applying Pinar's process of *currere*, the author aims to problematize the past in order to better understand his current relationships to identity, power, and resistance. Root's ecological framework of multiracial identity formation and Bhabha's theories of hybridity and Third Space are also utilized to argue that multiracial and transnational Canadians possess unique potential to destabilize hegemonic whiteness.

Valerie G. Damasco on "Transnational Labour Migration of Filipino Nurses to Canada: An Organized Historical, Institutional and Social Process" argues that a theoretical framework that comprises a single theory or one level of inductive theoretical analysis is insufficient for analyzing or explaining the labour migration process. Rather than simply claiming that macro-level developments, such as the liberalization of Canadian immigration policy, influenced the arrival of nurses, a deeper investigation is required, which underscores the complexity of the labour migration process. Damasco argues that it entails employing a more nuanced theoretical and conceptual framework, using a meso-level analytical framework, which examines the complexity as well as the *dialectical* and *bidirectional* manifestation of macro-level processes on micro-level findings.

Rose Ann Torres on "Theorizing Asian Canada" examines on how to theorize Asian Canada. The questions that she will be focusing on in this chapter are: What does it entail when we theorize Asian Canada? How do we know that when we theorize Asian Canada, we are not excluding other groups of people? What are the different sections that we need to include in theorizing Asian Canada?

## 2 Part 2: Race, Gender, Multiculturalism, Work

Sarah Alam on "South Asian Women Migrants Living in Canada: Prospects and Challenges in the Labor Market" draws on the cross-sectional analysis of gender and migration. It discusses post immigration experiences of first and second-generation South Asian women living in Canada and its impact on labor. The study focuses on Canada as a recipient country of women migrants from South Asian countries such as India, Pakistan, and Bangladesh. The perspectives shared by the author in the chapter are critical ethnographic lessons

INTRODUCTION 3

to learn from for future South Asian women migrants aspiring to migrate to Canada. It will not just assist South Asian women migrants in their adaptability to settle in but also enable the Canadian system to be more equitable and inclusive.

Rose Ann Torres and Dionisio Nyaga on "Unmapping Diasporic Pilipina Geographies" seeks to create and recreate peminism that speaks to the differences in terms of race, class, ethnicity, citizenship, nationhood, sexuality, and other identity politics. This is a poetic reconstitution of Asian imaginaries beyond a provincial conception of a normal pinay. The chapter complicates politics of negotiating boundaries in ways that come to imagine Asian bodies as being capable of circumventing a Western conceptualization of broken bodies.

Valerie G. Damasco on "Reciprocity Policies and Institutional Practices as Exclusionary Exceptions: Filipino Nurses as Recruited and Excluded Subjects" sheds light on how the process of racialization or ethnicization and the gendering of professions occur in practice and how they are reproduced and sustained. Using the case of the migration of Filipino nurses to Canada who attained mobility in the nursing profession between 1957 and 1969, Damasco illustrates how subsequent waves of Filipino women who entered the country are channelled into a continuous process of deskilling. Beginning with the lives of Filipino nurses point to the broader institutional and social relations that organized their migration. Damasco also demonstrates how these very same institutions and actors at the international, federal, and provincial level continuously adapt their policies to hire specific racialized groups, illuminating how the process of deskilling and exclusion occurs in practice.

Kailan Leung on "OutsourcEd: International Practicums as Responses to Internationalization in Canadian Teacher Education" suggests that these experiences are problematic on a number of fronts, particularly with regard to the unidirectional flow of knowledge, resources, and long-term benefits. Despite their imperfections, however, Leung believes international practicums (IPs) still hold innovative potential if program organizers and participants can recommit themselves to centering equity and reciprocity. provide a useful framework through which to understand the role of internationalization in driving innovation within Canadian teacher education programs.

Wallis Caldoza (in thought with Peyton Caldoza) on "Why I Don't Talk about Being Filipino (I Think)" captures a specific moment of conversations/non-conversations she herself trapped in about: resisting identity claiming; the contentious relationship between the un-assumed racialized identity of a Filipino-Trinidadian-Canadian scholar and her field of study rooted in social justice education; and the impossibility and instability of the inheritance of intergenerational identity under and within colonial neoliberalism and racial capitalism; the failure of be(long)ing to the nation-state.

## 3   Part 3: Citizenship, Multiculturalism, Culture, Identity

Vania Soepriatna on "The Multicultural Façade: A Colonial Performance of Diversity in Canada and Indonesia" analyzes multiculturalism in the context of two countries, Canada and Indonesia. Canada and Indonesia are two nations that have implemented multiculturalism in state policies, and this essay attempts to explore the historical factors and ways in which they apply multicultural laws. Soepriatna argues that adopting multicultural policies in Canadian and Indonesian legislature is an extension of colonialism that continues to reproduce colonial systems concealed by a façade of diversity and equality. As exemplified in the two nations, multiculturalism has further exacerbated racial, class, and economic inequality. It reduces conflicts rooted in colonial systems of injustice as mere cultural differences, removing any governmental responsibility to address them. In the Canadian context, the essay focuses on the experience of the "visible minorities," while the Indonesian context highlights the experience of the ethnic-Chinese minority.

Juanna Nguyen on "Impact and Implications of Rap and Hip-Hop Music as a Form of Resistance" first narrows the focus to South and Southeast Asian and Asian-American/-Canadian communities, introduces the concept of empowerment theory, defines music therapy and psychotherapy, and provides an overview of a history, background, and literature review of rap and hip-hop in America and in Asian communities as well as Asian exclusion, stereotypes and racial trauma.

Alison Lam on "'L'Autore Ha Musicato Fin Qui, Poi è Morto': Diversity, Inclusion and Equity in Modern Staging of Classical Orientalist Opera" states that what we present to our audiences today matters. Lam says that we cannot simply perform a piece that was written at a time of extreme bias and bigotry without finding a way to address the injustices of the piece. As a source of representation of the world today, the arts have a responsibility to put forward a depiction that does not feed into the marginalization and oppression of a bygone era.

Syed Fahad Ali on "South Asian Representations in the Media: Repetition or Progress?" discusses representations in television, film, and video games. He focuses on what 'progress' may look like and whether there a sense of repetition in these representations under the guise of inauthentic diversity.

Jasmine Pham on "The Fallacy of Native-Speakerism in English Language Education" addresses the impact of globalization and native-speakerism on the hiring practices and policies of South Korea's EPIK program and Japan's JET program. Pham discusses how native-speakerism not only undermines the professional identities of Korean and Japanese English teachers, but also the authenticity of NESTs of Asian descent and the English teaching profession in general. Pham finally offer policy suggestions and alternatives to native-speakerism that can improve the professional identities of both NESTs and NNESTs.

## 4 Part 4: Community Resistance and Activism

Rose Ann Torres on "Feminization of Pandemics: Experiences of Filipino Women in the Health Care System" explores the experiences of Filipino women in the health care system in the Philippines. Torres' objectives in focusing about them is to showcase their knowledge and she hopes that public health system will consult them about the on-going Covid-19 pandemic. Torres argues that they have the knowledge in addressing this Covid-19 pandemic. Torres includes recommendations for why we need to acknowledge and include the participation of the Indigenous healers in the local, national and global public health.

Tika Ram Thapa on "Multiculturalism: A Case for Continued Resistance for Space for Race" introduces migration-based entry points into discussion of multiculturalism, immigrant positioning and the politics of possible. Thapa's analysis will be primarily informed by anti-racism framework within Critical Race Theory.

Grace Garlow on "Brokering Belonging, Shattering Silences and Examining Erasures" presents a critique through embodiment anchoring lived experience with racism by expounding relations of power, oppression, and enslavement using the framework interpreted through the situatedness of a female Taiwanese Canadian. The framework is then applied to schooling to examine multiple resistances to inclusion and human rights education.

Rose Ann Torres on "Filipina Activism from a Transnational Theoretical Framework" focuses on her mother's activism. Torres begins by explaining the meaning of activism, followed by the meaning of transnational framework and how it is used in this chapter. Torres discusses the different forms of activism that her mother embodied and how her activism helped Torres to position her life in Canada and beyond.

Valerie G. Damasco and Rose Ann Torres on "Framework for Developing Resilience among Filipino-Canadian Youth during the Covid-19 Pandemic" introduce a new approach on youth resilience. Damasco and Torres hope that this chapter will be of used to others who also want to do the same talk/training/workshops on developing resilience.

# PART 1

## *Theorizing Asian Canada*

∴

CHAPTER 1

# Critical Reflexivity

*Re-imagining Asian Canada*

Rose Ann Torres and Dionisio Nyaga

## 1   Introduction

Asians' immigration to Canada increased in the late 18th century, largely as a result of "labour-hungry contractors looking for cheap and disposable workers to help build the transcontinental railroad" (Satzewitch & Liodakis, 2017, p. 77). By 2011, Chinese and Filipinos were among the top ethnic groups in Canada, providing disposable labour to corporations and private companies (Satzewitch & Liodakis, 2017). Yet in an educational context, as Coloma (2012) notes, "In spite of their strong numerical presence ... Asian Canadians remain relegated to the margins of research and teaching in the fields of education in general, and of curriculum studies in particular" (p. 119).

This chapter extends Coloma's (2012) work presented in "Theorizing Asian Canadians, Reframing Differences" that outlines a pan-ethnic and ethnic-specific, intersectional approach, a transnational lens, and a comparative view in addition to using research on the history of Asian Canadians' racial discrimination and social movements, and provides theories that explain the social, political, and economic locations of Asian Canadians. While we concur with Coloma's theoretical framework showcasing Asian Canadians' presence in Canada, we find it limiting in explaining different imperial mechanisms and technologies that continue to discriminate against Asian Canadians in Canada. Although we agree that the inclusion of race is important, sexuality and other forms of categories like spiritualities, class, disability, and nationhood are equally relevant in understanding, researching, and theorizing Asian Canadians.

As such, we use critical reflexivity to understand Asian Canadians' experiences more deeply, particularly in a metaphysical context. It is important to include spirituality as one of the frameworks that explain Asian Canadians' positions, power, knowledge, and practices. While Asian Canadians possess spiritualities, imperial spiritualities have been used to disempower them. When spirituality is frozen, nouned, and made accessible to people as a form of control rather than a means to achieve social justice, it imprisons and debilitates the receiver (Wane et al., 2017). This is the kind of spirituality (i.e., religion) that continues to play the role of colonizing the Asian Canadian. This chapter troubles such imperial and corporate spirituality and reimagines Asian spiritualities as power points of imagination and social justice. We need to refocus on the Asian fantasies brought about by their spiritualities in ways that disturb Canadian imaginaries. This point can only be relevant if we present their ways of spiritualities as a point of interrogating the racial erasure of Asian Canadian. The next section focuses on critical reflexivity in relation to Asian Canadians. Following this, we discuss spirituality and provide a conclusion.

## 2   Critical Reflexivity

We include into our conversation the importance of using critical reflexivity in teaching and researching Asian Canadians because it enriches an understanding of historical experiences and the normalizing state technologies on Asian Canadians bodies. While some may think that critical reflexivity has nothing to do with Asian Canadians, we argue that critical reflexivity is a relevant lens of interrogating the Asian continuum in the beyond. While it is important to interrogate the structure, it is equally imperative that we interrogate our own implicit participation in the oppression of ourselves laterally. In fact, to think and act in interrogating the structure reminds us that we are part of and embody the structure that we are investigating. Consequently, the decolonization of the structure is equally a representation of how we engage in reflexive exercise of our implication in colonization. To that extent, critical reflexivity plays the role of *outhabiting* us from ourselves in ways that we mourn and question the role we play in the elimination of others from national imaginaries. Through grief, we come to reimagine ourselves through others (Butler, 2006).

Critical reflexivity invites students and educators to be open about their identities without being fearful of homophobia while creating a space of acceptance. The space of acceptance is political and may reinvent colonial texts. Such a space is created in a way that all stakeholders come to participate in its creation. The creation of such a space is a violent encounter between and beyond stakeholders, in which case all those who participate are invited to be comfortable in the discomfort of space production. Such a space is reflexive in nature in that it cuts back and forth in ways that leave dents of imagination to all those invested in its production. The creation of such a space invites us to a moment of mourning and grief. To mourn is to identify our own vulnerabilities in ways that we call upon the community to participate in space production in ways that reimagine violence as a colonial pedagogy of space production. Grief has been used to justify violence against those others who inflict pain on our bodies. According to Butler (2006), there is a need to reinvent ways through which we imagine grief as a point of emergence. We need to look at mourning and space creation as political in ways that we come to question which bodies are grievable and which are not, which bodies are livable and which are not, and which bodies speak and which do not. These fundamental questions will guide a more cohesive space that sits within and without the discomfort of those investing their grief in such a space.

Such an orientation dismantles and reconfigures colonial ideologies and practices that form White supremacist, heteropatriarchal, and imperialist capitalist ideologies. The process of going back and forth in space creation feminizes the space in ways that everyone—regardless of sexuality, gender, class, and other forms of categorization—come to invest their ideas, feelings, and spirituality in the production of spaces. Such a spatial orientation informed by constant, consistent grief acknowledges diversity of strategies and tactics that expose, deflate, and demystify heteronormativity.

Critical reflexivity calls for recognition of these *funk* strategies that may seem abnormal to the dominant heteropatriarchal society and yet occupy a space of reimagining normativity in space production. It is unregulated in ways that reimagine possibilities and opportunities beyond the current occluded processes of space production, hence allowing the celebration of the fluidity of identities. It turns a neoliberal register of control, affirmation, and accommodation on its face to reimagine how such processes of producing spaces are in themselves invested in coloniality. To speak of "funk" is to invite the process of grief whereby in losing we come to reimagine a new world that never seeks violence as a reparative practice. It is a process of looking at that which has been disabled as central in production of space and knowledge.

Critical reflexivity provides us with the space of theorizing lived experiences of the inhabiting body (Ahmed, 2006). This activity is what critical reflexivity calls disidentification, a survival strategy that works simultaneously within and outside the dominant public sphere and provides "a lens to elucidate minoritarian politics that is not monocausal or monothematic, one that is calibrated to discern a multiplicity of interlocking identity components and the ways in which they affect the social" (Muñoz, 1999, p. 5). Asian Canadians apply these strategies and tactics in ways that come to reimagine research, teaching, and learning. How would one explain Filipino women who meet daily in the park with their employers' children? Such a park, while representing Whiteness, comes to be reconfigured in ways that open space for negotiating nationhood and citizenship. Such are the ways through which Filipino women out habit colonial spaces. Such social production of spaces gives a sense of how Asian

Canadians resist and continue to resist the colonial tools and mechanisms that sustain biopolitics—that they are needed when in need and that they are everlastingly deportable bodies.

Disidentificatory theory (or what we call outhabiting) provides us with new forms of theorizing Asian Canadians in teaching and researching. Disidentification according to Muñoz (1999) is meant "to be descriptive of the survival strategies the minority subject practices in order to negotiate a phobic majoritarian public sphere that continuously elides or punishes the existence of subjects who do not conform to the phantasm of normative citizenship" (p. 4). While Asian Canadians have a history of oppression (Satzewich & Liokadis, 2017), they also have a past that cites their resiliency and coping mechanisms (Belshaw, 2015). As researchers, we lose a lot when we represent them as weak, broken, and irredeemably disordered. The art of representing them as only receivers of violence without reimagining how they negotiate such violence places our representation within a colonial imagination of the other as fully frozen in the violent past. This has both material and symbolic investment in that we earn our space of exultation through their pain. It is important that we also identify ways in which they call out colonialism in ways that may not normally be called resistance. Could their vulnerability be the space through which they create community of purpose to reconfigure imperial oppression and marking of their bodies as broken? These strategies need to be included in the classroom discussion as much as we "explore" and "examine" Asian Canadians' history of oppression. It is interesting how we look at other histories as spaces of exploration and examination: How does such movement invest us with coloniality? How does such expedition place us in the midpoint of the colonial encounter in ways that we return to coloniality in decolonization? This questions our spatial investment in ways that we "funk" the colonial exploration to accommodate the other in ways that they come to speak to colonial spaces. It means that we do not only inhabit but out habit.

How would this be relevant to learning, research, and teaching? Offering a course on Asian Canadians in higher education is not enough. In fact, while such a process is necessary, it should not be an end. While we focus on the content and methodology of theorizing the other, it is equally necessary to include the discussion on negotiations between desire, identification, and ideology of Asian Canadians. Disidentification as a theory and praxis helps produce a space (Muñoz, 1999) for Asian Canadians in ways that speaks to their all-inclusive experience. It is a discussion wherein theory and practice are incorporated in complex ways that invoke the difference (read subjugated fantasies) as a point of emergence. The topic of desire, longing, sadness, and dreams are not included in classroom teaching and learning. As educators we need to encourage students' engagement with desires, frustration, and disappointments in ways that extend and break the canonical programming of teaching, learning, and research. This can only if we become vulnerable and present our very own point of desires in ways that encourage others to be true to themselves. We argue that the classroom can provide a space where students and educators alike return to their psychic selves in ways that they gather the repressed self for the purpose of representing it in the public space. This way of presenting ourselves in the public does not negate the fact that our own marginality is a point of power and knowledge; it also comes to re-orient the canons of teaching, learning, and research through our different vulnerable self-presentation. We argue and concur with Butler (2006) that vulnerability can become a site of marshalling marginalized knowledges in ways that disassembles the public space. This is our point of investing spaces with new forms of imagining spaces as negotiable rather than unilaterally drawn for the marginalized communities. Such a process needs to be placed in a platform of authenticity, honesty, and reciprocity, which are key spiritual values (Wane et al., 2017).

It is imperative that Asian Canadians, as speaking subjects, should present their desires, frustrations, and disappointments in ways that outhabit colonial spaces. Inhabiting a White space is psychically disorienting (Ahmed, 2006) and has a material and symbolic influence in space production and investment. Through the discussion of desire, these repressed selves come to be manifested in ways that decolonize the public space. The decolonization process cannot happen when repression and securitization of space authorized by the state through psychiatric centres is occupying the watchtower. In an era of acceleration of information and knowledge, the once emotional beings cannot be wished away in classroom politics.

The question remains on how a professor can address the issue of psychic doubts historically invested on the student. First, it is necessary to ask students of the need to undress and address their repressed selves. To unmask (read undress) remains a contested issue of who makes one public and for what purpose? When does undressing the repressed self-trouble the making of the colonial space in ways that we exteriorize (read address) space of exception through presentation of our desires and fantasies? In this way, power to decide one's life belongs to the owner of the body, whereby according to Butler (2006), such bodily territories are the community's spaces of emergence. To disallow students to emerge and therefore recolonize and normalize spaces of knowledge production denies the students the ability to undress and address their repressed selves in ways that help them reimagine violence and their place in colonial grounds. Disidentificatory theory tells us that every individual can find a strategy that will work against the situation that needs to be destabilized.

### 2.1 Implications of Critical Reflexive Imaginations to Asian Studies

Chinese head tax, the Japanese gentlemen's agreement, and the continuous journey requirement (Belshaw, 2015) remain relevant in our theorizing of Asian studies in Canada. This history speaks of how some bodies are livable while others come to be considered as broken and monstrous. The life of the Asian other has historically been marked as a space invader, eliciting a hysterical process of securing the state from the emotional Asian other. While we may discuss this as just something in the past, we are again informed of how that history comes to be invested in the class and academic spaces when sentiment of a Canadian university marked as being too Asian (Coloma, 2012; Gilmour et al., 2012) is made normal. In Toronto's Bathurst–Wilson neighbourhood, Filipinos thrive in business, as they do elsewhere in Toronto, and in other Canadian cities such as Vancouver, Asian Canadians have a significant role in Canada's economy. This is a

> response to state and global power apparatuses that employs systems of racial, sexual, and national subjugation. The routinized protocols of subjugation are brutal and painful. Disidentification is about managing and negotiating historical trauma and systemic violence. ... Such processes of self actualization come into discourse as a response to ideologies that discriminate against, demean, and attempt to destroy components of subjectivity that do not conform or respond to narratives of universalization and normalization.
> 
> MUÑOZ 1999, p. 161

Asian Canadians developed their own respective strategies to secure survival at least and prosperity at best (Belshaw, 2015) in ways that come to reimagine Canadian geographies through migrant intimacies. Of course, such low presentation erects physical and psychic borders, which reminds them of their original place. To decide to settle in such a colonial imagination of the Asian other is to be a colonial accomplice. How would one explain Asian success in times of erasure if we don't factor their desire as a means of negotiating colonial violence? Speaking of negotiating violence, there is a need to retheorize success in ways that we don't extinct marginal forms of success. And all these things need to be integrated in teaching and researching Asian Canadians through critical reflexivity.

## 3 Spirituality

Colonization has affected the Indigenous spiritualities that seek to look at relationships as fundamental in the making of bodies and spaces they occupy. Colonial spaces are individualistic and pegged on the discourse of competition as opposed to community and relationality. The real self-born out of the community exists in ways that are in congruence with nature and nurture. In African societies, the discourse of *ubuntu* is relevant in terms of how the individual's progress is a replication of the social fabric. The colonial technology of control and rational thinking seems to have acted upon these Indigenous ways but not without resistance from an Indigenous perspective steeped in spirituality. We have discussed elsewhere (see Wane et al., 2017) the role of African spirituality in governance and ways in which we speak of damage and the need to bring forth the essence of marginal fantasies as points of resistance.

Among the Asian Indigenous peoples, colonialism instilled the idea that a man-as-body was prone to punishment (Torres, 2012; Torres & Nyaga, 2016). It looked at the body as being controlled and the property of the colonizer. It changed the practices of the community from a loving community to a competitive one. However, the spirit cannot be colonized and will always reinvent itself in ways that are monstrous and unrecognizable to the colonizer. This community used their spirituality to resist colonialism. The same form of spirituality continues to be applied by Filipina/o in the diaspora in terms of reimagining White Canadian spaces. To speak of Filipino caregivers bringing their employers' children in the park and having their Filipino delicacies in the park (Torres, 2019) is a point of reimagining the White space using food as their point of spiritual emergence.

Asian Canadians experience colonization in a painful and brutal way. As they inhabit a White settler society, they experience new form of racisms. These new forms of racisms according to Henry and Tator represent democratic racism, an ideology in which two conflicting sets of values are made congruent to each other. Commitments to democratic principles such as justice, equality, and fairness conflict but coexist with attitudes and behaviours that include negative feelings about minority groups (as cited in Satzewich & Liodakis, 2017). Some of the discourses of democratic racism are predicated on colour-blindness, equal opportunity, victim blaming, and multiculturalism. The belief that the current spatial inequality, multiculturalism, and diversity can resolve historical injustices is far-fetched. The question of colour-blindness brought about by affirmative action and the cultural sensitivity project reimagines racism in what Pon (2009) calls the ontology of forgetting. It is another technology of disremembering the Asian body as capable of renegotiating space and consequently the White body negotiates such space on their behalf. When the Asian body fails to walk through such charitable space they are blamed for their inadequacy, therefore affirming the stereotype of the Asian as irredeemably broken and unable to enter the modern age.

We argue that while such forms of erasure are present and prescient, to continue affirming them is an implication if we deny the space of low forms of resistance. To this point, we affirm the role of spirituality as a form of agency and resistance for the Asian body in the beyond. Spirituality for some Asian Canadians is about their relationship to a Higher Being, and that connects them to their ancestors, culture and traditions, language, and communities. Spiritualities help them navigate and reimagine racism, classism, and other forms of social differences in ways that "rupture the dominant Euro-American conventional approaches to knowledge production" (Shahjahan, 2005 p. 214).

In teaching and researching Asian Canadians, there is a need to incorporate a discussion of spiritualities as subversive low technologies and theories. Asian Canadians are diverse in many ways, including their spiritualities. There is no single meaning of spirituality to Asian Canadians. Asian Canadians express their own meanings and understanding of spiritualities in ways that are contextual and informed by a particular historical happening. Some students say that spirituality for them is about their religion—about being a Christian, Buddhist, Hindu, Catholic, among others. Some say that it has nothing to do with the organized religion, and that it is about love, respect, generosity, and kindness. It is about having a relationship with God or Higher Being. It is also about practising yoga or other forms of meditation. Spirituality is something personal and political (Wane et al., 2017). The White settler society limits the existence of Asian Canadians in public space while in returning back such White eviction, the Asian bodies apply their multiple spiritualities to affirm their place in White spaces. For example, an Indian woman wearing hijab was assaulted in the subway. To speak of the hijab is to identify the question of spiritualities and the politics of unveiling and veiling. A woman assaulted because she is wearing hijab in public speaks of the levels of islamophobia in the city. Phobia or what is called fear is a point to engage with in order to interrogate why the city is in the state of hysteria. What is in the hijab that the White city engages in violence against the Muslim woman? Could the hijab be the reversal of the panoptic technology that sets the Muslim woman as unrecognizable while their capacity to watch the other puts the Muslim woman in the watch tower? What would this inverted surveillance speak of in terms of spiritualities? Does spirituality work towards inverting racial surveillance of the Muslim other? While we may work with this thesis, we are conscious of how spiritualities cannot be reduced in the hijab. It is more than the visible.

Discussing the essentialist aspect of White feminism, for which we lay our claim on going beyond the Western construction of the other as just broken and in need of a saviour, Butler (2006), quoting Mohanty on the topic of the veil and burka, says:

> The imposition of versions of agency signified by the veil and burka, not only misunderstands the various cultural meanings that the burka might carry for women who wear it, but also denies the very idioms of agency that are relevant to for such women. (p. 47)

The use of hijab is to extend our orientation in reimagining how spirituality is a form of resistance. This may sound far away from academic spaces but in an era referred to as imperial and global in nature, the current classroom is fused with this colonial process of evicting the Muslim other. With this in mind, we seek to ask for a place of spirituality in teaching and learning as a form of inversing the panoptic nature of the colonial classroom.

Theorizing Asian Canadians is incomplete if spirituality is not included in the pedagogical discussion of classroom production. To speak of spirituality as an instrument of reimagining the classroom is to embrace diversity of belief systems as they come to define and orient learning and teaching. It means reimagining the colonial curriculum and its vertical praxis of power (Nyaga, 2017). It means bringing on board the view of learners and educators in ways that they speak to each other with respect, love, and vulnerability. It is time to allow the art of spiritual vulnerability as a praxis of decolonization and reimagination of learning and teaching. Rose says that after many years of teaching spirituality and education, students come to embrace course materials when their stories are appreciated and made to walk through the classroom. Otherwise, students become passive and not active in the learning spaces if we continue to verticalize learning and teaching. The presence of spirituality as teachable is violent and necessary for opening new forms of reimagining teaching and learning. Such a move disassembles the class, opening cracks of imagining the class beyond the colonial industrial complex. For example, Rose recounts a story of her grandmother's colonial experience with Japanese soldiers in 1940 in ways that emphasize the role of spirituality as a decolonial praxis of Indigenous women of the Philippines. The fact that her grandmother focused on healing the other even after such a violent encounter with the Japanese soldiers speaks of resiliency and vulnerability as necessary in anti-colonialism.

The impact of colonization in one's life is an ongoing process (Fanon, 1968; Memmi, 1967; Simmons & Dei, 2012). Spirituality as a process of decolonization helps us to go deep into our soul and search for the real meaning of transformation that understands our pain through the other while acknowledging the agony of others. It helps us understand the issues that we are facing in our everyday acts of survival. Teaching Asian Canadians must include this kind of open, fluid, flexible, and volatile discussion that goes beyond the colonial definition of the other as broken. It is time to reimagine accountability in the classroom in ways that we don't only count but also imagine how bodies that are counted count as grievable, speakable, and livable. Otherwise, theorizing Asian Canadians will remain a tokenistic exercise that removes bodies from one prison to another.

## 4 Conclusion

This chapter showcased subjugated knowledges as not only damaged but also as necessary in orienting spaces. It centres ideas, impressions, notions, sense, conception, images, and perception from Asian Canadians in ways that come to imagine White space as alterable. These ideas may perhaps sound senseless, unwise, and heedless and yet to Asian Canadians they are a prudent and necessary art of imagined livability and speakability. These are the reasons why there is a need to amalgamate them in teaching and researching Asian Canadians. When we say resisting mastery, it is about letting the Asian Canadians inform or speak to the curriculum. It is the notion of Asian as the speaking subject in defining who counts in an environment of learning and teaching. Spirituality seems to have taken the central role in defining how spaces should be mapped in ways that acknowledge the Asian other as a speaking subject with needs and aspirations.

Critical reflexivity intimates the art of disidentificatory strategies and tactics informed by a spiritual point of view that can help reimagine how we learn and teach in the classroom. It is a space where there is recognition of pain and suffering as well as joy and happiness. In negotiating classroom space, we as educators should take the role of facilitating the coming out of other forms of knowing in ways that are strategic, skeptical, and affirming. The act of Asians negotiating Western geographies needs to be messy and dirty. There is no one framework that surveys a neat form of transgressing the now, which is ordered and systematic, other than the unpreparedness of the messy theory from below. This is a key perspective that need to define the processes of queering the space of learning, teaching, and researching. In fact, as Butler (2006) says, indeed, an international coalition of feminist activists and thinkers—a coalition that affirms the thinking of feminist activists and the activism of thinkers and refuses to put them into distinctive categories that denies the actual complexity of the lives in questions—will have to accept the array of sometimes incommensurable epistemological and political beliefs and modes and means of agency that bring us into activism. (p. 48)

## References

Ahmed, S. (2006). *Queer phenomenology: Orientations, objects, others*. Duke University Press.

Belshaw, J. D. (2015). *Canadian history: Pre-Confederation*. BCCampus. https://opentextbc.ca/preconfederation/

Butler, J. (2006). *Precarious life: The powers of mourning and violence*. Verso.

Coloma, R. S. (2012). Theorizing Asian Canada, reframing differences. In N. Ng-A-Fook & J. Rottmann (Eds.), *Reconsidering Canadian curriculum studies: Provoking historical, present, and future perspectives* (pp. 119–135). London: Palgrave Macmillan. https://doi.org/10.1057/9781137008978_7

Fanon, F. (1968). *Black skin, white masks*. New York: Grove Press.

Gilmour, R. J., Bhandar, D., Heer, J., & Ma, M. C. K. (Eds.). (2012). *"Too Asian?": Racism, privilege, and post-secondary education*. Between the Lines.

Memmi, A. (1967). *The colonizer and the colonized*. Boston: Beacon Press.

Muñoz, J. E. (1999). *Disidentifications: Queers of color and the performance of politics*. Minneapolis: University of Minnesota Press.

Nyaga, D. (2017). New possibilities for school curriculum: Praxis of Indigenous peoples in Kenya. In N. Phasha, D. Mahlo, & G. J. S. Dei (Eds.), *Inclusive education in African contexts: A critical reader* (pp. 139–149). Sense.

Pon, G. (2009). Cultural competency as new racism: An ontology of forgetting. *Journal of Progressive Human Services, 20*(1), 59–71. https://doi.org/10.1080/10428230902871173

Satzewich, V., & Liodakis, N. (2017). *"Race" and ethnicity in Canada: A critical introduction* (4th ed.). Oxford: Oxford University Press.

Shahjahan, R. A. (2005). Mapping the field of anti-colonial discourse to understand issues of indigenous knowledges: Decolonizing praxis. *McGill Journal of Education, 40*(3), 213–240. https://mje.mcgill.ca/article/view/566/455

Simmons, M., & Dei, G. J. S. (2012). Reframing anti-colonial theory for the diasporic context. *Postcolonial Directions in Education, 1*(1), 67–99. https://core.ac.uk/download/pdf/83023007.pdf

Torres, R. (2012). *Aeta Indigenous women healers in the Philippines: Lessons and implications* [Doctoral dissertation, University of Toronto]. TSpace. https://tinyurl.com/y4lnahlo

Torres, R. (2019, April 18). *Re-imagining Peminist development* [Paper presentation]. Pinay Power II Conference, Montreal, QC, Canada.

Torres, R., & Nyaga, D. (2016). Discussion of power through the eyes of the margins: Praxis of post-colonial Aeta indigenous women healers in the Philippines. *International Journal of Asia Pacific Studies*, *12*(2), 31–56. https://doi.org/10.21315/IJAPS2016.12.2.2

Torres, R., & Nyaga, D. (2017). Gendered citizenship: A case study of paid Filipino male live-in caregivers in Toronto. *International Journal of Asia Pacific Studies*, *13*(1), 51–71. http://dx.doi.org/10.21315/ijaps2017.13.1.3

Wane, N., Torres, R., & Nyaga, D. (2017). African Indigenous governance from spiritual lens. In E. A. McKinley & L. Tuhiwai Smith (Eds.), *Handbook of Indigenous education* (pp. 1–15). Springer. https://doi.org/10.1007/978-981-10-1839-8_45-1

CHAPTER 2

# Mixture and Movement

*Reflections on Identity, Power and Border Crossing through the Process of Currere*

Kailan Leung

## 1      Introduction

I first read Fred Wah's *Diamond Grill* in 2008, halfway through my Literature BA at McGill University. Reading Wah's biotext, I felt for the first time in my life that I was being *written to*. In each of the poet's vignettes, I saw my own oppressions and contradictions. I felt validated at times and shamed at others. *Diamond Grill* suggested both the power and pain of hybridity and encouraged me to envision myself as a member of a broader community with similar lived experiences. To discover oneself on the page for the first time is a powerful experience, and my initial encounter with Wah's work pushed me to reexamine and reconceptualize the hyphenated spaces of my own identity. Since then, I have been introduced—over the course of my academic and professional career—to a variety of new fields, theories, and pedagogies which have helped provide me with some (but not all) of the language, history, and thinking needed to critically engage with a multiracial, transnational Canadian identity.

In this chapter, I apply elements of Pinar's (2004) framework of *currere* in reflecting on past, current, and future positionalities with the goal of better understanding my relationship to identity, power, and resistance. I understand *currere* as a form of self-analysis through autobiography, in which particular focus is paid to past educational experiences as a means of gaining insight into one's life "and how both are imbricated in society, politics, and culture" (p. 36). Pinar states that for educators, *currere* becomes "an ongoing project of self-understanding in which one becomes mobilized for engaged pedagogical action—as a private-and-public intellectual—with others in the social reconstruction of the public sphere" (p. 37). Autobiography, according to Pinar, is an inherently revolutionary act: it rejects the primacy of systematized and established epistemologies in favor of individual knowledge and subjectivities. On a macro level, autobiography also challenges national mythologies that serve to propagate unjust power structures and societal behaviors, stories that "[create] the illusion of truth being on the social surface, when it is nearly axiomatic that [those stories] mask other, unacceptable truths" (p. 38).

Pinar (1975, 2004) envisioned *currere* as a way to reconceptualize curriculum, and as a pathway for teachers to become what Said (1996) called "amateur intellectuals" (p. 81). Through critical self-examination, Said (1996) suggested individuals could "transform the merely professional routine most of us go through into something more lively and radical" (p. 82). Drawing heavily from psychoanalytic theory, Pinar (1975, 2004) divides the method of *currere* into four successive parts: regressive, progressive, analytical, and synthetical. In the regressive, the writer draws upon formative memories to "re-enter the past, and to thereby enlarge—and transform—one's memory" (p. 36). The progressive step provides opportunities to reimagine possible futures and positionalities, while the analytical moment entails "one's distantiation from past and future [...] to create a subjective space of freedom in the present" (p. 36). Lastly, in the synthetical stage, the writer "re-enters the lived present" (p. 37) better equipped to make sense of one's experiences in the hopes of renewed "self-mobilization for social reconstruction" (p. 37).

Here, I have attempted to follow Pinar's (2004) methodology for the sake of structural coherence, with the understanding that gaps occur naturally, and that some connections cannot and should not be confined to a particular narrative format. In writing *currere*, my aim is not "self-scrutiny for the sake of public performance" (p. 37), but rather to offer up lived experience for collective witnessing. By problematizing the past, I hope to contribute to what Freire (1970) called a "revolutionary futurity", a "movement that engages people as beings aware of their incompletion—an historical movement which has as its point of departure, its Subjects and its objective" (p. 84).

## 2 The Regressive: Multiracial Identity Formation in a Transnational Context

The first friend I made without the assistance of my parents was Dan O'Brien, a tall, lanky boy who called his father Neil and his mother Yoko. We gravitated toward each other on the first day of second grade, and a week later had made a pact to be best friends. Dan and I certainly got along, but I also recall the pragmatic origins of our friendship: we looked the same—which was to say that we looked different from our peers and teachers—and thus needed to stick together. In our class photograph from that year, the two of us stand beside each other amid a sea of white faces: half-Asian, half-White, half-smiling.

Other memories that stand out from my three years at a public elementary school in small-town Washington State: a classmate snatching the 'flesh' crayon out of my fist and handing me 'yellow' instead; a girl in the line to assembly being struck by a red-haired boy standing next to me, and then bursting into tears and pointing a finger at my face when the teacher approached; the traditional taunts involving slanted eyes and mock-Chinese gibberish on the playground at recess. Each of these "biographic situations" (Pinar 2004, p. 36) elicited a combination of anger and shame that was also intensely confusing. My parents and I spoke English, watched sports, and ate at McDonald's like everyone else in town. If the differences between my peers and I were minimal, why was I the target of their aggressions and exclusions? This thought wormed its way into my seven-year-old psyche and began to fester.

While unique in some ways, the memories catalogued above correspond with much of the research that has emerged in the past thirty years on multiracial identity formation. In a study on identity development in biracial siblings, Root (1998) found that like me, "most [participants] reported an awareness of racial difference by 5 or 6 years of age" (p. 242). After that initial realization, however, the process of racial identification among multiracial individuals is extremely varied. Rockquemore, Brunsma, and Delgado (2009) review the empirical literature on mixed-race children to suggest that "racial identity often changes over the life course, racial identity development is not a predictable linear process with a single outcome, and social, cultural, and spatial context are critical" (pp. 20–21).

This notion of fluidity is central to the ecological framework of identity formation first proposed by Root (1998) in the early 1990s, a framework widely accepted and utilized in the field of Mixed-Race Studies today. The ecological framework posits that contextual "macrolenses" and "microlenses" combine to "filter the meaning of situations and experiences to which people are exposed" (Root 1998, p. 238). Macrolenses include factors such as class, gender, generation, and regional racial histories. Root divides microlenses into three separate categories: inherited influences, traits, and social environments. These 'filters' interact constantly, and the various influences of one lens on another shape the multiracial individual's self-conception of identity. One foundational aspect of the framework is the multiracial individual's conscious choice to "sit on the border and [experience a] border identity as a central reference point" (Rockquemore et al. 2009). Root does not suggest, however, that this particular agency makes the process of navigating new ecological environments easier for multiracial individuals; in fact, it may complicate interpretations of exclusion or belonging (Root 1998).

Whatever trajectory my racial identity had been following in the United States, it was ruptured when my family moved to the Philippines—where I had been born seven years earlier—in 1996. My father, an agricultural scientist, was returning to a position at the International Rice Research Institute (IRRI) in the countryside south of Manila. My mother, a teacher and school administrator, had been asked to lead a new K-5 school for the children of IRRI's expatriate staff. What was meant to be a brief sabbatical from American life ended up lasting 25 years, and while it would be presumptuous of me to claim a Filipino identity outright, my most powerful memories and emotional attachments are without question located in the Philippines.

In the postcolonial context of the Philippines, my mixed-race heritage both conveyed and produced privilege. A residual effect of five hundred years of Spanish and American imperialism has been the widespread "colonial mentality" apparent in much of contemporary Philippine life (David & Okazaki 2006). David and Nadal (2013) suggest that this "specific form of internalized oppression [is] perhaps the most insidious psychological legacy of colonialism" (p. 299), serving to automatically privilege anything Western while simultaneously denigrating all things Filipino. It did not take long for me to realize that my *mestizo* appearance—in contrast to my early childhood in the United States—was desirable and celebrated in the Philippines. By learning fragments of the language, I found I could easily 'pass' as Filipino: my hybridity, in this case, allowed me to navigate an in-between world in which I was privileged enough to opt in and out of the experiences and agencies associated with both the local and the foreign.

Over the course of my adolescence and early adulthood, I became more aware of the assumptions of power made about me and was subsequently faced with the uncomfortable realization that many of those assumptions were true. No matter how Filipino I feel today, when I return to the Philippines my positionality remains that of a cisgender male, English-speaking foreigner whose passport, money, education, and social connections allow far greater access to power (and refuge from oppression) than the vast majority of Filipino citizens.

My secondary education took place at an elite American international school on the outskirts of Manila. With few exceptions, the parents of my peers were either employees of the school, expatriate workers, or the very wealthiest and most influential members of Philippine society. Up until the tenth grade, we followed a patchwork American curriculum cobbled together from multiple state standards, before transitioning to the International Baccalaureate (IB) Diploma Program for the final two years of high school.

In English class, we learned about chattel slavery and Jim Crow laws through Richard Wright's *Native Son* and Toni Morrison's *Beloved*. In History,

I memorized the economic, social, and political conditions that contributed to the Scramble for Africa. Once, I attended a field trip to the World War II battlefield of Corregidor Island in Manila Bay. Over the course of the day, we learned about General MacArthur's heroic last stand and the present-day importance of a military relationship between the United States and the Philippines. We nodded as we sipped our bottled water and ate pre-packaged sandwiches, surrounded by an army of security guards and tour guides making less than five dollars a day. As Freire (1970) suggests, a banking model of education delivered by the elites "stimulates the credulity of students, with the ideological intent (often not perceived by educators) of indoctrinating them to adapt to the world of oppression" (p. 78). Never once did my international schooling explicitly engage with the structural inequities of our surroundings or challenge our complicity in a meaningful way.

When I left the Philippines to pursue a university education in Canada, the negative racialization I had experienced as a young child resumed. At orientation, I was complimented on the fluency of my English by a host of well-meaning White students. During my second year in Montreal, I was denied a rental application—along with my Chinese roommate—for being "too oriental". To complete my degree, I was required to take a two-term survey course of the Western canon, a Shakespeare seminar, and an introductory course on (White) poetics. In my third year, I finally stumbled upon a postcolonial literature course, albeit one taught by a White professor. There, I was introduced to Frantz Fanon, Edward Said, Ngugi Wa Thiong'o, and Benedict Anderson. In another class that semester, I encountered the poetry of Fred Wah and Roy Miki. I could feel, quite viscerally, the onset of an ontological shift as these authors and texts began to inform my understanding of reality.

## 3  The Progressive: (Re)Imagining Possible Futures

When I consider the future with regards to multiracial, transnational identities, I take comfort in the fact that upbringings similar to mine are becoming more common. Within Canada, census data points to an exponential rise in interracial marriages and multiracial families over the past two decades (Statistics Canada 2019; Bascaramurty 2018). Globalization, of course, has directly impacted the growth of a multiracial population worldwide (Osanami Torngren et al. 2019), which in turn has fueled a demand for new research within the field of Mixed-Race Studies. Many multiracial scholars have also recognized the dangers of essentializing complex narratives of identity through global frameworks, and I hope that as its representation grows in the academic literature, multi-raciality may avoid portrayal as a panacea for racial inequity—or worse—as evidence of a post-racial world (Childs 2014).

In my professional occupation as an educator, I recognize a personal obligation to reimagine the ways in which I can use my platform to pursue the *conscientization* of my students (Freire 1970), while agitating for change within and outside of my own educational institution. In teaching and learning, I imagine conflict as a necessary ingredient for change: I find myself persuaded, for instance, by Lo's (2017) call for agonistic deliberation—"an approach to the political that accepts the pervasiveness of political conflict and seeks to channel that conflict positively" (p. 5)—as a means of enacting a liberatory and decolonial praxis.

In Canadian education, I anticipate that the actions undertaken to challenge hegemonic structures will look different for each practitioner. For me, my privilege gives me pause when I consider possible futures for myself and other multiracial, transnational educators. I know there will be times when my lived reality contradicts my convictions. In those instances, I aspire toward humility in accepting the limits of my own perspectives, and to consciously make room for other epistemologies, ontologies, and axiologies (Carson 2017).

When it comes to theory, I share Bhabha's (1994) conviction that hybridity offers potential as a site of power and resistance. For Bhabha, hybridity results from contact between uneven powers—the colonizer and the colonized—in which attempts by the dominant group to subdue and 'translate' the identity of the subordinate instead result in the creation of something entirely new. Bhabha attributes power to the hybrid form because it becomes inaccessible (and desirable) to the dominant group, while also possessing intimate knowledge of its would-be oppressor. Hybridity refuses and refutes an essentialist binary (us/them), inhabiting instead "the cutting edge of translation and negotiation, the in-between space" (Bhabha 1994, p. 56) in which meaning can be found. While Papastergiadis (1995) suggests that "Bhabha has divorced the term hybridity from the context of miscegenation" (p. 17), I contend that the former's theory remains applicable here, especially as multiracial experiences become transnational *and* transcultural.

Bhabha sets himself apart from other theorists of hybridity through a consistently optimistic framing of its power. To Bhabha, any culture that emerges from the colonial encounter must be in a constant state of flux, and he rejects any narrative (for example, nation-building mythologies) promoting "primordial unity or fixity" (Bhabha 1994, p. 37). Instead, Bhabha argues, "even the same signs can be appropriated, translated, rehistoricized, and read anew" in the margins of multiple cultures. In this liminal Third Space, ambivalence is welcome, and Bhabha suggests that "a willingness to descend into this [Third Space] [...] may open the way to conceptualizing an *inter*national culture, based not on the exoticism of multiculturalism or the *diversity* of cultures, but on the inscription and articulation of culture's *hybridity*" (p. 38, original emphasis).

If we consider multiracial individuals as one manifestation of hybridity, I argue they are also imbued with the power to subvert and renegotiate culture through a Third Space. In an officially multicultural context such as Canada, the very concept of diversity exists only in relation to normalized, hegemonic Whiteness, much in the way Said (1978) suggests that the identity of the Occident relies on its opposition to the Orient. However, the hybrid, multiracial individual bridges the gap between assumptions of dominance and subordination with regards to race and culture. Lowe (1991) suggests:

> "[Hegemony] is not only the political process by which a particular group constitutes itself as 'the one' or 'the majority' in relation to which 'minorities' are defined and know themselves to be 'other', but it is equally the process by which positions of otherness may ally and constitute a new majority, a 'counter-hegemony' " (p. 29).

Multiraciality is a position of otherness, and transnational multiraciality is an amplified otherness. In both cases, the potential for counter-hegemonic resistance exists; individuals may use their hybridity to 'translate and negotiate' culture, while groups might come together to enact what Gaztambide-Fernández (2012) calls a "creative solidarity" that "[insists] on a more complex and more accurate conception of culture than the one that informs multiculturalism or even cosmopolitanism" (p. 57).

## 4   The Analytical: Locating the Self Betwixt and Between

In the analytical moment, Pinar (2004) encourages a "phenomenological bracketing; one's distantiation from past and future functions to create a subjective space of freedom in the present" (p. 36). To turn procedure into a question, one might ask: who am I at the moment?

The term 'Third Culture Kid' (TCK) was coined nearly sixty years ago but has received renewed attention in the era of globalization. Pollock and Van Reken (1999) characterize TCKs as individuals who have "spent a significant part of their developmental years in a culture other than the parents' culture, [and develop] a sense of relationship to all of [their] cultures while not having full ownership in any" (p. xi). Qualitative research suggests TCKs experience a sense of rootlessness throughout their lives, but that they are also well equipped to adjust to new environments and socio-cultural norms (Fail et al. 2004). Reverse culture shock upon returning to their home (i.e., passport) country is also common. While these definitions of identity are not totalizing, they speak to many of my lived experiences. More than anything else at the moment, I consider myself a TCK.

A common adage among self-identified TCKs is that they belong to people, not places. Anderson's (1983) definition of the nation as "an imagined political community" (p. 6), then, is an easy sell for those with transnational upbringings like mine. Nationalism and patriotism have never come naturally to me, and to some extent, my dual role as both insider and outsider—racially and culturally—while living in the United States, the Philippines, and Canada has allowed me to be more attuned to "the actual inequality and exploitation that may prevail in each [nation]", while being skeptical of any state-led efforts to promote "deep, horizontal comradeship" (p. 7).

In the current moment, I write from a position in which different signifiers of mixture—half-Asian, half-White, cross-cultural, Asian-Canadian, Canadian Chinese—can only insinuate the movement that has been so critical to my identity. In *Mixed Race Amnesia: Resisting the Romanticization of Multiraciality*, Mahtani (2002) draws on Fred Wah to help explore the complexity of hyphenated identities with regard to national belonging:

> "The hyphen marks a distance from potential claims to nation. It is a troubling symbol that refuses to admit the possibility of the comingling of ethnicities and national citizenship, compounding difference as 'a property marker, a boundary post, a knot, a chain, a bridge, a foreign word, a nomadic, floating magic carpet' (Wah 1996, 60). [...] The hyphen holds a particular tension, articulating a union of contradictions, each word symbolizing the inverted contradiction of the other. Consequently, the hyphen marks places of ambiguity and multiplicity. More attention needs to be paid to the hyphen itself rather than to the words—and subsequent places—on either side of it." (p. 119)

I still feel the tension of the hyphen, but it no longer elicits feelings of confusion or shame. I come from a multitude of places, peoples, contexts, and perspectives. At times, I feel neither here nor there. However, this feeling is not one of absence, but rather of fullness; the mixtures and movements of my life story bring me closer to *everywhere* than they do to *nowhere*.

## 5  The Synthetical: Engaging with Context and Complicity

In her theoretical review of democratic education, Sant (2019) outlines two spectrums in which "distinctive normative aims [in political and educational discourses] are grounded in different ontological assumptions" (p. 680). The first spectrum places *individualism* on one end and *communitarianism* on the other, while the second places *particularism* and *universalism* in opposition. Imagined as intersecting axes, we might plot—albeit crudely—one's aims, assumptions, and solutions to various social questions in different quadrants. A combination of particularism and individualism, for instance, is a hallmark of neoliberal thinking. Socialist ideologies, on the other hand, might be associated with universalism and communitarianism. One byproduct of my own transnational upbringing has been an appreciation for how the circumstances and opportunities of one's life contribute to one's positioning along each axis. For me, my experiences in and across different physical, cultural, and educational spaces as a multiracial individual have underscored the importance of the collective, and a belief that achieving universal outcomes—especially with regard to education and social justice—often depends on adapting to the needs of particular contexts.

Throughout my international education, I was encouraged to think of myself as a 'global citizen', or a 'citizen of the world'. These labels express the privilege of mobility, access, and a relative freedom from oppression. Globalization has propelled my transnational life, and unlike so many others, I have had the freedom as an adult to choose and control my movement around the world. While the oppressions and discomforts I have encountered are real, I have also benefited from a global capitalist society rooted in systemic oppression and the erasure of Indigenous peoples. The privilege I experience today, especially as a citizen and settler of Canada, thus demands a reckoning with my own complicity.

In "Decolonization is Not a Metaphor", Tuck and Yang (2012) outline a series of "settler moves to innocence" which serve to prop up settler colonialism through "a framework of excuses, distractions, and diversions from decolonization" (p. 10). All settlers, the authors contend, seek to "deny and deflect their own complicity in settler colonialism" (p. 10), thus removing themselves from the hard work of "breaking the settler colonial triad [through] repatriating land to sovereign Native tribes and nations, [abolishing] slavery in its contemporary forms, and [dismantling] the imperial metropole" (p. 31). Accepting my own settler status in Canada and attending to my complicity in Indigenous erasure is an ongoing process. I am a racialized body who remains subjected to colonial, neoliberal institutions and policies, and my powers and privileges within the boundaries of the nation-state are typically different than those of my White fellow citizens. At the same time, my participation in a capitalist consumer society, my 'ownership' of land, and my access to exploitative institutions of knowledge-production make it impossible to deny my role in the oppression of Indigenous people, cultures, and power.

Sium, Desai, and Ritskes (2012) suggest "decolonization is a messy, dynamic, and contradictory process" (p. 2), and that while "[there] is no escaping complicity within a settler colonial state [...] complicity cannot be collapsed into simple and neat categories without historicizing the political legacy of colonialism" (p. 3). I tend to agree; complicity is a spectrum, but where we fall on this spectrum cannot relativize the amount of work each individual must contribute to reimagining a decolonial future.

Canada remains a hegemonically white nation-state, in which 'ethnicity' is attributed only to those of non-European descent, and the celebration of 'visible minorities' is more likely to come in the form of festivals and food than the redistribution of wealth and power. The non-white Canadian is both a necessity and a threat to white supremacy. Racialized bodies must be controlled for the maintenance of a specifically white culture, and Canada's history provides a playbook for ensuring this status quo. However, the blueprint for dealing with the hybrid subject is far less clear. Multiracial Canadians are unusual yet familiar, intriguing yet discomfiting to those who feel entitled to power. Through their successful transgression of racial boundaries, multiracial Canadians are an inescapable reminder that traditional racial hierarchies cannot exist forever.

Bhabha (1994) suggests that transnational movement results in a process of cultural translation, through which the new arrival "becomes increasingly aware of the construction of culture and the invention of tradition" (p. 247). The transnational arrival, I would suggest, thus comes equipped with a level of critical discernment lacking in the native-born, lifelong resident of Canada. Taylor (1991) describes this process as 'transculturation', which she envisions as "a shifting or circulating pattern of cultural transference" (p. 93). While power imbalances are always present when boundaries are crossed, Taylor (1991) contends that through this act of transgression, the transnational border-crosser gains agency in knowing that their presence—in some small way—alters the dominant power forever.

## 6   (In)Conclusion

Through the process of *currere*, I have attempted to interrogate my own subjective past, present, and future in the pursuit of theorizing multiracial and transnational identity in Canada. At the end of this reflective exercise, it would be arrogant—and frankly, impossible—to offer any conclusion other than the following: self-examination leads in unexpected directions, and the best one can hope for at any pause in their journey is a firmer understanding of their beliefs, allegiances, and accountabilities.

My subjectivities have led me to believe that in a Canadian context, multiracial and transnational individuals are poised to navigate and renegotiate previously inaccessible or unknown Third Spaces between cultural, historical, and political borders. Their bodies are already a symbolic form of resistance against hegemonic whiteness, and by embracing their border identities they become powerful agents for change. Those committed to reimagining the future must continue to engage in reflection and conversation to identify what the mobilization of hybridity for resistance might look like in different settings.

Reyes (2019) sees "the process of becoming comfortable with being uncomfortable" as essential to "developing the tools to be radically mindful in the moment" (p. 5). *Currere*, I believe, is one such tool to assist in building an ethic of radical mindfulness. The articulation of my positionality/ies has afforded me a new vantage point from which to assess my relationships with power, privilege, and resistance. I encourage others to seize on this (in)conclusion and embrace *currere*—however they might interpret it—as a means to unsettle and unlearn.

### References

Anderson, B. (1983). *Imagined Communities: Reflections on the Origin and Spread of Nationalism*. Verso.

Bascaramurty, D. (2018, January 2). As multi-ethnic population in Canada rises, complications arise. *Globe and Mail*. Retrieved from https://www.theglobeandmail.com/news/national/multi-ethnic-mixed-race-canada-census-2016/article37475308/

Bhabha, H. K. (1994). *The Location of Culture*. London & New York: Routledge.

Carson, Q. (2017, August 25). *Pedagogy of the Decolonizing* [Video]. YouTube. https://www.youtube.com/watch?v=IN17Os8JAr8

Childs, E. C. (2014). A global look at mixing: Problems, pitfalls and possibilities. *Journal of Intercultural Studies*, 35(6), 677–688.

David, E. J. R., & Okazaki, S. (2006). Colonial mentality: A review and recommendation for Filipino American psychology. *Cultural Diversity and Ethnic Minority Psychology*, 12(1), 1–16.

David, E. J. R., & Nadal, K. L. (2013). The colonial context of Filipino American immigrants' psychological experiences. *Cultural Diversity and Ethnic Minority Psychology*, 19(3), 298–309.

Fail, H., Thompson, J., & Walker, G. (2004). Belonging, identity and Third Culture Kids: Life histories of former international school students. *Journal of Research in International Education*, *3*(3), 319–338.

Friere, P. (1970). *Pedagogy of the oppressed*. Ch 12 in Flinders, David & Thornton, Stephen. (Eds.) *The Curriculum Studies Reader*, 2nd ed. New York: Routledge.

Gaztambide-Fernández, R. A. (2012). Decolonization and the pedagogy of solidarity. *Decolonization: Indigeneity, Education & Society*, *1*(1). 41–67.

Lo, J. (2017). Empowering young people through conflict and conciliation: Attending to the political and agonism in democratic education. *Democracy & Education*, *25*(1), 1–9.

Lowe, L. (1991). Heterogeneity, hybridity, multiplicity: Marking Asian American differences. *Diaspora*, *1*(1), 24–44.

Mahtani, M. (2002). "Interrogating the hyphen-nation: Canadian multicultural policy and 'mixed race' identities". *Social Identities*, *8*(1), 67–90.

Osanami Törngren, S., Irastorza, N. & Rodríguez-García, D. (2019). Understanding multiethnic and multiracial experiences globally: towards a conceptual framework of mixedness. *Journal of Ethnic and Migration Studies*, 1–19.

Papastergiadis, N. (1995). Restless hybrids. *Third Text*, *9*(32), 9–18.

Pinar, W. (2004). *What Is Curriculum Theory?* L. Erlbaum Associates.

Pinar, W. (1975). *Currere: Toward reconceptualization*. In W. Pinar (Ed.), *Curriculum theorizing: The reconceptualists* (pp. 396–414). Berkeley, CA: McCutchan.

Pollock, D.C. and Van Reken, R.E. (1999). *The Third Culture Kid Experience: Growing Up among Worlds*. Intercultural Press.

Reyes, G. T. (2019). Pedagogy of and towards decoloniality. *Encyclopedia of Teacher Education*. Singapore: Springer.

Rockquemore, K.A., Brunsma, D.L. and Delgado, D.J. (2009), "Racing to theory or retheorizing race? Understanding the struggle to build a multiracial identity theory." *Journal of Social Issues*, *65*: 13–34.

Root, M. P. P. (1998). Experiences and processes affecting racial identity development: Preliminary results from the biracial sibling project. *Cultural Diversity and Mental Health*, *4*, 237–247.

Said, E. (1996). *Representations of the Intellectual. The 1993 Reith Lectures*. New York: Vintage.

Said, E. W. (1978). *Orientalism*. New York: Pantheon Books.

Sant, E. (2019). Democratic education: A theoretical review (2006–2017). *Review of Educational Research*, *89*(5), 655–696.

Sium, A., Desai, C., & Ritskes, E. (2012). Towards the 'tangible unknown': Decolonization and the Indigenous future. *Decolonization: Indigeneity, Education & Society*, *1*(1), I–XIII.

Statistics Canada. (2019, June 17). Data tables, 2016 Census. Retrieved from https://www12.statcan.gc.ca/census-recensement/2016/dp-pd/dt-td/Rp-eng.cfm?.

Taylor, D. (1991). Transculturating transculturation. *Performing Arts Journal, 13*(2), 90–104.

Tuck, E., & Yang, K. W. (2012). Decolonization is not a metaphor. *Decolonization: Indigeneity, Education & Society, 1*(1). 1–40.

Wah, F. (1996). Half-bred poetics. *Absinthe*, 9 (2), 60–66.

CHAPTER 3

# Transnational Labour Migration of Filipino Nurses to Canada

*An Organized Historical, Institutional and Social Process*

Valerie G. Damasco

## 1     Introduction

Scholars who have investigated the labour migration history of Filipinos who arrived in Canada during the mid-twentieth century, which includes those who were hired in nursing, employed conventional theoretical approaches to explain the macro-level factors that have caused their movement. Such frameworks include grounded theory (see Glaser & Strauss, 1967; Ralph, Birks, & Chapman, 2015; Strauss & Corbin, 1994), dual labour market theory (see Arango, 2000; Castles & Miller, 1998; Goss & Lindquist, 1995; Massey et al.,1993, 1994; Portes & Böröcz, 1989), and neo-classical economic theory (see Arango, 2000; Castles, 2000, 2002; de Haas, 2010a; de Haas,2010b;, 2011).

Common to all the studies, micro-level findings have been explained by macro-level processes. Macro-level developments, including amendments to Canadian immigration and healthcare policy, have been considered principal factors that prompted micro-level findings, including the labour mobility of Filipino immigrants, their patterns of employment, and the occupations in which they were hired. More importantly, analyses have principally been fixated on the period of the 1960s. Indeed, while these frameworks are useful for understanding the broader trends pertaining to the movement of Filipino nurses to Canada. However, the same methodological and analytical approaches cannot be applied to the complex and interrelated nature of, for example, *how* the liberalization of Canadian immigration policy and *how* the expansion of the healthcare system prompted the enlistment of Filipino nurses to Canada during the 1950s and 1960s (see Damasco, 2012).

In explaining how their transnational labour migration process was organized during the mid-twentieth century, I applied five distinct theoretical foundations: (i) stratification theory (Castles, de Haas, & Miller, 2013; de Haas, 2007); (ii) historical-structural theory of immigration (Wood, 1982), particularly dependency theory (Frank, 1966; 1969) and world systems theory (Wallerstein, 1974, 1979, 1980); (iii) social networks theory, as it pertains to migrant social networks (i.e., personal and professional networks) (Boyd, 1989) and migrant networks as a form of social capital (Coleman, 1988; Ryan et al., 2008; Paloni et al., 2001; Portes, 1998; Portes & Landolt, 2000); and (iv) systems theory of migration (Boyd, 1989; Fawcett, 1989; Kritz, Lim, & Zlotnik, 1992; Mabogunje, 1970; Zlotnik, 1992).

I argue that a theoretical framework that comprises a single theory or one level of inductive theoretical analysis is insufficient for analyzing or explaining the labour migration process. Rather than simply claiming that macro-level developments, such as the liberalization of Canadian immigration policy, influenced the arrival of nurses, a deeper investigation is required, which underscores the complexity of the labour migration process. This entails employing a more nuanced theoretical and conceptual framework, using a meso-level analytical framework, which examines the complexity as well as the *dialectical* and *bidirectional* manifestation of macro-level processes on micro-level findings.

## 2  Complementary Approaches: Using *A Priori* and *A Posteriori* Theorization in Analyzing Transnational Labour Migration Processes

### 2.1  *Challenging* A Priori *Theorization*

The manner by which I investigated and discovered the historical social processes that manifested during the 1950s and 1960s was prompted by my interest to understand how knowledge is produced. Elsewhere in my writings, I have argued that recognizing the origins of knowledge production is crucial for determining how particular conditions or situations in society have materialized, including how the labour migration of Filipino nurses to Canada was organized during the 1950s and 1960s (see Damasco, 2012), a period when efforts have mainly been focused on recruiting 'white' immigrants. How we conceive of social phenomena can be characterized by *a priori* or *a posteriori* theorization.

According to Lash (2009), *a priori* to *a posteriori* theorization "moves from the question of how knowledge is possible to the question of how society is possible" (p. 175). Scholars who have examined the labour migration history of skilled workers and professionals from the Philippines who arrived in Canada during the mid-twentieth century, which include those who were hired in the nursing profession, argue that the liberalization of Canadian immigration policy enabled the admission and employment of Filipino nurses in teaching and municipal hospitals across the country during the 1960s (see Aranas, 1983;

Bejar, 2006; Boschma et al., 2012; Bustamante, 1984; Chen, 1998a; Cusipag & Buenafe, 1993; Kelly, 2006; Laquian, 1973; Ronquillo, 2010, 2012; Ronquillo et al., 2011). However, the data from my study confirm that several Filipino nurses began working in Canadian hospitals prior to this period, commencing in the late 1950s.

Thus, I questioned why there has been a continuous preoccupation with the period of the 1960s and why the liberalization of Canadian immigration policy has been deemed as the cause of this movement. I characterize this presumption as an *a priori* theorization of migration, whereby immigration policy is assumed to have initiated the admissibility of prospective immigrants. More importantly, an analysis as such is *independent of* exhaustive empirical evidence, since macro-level factors are perceived to be the ultimate, and often, the only cause of what predisposed the enlistment of workers. According to Lash (2009),

> [A] *priori* thinking starts from axioms that are self-evident, that are most indubitable, and proceeds analytically, without undue reference to experience, to making statements. It of course makes arguments as to why those assumptions are more or less indubitable (p. 176).

Examples of what constitutes ideological definitions, for instance, are macro-level factors, such as the liberalization of Canadian immigration policy.

The immigration policy of 1962 supposedly eliminated racial discrimination in the evaluation of prospective immigrants. Applicants supposedly were no longer assessed according to race or national origin (see Abu-Laban, 1998; Borjas, 1990; Corbett, 1963; Hawkins, 1988; Kelly & Trebilcock, 1998; Parai, 1975; Satzewich, 1989). Instead, the skill set of the individual determined their admittance in Canada. This also applied to how Filipino nurses were evaluated (see Bustamante, 1984; Chen, 1998a, 1998b; Cusipag & Buenafe, 1993; Laquian, 1973). Turning to the Canadian Points System of 1967, prospective immigrants were evaluated based on an objective measure. Immigration authorities prioritized individuals according to level of education achieved, occupational skills, employment prospective, age, proficiency in English, and other characteristics (see Abu-Laban, 1998; Borjas, 1990; Coulson & Devoretz, 1993; Green & Green, 1995, 1999; Hawkins, 1988; Knowles, 2016).

I argue that macro-level arguments are only useful to a certain degree for explaining micro-level findings. According to the data from my study, provisions under the liberal Canadian immigration policy of the 1960s were not the only method of evaluation or assessment that were used to determine the admissibility and suitability of prospective Filipino nurses for the nursing profession in Canada. Further, I maintain that Canadian immigration policy or amendments to the healthcare system were not solely the conditions responsible for substantiating the migration of my participants to Canada. My analysis reveals that Canadian immigration authorities and officials employed *nonstandardized practices* in the evaluation of their admissibility. More importantly, other salient factors, including the colonial history of the Philippines (i.e., development of American colonial nursing education in the Philippines), social class and processes of stratification, the accumulation and conversion of capital into other forms (i.e., human, economic, cultural, and social capital), and social networks (i.e., personal and professional networks), contributed to their migration and mobility to Canada and the United States.

Thus, analyzing the transnational labour migration process according to *a priori* principles of theorization is problematic as it renders a limited understanding of, for example, *how* immigration authorities and officials evaluated cases. Claiming that the liberalization of Canadian immigration policy determined their successful admission prompts the false assumption that the only method of evaluation that was utilized to assess their suitability in the nursing profession in Canada were the stipulations associated with the immigration regulation to which they were obliged to adhere. Further, it propagates the belief that simply satisfying the requirements of the immigration policy and the labour market demands would consider them suitable employees. If in fact this were the case, then foreign-trained nurses from countries other than the United States and the Philippines should have similarly been granted immediate admission and employment in Canada.

My review of historical documents from Canadian provincial and federal archival repositories reveals that nurses from Eastern Europe were granted immediate admission. However, they faced issues in their attempt to provide healthcare services since they lacked the ability to converse with their patients in English. Filipino nurses, on the other hand, were equipped with the training and skills to successfully function in Canadian healthcare institutions or, in other words, possessed the cultural and human capital. Canadian immigration authorities and officials as well as hospital administrators regarded Filipino nurses a valuable source of skilled labour and ideal employees to assume positions that needed to be promptly filled (see Bustamante, 1984).

For example, while reviewing historical documents I obtained from provincial and federal archival repositories, I learned that Canadian hospitals began recruiting nurses from Eastern Europe during the labour shortage. However, as I discussed above, the nurses could not perform efficiently as they lacked the ability to communicate with patients in English. Consequently, translators were hired to assist them (Archives of Ontario, RG 76-3-0-593). A workplace arrangement or accommodation as such, however, did not suffice since it resulted in delays in healthcare service delivery. Thus, resorting to other effective and efficient solutions to alleviate the labour shortages of the 1950s and 1960s was crucial. It was not long after Filipino nurses arrived, all of whom easily transitioned into the North American healthcare setting.

### 2.2 Incorporating A Posteriori *Theorization*

Based on the findings from my research (see Damasco, 2012) and my analysis of the data from this study, I argue that federal and provincial authorities in immigration and healthcare institutions, despite the policies and regulations that were enforced, *adapted* their practices informally to enable Filipino nurses enter the country. In my research, for example, I conducted life history interviews with retired nurses who were hired from the Philippines to work in hospitals in Toronto during the mid to the late 1960s. Further, I analyzed historical documents which I obtained from the Archives of Ontario. The correspondence revealed that Canadian immigration authorities along with airline officials, and in coordination with hospitals in the Philippines, strategically organized recruitment practices to enlist nurses from the Philippines. However, this would not have been possible without the intervention of former Ontario health minister, Dr. Matthew Dymond and the initiatives performed by representatives of Canadian Pacific Airlines, as the College of Nurses of Ontario had initially denied them from writing the registration and licensure examination (see Damasco, 2012).

Similarly, the data from my doctoral research suggest that from the late 1950s to the latter years of the 1960s, Canadian federal immigration authorities administered policies, practices, or recommendations based on the success or, in other circumstances, the failure of previous regulations that were utilized in the recruitment of former waves of foreign-trained nurses. I characterize this presumption as an *a posteriori* theorization of immigration, whereby policies or regulations are analyzed to determine their influence on the admissibility of prospective skilled immigrants. More importantly, an analysis as such is *dependent on* experience and exhaustive empirical evidence, and macro-level factors are not considered the ultimate cause of, for example, what predisposed the enlistment of workers. As Lash (2009) explains, "*a posteriori* judgements proceed in the opposite direction. You start not from indubitable assumptions but from experience […] You begin from sense-impressions. Then you reason synthetically and make judgements" (p. 176).

Calliste (1993), for example, examined the manner by which Canadian authorities and officials enforced immigration policies and explains that they evaluated prospective nurses based on race and country of origin. Caucasian nurses, she emphasizes, were admitted as permanent settlers while Caribbean nurses were permitted "as cases of exceptional merit" (p. 87). Additionally, to further Canada's trade interest in the British Caribbean, she argues that Canadian immigration policies were subsequently altered. This is similar to the findings of my doctoral research whereby immigration practices during the 1950s and 1960s were altered and tailored to enable Filipino nurses to work in the country, despite Canada's efforts in prioritizing immigrants from Europe and the United States. Employing a practice as such, ironically, enabled Canada to maintain access to mining initiatives in the Philippines. At the same time, the data confirm that Filipino nurses were admitted under *both* provisions, as permanent settlers and as cases of exceptional merit.

Although several scholars argue that the liberalization of Canadian immigration policy facilitated the enlistment of Filipino nurses in Canada (see Bustamante, 1984; Chen, 1998a, 1998b; Cusipag & Buenafe, 1993; Laquian, 1973), I argue that institutional practices, which I define as *latent amendments*, expedited their admission and appointment in hospitals. The data in my study confirm that, what I characterize as *interdependent migration systems*, which comprise *formal practices* and *informal practices*, facilitated the movement of my participants. I define *formal practices* as activities that simply operate in the background of the labour migration process. They are institutional and bureaucratic in nature and comprise the work or activities of: (i) *immigration authorities and officials* who are visible or invisible actors in the process; and (ii) *other institutional authorities and officials* who are predominantly invisible actors. *Informal practices*, on the other hand, are activities that operate in the foreground. They constitute the work or activities of, for example, travel or recruitment agents in the Philippines who were mainly invisible in the process. Although their work was invisible, according to the data, they were actively involved in the labour migration process and served an important function. They processed the immigration and employment applications of my participants in conjunction with American or Canadian immigration officials and administrators of hospitals to which they applied.

Further, I argue that other crucial factors, in addition to those prescribed by Canadian immigration policy, which were unrelated to the formal evaluation procedure, nonetheless dictated the labour migration process of my participants. Such influences predisposed them to be suitable employees for positions in the nursing profession in Canada. For instance, colonial relations between the Philippines and the United States since the early 1900s prompted the development of nursing education. Several of my participants pursued a diploma or baccalaureate program in nursing and eventually a career in nursing. They were trained in first-tier and second-tier private nursing schools in the Philippines, which were founded according to an American model of curriculum and clinical practice. In addition to the training they received, other factors, which were pertinent for their social and labour mobility, involve the accumulation and aggregate of capital (e.g., economic, cultural, human), the mobilization of social capital, as well as access to personal and professional networks. I refer to these influences as *latent prerequisites*, which not only influenced how they navigated the labour migration process but also the trajectories they assumed.

## 3 Macro-, Meso- and Micro-level Relations in the Transnational Labour Migration Process

As I stated elsewhere, I argue that the transnational labour migration of my participants was not prompted solely by *macro-level structural factors* (e.g., colonial relations between nation states, immigration policy, healthcare policy) or by *micro-level individual decisions* (e.g., expectations, decisions, personal motivations to immigrate) but by the interaction of both and, more importantly, the incorporation of *meso-level social interactions* (e.g., accumulation and aggregate of capital, mobilization of social capital, migrant social networks, as well as access to professional and personal networks) (see Deaux, 2006).

My decision to use a methodological framework that comprises institutional ethnography (Campbell & Gregor, 2008; Smith, 1987, 2005a, 2005b, 2006, 2014) and historical methods (see Ginzburg, 2013), including oral history interviews (see Anderson et al., 1987; Boyd, 2015; Gluck & Patai, 2013; Layman, 2009; Smith, 2003; Summerfield, 2004; Thompson & Bornat, 2017) and archival research methods (see Brothman, 2002; Cook, 2001; Derrida, 1996; Ketelaar, 2001; Menninger, 1996; Millar, 2006; Schwartz & Cook, 2002) complements the complexity and multi-level analysis of the study.

More importantly, utilizing a multi-method approach as such enabled meso-level social and institutional relations to emerge. DeVault (2008a) explains the analytical objectives of utilizing institutional ethnography as a methodology,

> The goal [of institutional ethnographic research] is not simply to assert a macro sociological (or structural) argument to frame micro sociological findings: [sic] institutional ethnographers reject that distinction, and, as the analysis moves from one setting to another, the researcher strives always to attend to the activities of the people constituting and operating institutional machinery (p. 4).

First, at the *macro-level*, how institutions within a society affect the population in general is examined. For example, institutions including the economy, government, and education, which are interrelated and closely associated in their values, form the boundaries of the macro-level of society, the culture from which a society originates. The *micro-level*, in contrast, comprises the daily actions or activities and interactions of individuals. At this level of analysis, for example, social roles or positions that individuals assume, in addition to how they respond to and understand the institutions in which they are implicated, are examined. The focus therefore is on how people within a society or institutions interact as opposed to analyzing their social behaviour. For example, social institutions such as the family and education, which are the more intimate societies that individuals automatically identify with first, are micro-level groupings. Lastly, at the *meso-level*, divisions within societies and how they are segregated or stratified by, for example, ethnicity and social class, are examined. More importantly, the meso-level is the reconciliation between macro and micro level factors and how divisions and associations within societies form is analyzed. For example, communities or neighbourhoods, which are mid-sized groups, constitute meso-level societies.

Given the complexity of transnational labour migration processes, Guarnizo and Smith (1998) argue that a more successful approach for future transnational research would be to begin from "a meso-structural vantage point, the point at which institutions interact with structural and instrumental processes" (p. 25). Due to the limitations of macro-level definitions or arguments, which have defined the labour migration of professionals and skilled workers from the Philippines to Canada during the mid-twentieth century, I thus applied a meso-level analytical framework to examine the data in the study. Returning to the argument made by Guarnizo and Smith (1998), they maintain that using a meso-structural vantage point "would facilitate incorporating the effects of macro-structural processes and those generated by micro-structures and practices" (p. 25).

Further, they emphasize that beginning from a macro-structural vantage point may lead to an overgeneralization that produces "grand theories" (p. 25, emphasis in original). Equally, analyses that begin at the micro-structural level, whereby "personal knowledge" is privileged, fail to connect human intentions to social structure and historical change (Guarnizo & Smith, 1998, p. 26). They argue that one of the most complicated components to examine is the meso-dimension of transnationalism. Understanding transnationalism from below and above, they emphasize, requires a systemic study the of the trans-local micro-reproduction of transnational ties which shows how transnational networks function.

## 4 Importance of Meso-level Social Relations in the Transnational Labour Migration Process

As I discussed in previous sections of this chapter, a micro and macro framework of investigation and analysis prevails in studies that have examined the labour migration of professionals and skilled workers from the Philippines to Canada. As Faist (2010) explains, "Most theoretical efforts have mostly focused either on global structural factors including migration and refugee movements (macro-theories) or on factors motivating individuals to move (micro-theories)" (p. 60). Further, he emphasizes, "the importance of the meso-level in international migration," the level of analysis between individuals and larger structures (Faist, 2010, p. 60). As I noted elsewhere in this chapter, a meso-level of analysis focuses on the social relations or social ties between individuals in kinship groups, educational institutions, workplaces, and formal organizations in a nation state.

There are bodies of literature that focus on meso-level analyses of transnational labour migration. For instance, according to Portes (1998), the processes of immigrant incorporation are studied largely in economic sociology. There is also vast literature on migrant social networks (see Boyd, 1989; Castles & Miller, 2003; Faist & Ozveren, 2004; Jordan & Duvell, 2003; Massey et al., 1993) and how such associations are implicated in migration systems (see Boyd, 1989; Fawcett, 1989; Kritz & Zlotnik, 1992; Kritz, Lim, & Zlotnik, 1992; Zlotnik, 1992), both which, I argue, are crucial elements in explaining transnational migration. Using a meso-level of analysis, in addition to focusing on the social relations between individuals and institutions, how intermediate structures (e.g., migrant networks) systemically pattern decision making, which are shaped by the actions of potential and actual migrants as well as by larger social structures (Faist, 2010), are examined. Regarding social capital, Faist (2010) explains that at the meso-level, how social capital is created, accumulated, and mobilized by collectives and networks within particular macro-conditions is investigated. Additionally, how social capital is made available to individuals, members, and non-members of each collective is also examined. Additionally, he argues that "answers to pressing issues of international migration can be found in supplementing the dominant micro- and macro-sociological theories and including an explicit social relational perspective" (Faist, 2010, p. 89).

### References

Abu-Laban, Y. (1998). Welcome/Stay Out: The Contradiction of Canadian Integration and Immigration Policies at the Millennium. *Canadian Ethnic Studies Journal, 30*(3), 190–211.

Anderson, K., Armitage, S., Jack, D., & Wittner, J. (1987). Beginning Where We Are: Feminist Methodology in Oral History. *The Oral History Review, 15*(1), 103–127.

Aranas, M. Q. (1983). *The Dynamics of Filipino Immigrants in Canada.* Edmonton, Alberta: Coles Printing Co. Ltd.

Arango, J. (2000). Explaining Migration: A Critical View. *International Social Science Journal, 52*(165), 283–296.

Bejar, J. (2006). *Transnational Communities: Filipina Nurses in Rural Manitoba, 1965–1970.* Unpublished Master's Thesis. Immigration and Settlement Studies. Ryerson University. Toronto.

Boschma, G., Santiago, M. L., Choy, C. C., & Ronquillo, C. (2012). Health Worker Migration in Canada: Histories, Geographies, and Ethics. 1–30. http://mbc.metropolis.net/assets/uploads/files/wp/2012/WP12-02.pdf.

Boyd, J. (2015). His Narrative, My History: Problematising Subjectivity and the Uses of Oral History Interviews. *Oral History, 43*(2), 62–69.

Boyd, M. (1989). Family and Personal Networks in International Migration: Recent Developments and New Agendas. *International Migration Review, 23*(3), 638–670.

Brothman, B. (2002). Afterglow: Conceptions of Record and Evidence in Archival Discourse. *Archival Science, 2*, 311–342.

Bustamante, R. E. (1984). Filipino Canadians: A Growing Community. *Polyphony, 6*, 168–171.

Campbell, M. L., & Gregor, F. (2008). *Mapping Social Relations: A Primer in Doing Institutional Ethnography.* Toronto, Ontario: University of Toronto Press.

Castles, S. (2000). International Migration at the Beginning of the Twenty-First Century: Global Trends and Issues. *International Social Science Journal, 52*(165), 269–281.

Castles, S. (2002). Migration and Community Formation Under Conditions of Globalization. *International Migration Review, 36*(4), 1143–1168.

Castles, S., de Haas, H., & Miller, M. J. (2013). *The Age of Migration: International Population Movements in the Modern World* (5th ed.). London: Palgrave Macmillan.

Castles, S., & Miller, M. J. (1998). *The Age of Migration: International Population Movements in the Modern World.* London: Macmillan.

Castles, S., & Miller, M. J. (2003). *The Age of Migration: International Population Movements in the Modern World.* Basingstoke: Palgrave.

Chen, A. B. (1998a). *From Sunbelt to Snowbelt: Filipinos in Canada.* Calgary, Alberta: Canadian Ethnic Studies Association, University of Calgary.

Chen, A. B. (1998b). Filipinos. In *Encyclopedia of Canada's Peoples*.

Coleman, J. S. (1988). Social Capital in the Creation of Human Capital. *American Journal of Sociology, 94*, S95–S120.

Cook, T. (2001). Archival Science and Postmodernism: New Formulations for Old Concepts. *Archival Science, 1*, 3–24.

Corbett, D. (1963). Canada's Immigration Policy, 1957–1962. *International Journal, 18*(2), 166–180.

Coulson, R. G., & Devoretz, D. J. (1993). Human Capital Content of Canadian Immigrants: 1967–1987. *Canadian Public Policy / Analyse de Politiques, 19*(4), 357–366.

Cusipag, R. J., & Buenafe, M. C. (1993). *Portrait of Filipino Canadians in Ontario (1960–1990)*. Etobicoke, Ontario: Kalayaan Media Ltd.

Damasco, V. (2012). The Recruitment of Filipino Healthcare Professionals to Canada in the 1960s. In R. S. Coloma, B. McElhinny, E. Tungohan, J. P. C. Catungal, & L. M. Davidson (Eds.), *Filipinos in Canada: Disturbing Invisibility*. Toronto: University of Toronto Press.

de Haas, H. (2007). *Migration and Development: A Theoretical Perspective*. Paper presented at the Transnationalisation and Development(s): Towards a North-South Perspective, Center for Interdisciplinary Research, Bielefeld, Germany.

de Haas, H. (2010a). Migration and Development: A Theoretical Perspective. *The International Migration Review, 44*(1), 227–264.

de Haas, H. (2010b). The Internal Dynamics of Migration Processes: A Theoretical Inquiry. *Journal of Ethnic and Migration Studies, 36*(10), 1587–1617.

de Haas, H. (2011). The Determinants of International Migration: Conceptualizing Policy, Origin and Destination Effects. *IMI Working Papers*, 1–35. https://ora.ox.ac.uk/objects/uuid:0b10d9e8-810e-4f49-b76f-ba4d6b1faa86.

Deaux, K. (2006). *To Be an Immigrant*. New York: Russell Sage Foundation.

Derrida, J. (1996). *Archive Fever: A Freudian Impression*. Chicago: University of Chicago Press.

DeVault, M. L. (2008a). Introduction. In M. L. DeVault (Ed.), *People at Work: Life, Power, and Social Inclusion in the New Economy* (pp. 1–22). New York: New York University Press.

Faist, T. (2010). The Crucial Meso-Level. In M. Martiniello & J. Rath (Eds.), *Selected Studies in International Migration and Immigrant Incorporation* (pp. 59–90): Amsterdam University Press.

Faist, T. (2010). Towards Transnational Studies: World Theories, Transnationalisation and Changing Institutions. *Journal of Ethnic and Migration Studies, 36*(10), 1665–1687.

Faist, T., & Ozveren, E. (Eds.). (2004). *Transnational Social Spaces: Agents, Networks and Institutions*. Aldershot: Ashgate.

Fawcett, J. T. (1989). Networks, Linkages, and Migration Systems. *International Migration Review, 23*(3), 671-680.

Frank, A. G. (1969). *Capitalism and Underdevelopment in Latin America*. New York: Monthly Review Press.

Ginzburg, C. (2013). *Clues, Myths, and the Historical Method*. Baltimore: Johns Hopkins University Press.

Glaser, B. G., & Strauss, A. L. (1967). *The Discovery of Grounded Theory: Strategies for Qualitative Research*. New Jersey: Aldine.

Gluck, S. B., & Patai, D. (Eds.). (2013). *Women's Words: The Feminist Practice of Oral History*. New York: Routledge.

Goss, J., & Lindquist, B. (1995). Conceptualizing International Labor Migration: A Structuration Perspective. *The International Migration Review, 29*(2), 317–351.

Green, A. G., & Green, D. A. (1995). Canadian Immigration Policy: The Effectiveness of the Point System and Other Instruments. *Canadian Journal of Economics, 28*(4b), 1006–1041.

Green, A. G., & Green, D. A. (1999). The Economic Goals of Canada's Immigration Policy: Past and Present. *Canadian Public Policy / Analyse de Politiques, 25*(4), 425–451.

Guarnizo, L. E., & Smith, M. P. (1998). The Locations of Transnationalism. In M. P. Smith & L. E. Guarnizo (Eds.), *Transnationalism from Below* (pp. 3–34). New Jersey: Transaction Publishers.

Hawkins, F. (1988). *Canada and Immigration. Public Policy and Public Concern.* Kingston and Montreal: McGill-Queen's University Press.

Jordan, B., & Düvell, F. (2003). *Migration: The Boundaries of Equality and Justice.* Cambridge: Polity.

Kelly, N., & Trebilcock, M. J. (1998). *The Making of the Mosaic: A History of Canadian Immigration Policy.* Toronto, Ontario: University of Toronto Press.

Kelly, P. F. (2006). Filipinos in Canada: Economic Dimensions of Immigration and Settlement. *CERIS Working Paper No. 48*, 1–43. http://www.ceris.metropolis.net/wp-content/uploads/pdf/research_publication/working_papers/wp48.pdf.

Ketelaar, E. (2001). Tacit Narratives: The Meaning of Archives. *Archival Science, 1*, 131–141.

Knowles, V. (2016). *Strangers at Our Gates: Canadian Immigration and Immigration Policy, 1540–2015* (4th Ed.). Toronto: Dundurn Press.

Kritz, M. M., Lim, L. L., & Zlotnik, H. (Eds.). (1992). *International Migration Systems: A Global Approach.* Oxford: Clarendon Press.

Laquian, E. R. (1973). *A Study of Filipino Immigration to Canada, 1962–1972* (Vol. Publication 2). Ottawa: United Council of Filipino Associations in Canada.

Lash, S. (2009). Afterword: In Praise of the A Posteriori. Sociology and the Empirical. *European Journal of Social Theory, 12*(1), 175–187.

Layman, L. (2009). Reticence in Oral History Interviews. *Oral History Review, 36*(2), 207–230.

Mabogunje, A. L. (1970). Systems Approach to a Theory of Rural–Urban Migration. *Geographical Analysis, 2*(1), 1–18.

Massey, D. S., Arango, J., Hugo, G., Kouaouci, A., Pellegrino, A., & Taylor, J. E. (1993). Theories of International Migration: A Review and Appraisal. *Population and Development Review, 19*(3), 431–466.

Massey, D. S., Arango, J., Hugo, G., Kouaouci, A., Pellegrino, A., & Taylor, J. E. (1994). An Evaluation of International Migration Theory: The North American Case. *Population and Development Review, 20*(4), 699-751.

Menninger, W. W. (1996). Memory and History: What Can You Believe? *Archival Issues, 21*(2), 97–106.

Millar, L. (2006). An Obligation of Trust: Speculations on Accountability and Description. *The American Archivist, 69*, 60–78.

Palloni, A., Massey, D. S., Ceballos, M., Espinosa, K., & Spittel, M. (2001). Social Capital and International Migration: A Test Using Information on Family Networks. *American Journal of Sociology, 106*(5), 1262–1298.

Parai, L. (1975). Canada's Immigration Policy, 1962–74. *International Migration Review, 9*(4), 449–477.

Portes, A. (1998). Social Capital: Its Origins and Applications in Modern Sociology. *Annual Review of Sociology, 24*(1), 1-24.

Portes, A., & Böröcz, J. (1989). Contemporary Immigration: Theoretical Perspectives on Its Determinants and Modes of Incorporation. *The International Migration Review, 23*(3), 606–630.

Portes, A., & Landolt, P. (2000). Social Capital: Promise and Pitfalls of its Role in Development. *Journal of Latin American Studies, 32*(2), 529-547.

Ralph, N., Birks, M., & Chapman, Y. (2015). The Methodological Dynamism of Grounded Theory. *International Journal of Qualitative Methods, 14*(4), 1–6.

Ronquillo, C. (2010). *Immigrant Filipino Nurses in Western Canada: An Exploration of Motivations and Migration Experiences Through Oral History.* (Unpublished Master's Thesis), University of British Columbia, Vancouver.

Ronquillo, C. (2012). Leaving the Philippines: Oral Histories of Nurses' Transition to Canadian Nursing Practice. *CJNR (Canadian Journal of Nursing Research), 44*(4), 96–115.

Ronquillo, C., Boschma, G., Wong, S. T., & Quiney, L. (2011). Beyond Greener Pastures: Exploring Contexts Surrounding Filipino Nurse Migration in Canada through Oral History. *Nursing Inquiry, 18*(3), 262–275.

Ryan, L., Sales, R., Tilki, M., & Siara, B. (2008). Social Networks, Social Support and Social Capital: The Experiences of Recent Polish Migrants in London. *Sociology, 42*(4), 672–690.

Satzewich, V. (1989). Racisms: The Reactions to Chinese Migrants in Canada at the Turn of the Century. *International Sociology, 4*(3), 311–327.

Schwartz, J. M., & Cook, T. (2002). Archives, Records, and Power: The Making of Modern Memory. *Archival Science, 2*, 1–19.

Smith, D. E. (1987). *The Everyday World as Problematic: A Feminist Sociology.* Athens: Northeastern University Press.

Smith, D. E. (2005a). Institutional Ethnography: *A Sociology for People*. Lanham, Maryland: AltaMira Press.

Smith, D. E. (2005b). Where We've Got To and Where We Can Go. In *Institutional Ethnography: A Sociology for People* (pp. 205–222). Lanham, Maryland: AltaMira Press.

Smith, D. E. (Ed.) (2006). *Institutional Ethnography as Practice*. Lanham, Maryland: Rowman & Littlefield Publishers, Inc.

Smith, D. E. (2014). Discourse as Social Relations: Sociological Theory and the Dialogic of Sociology. In D. E. Smith & S. M. Turner (Eds.), *Incorporating Texts into Institutional Ethnographies*. Toronto: University of Toronto Press.

Smith, R. C. (2003). Analytic Strategies for Oral History Interviews. In J. F. Gubrium & J. A. Holstein (Eds.), *Postmodern Interviewing* (pp. 203–224). Thousand Oaks, CA: SAGE Publications.

Strauss, A. L., & Corbin, J. (1994). Grounded Theory Methodology: An Overview. In N. K. Denzin & Y. S. Lincoln (Eds.), *Handbook of Qualitative Research* (pp. 273–284). Thousand Oaks: Sage Publications.

Summerfield, P. (2004). Culture and Composure: Creating Narratives of the Gendered Self in Oral History Interviews. *Cultural and Social History, 1*(1), 65–93.

Thompson, P., & Bornat, J. (2017). *The Voice of the Past: Oral History* (4th ed.). New York: Oxford University Press.

Wallerstein, I. (1974). *The Modern World System I, Capitalist Agriculture and the Origins of the European World Economy in the Sixteenth Century*. New York: Academic Press.

Wallerstein, I. (1979). *The Capitalist World Economy*. Cambridge: Cambridge University Press.

Wallerstein, I. (1980). *The Modern World System II, Mercantilism and the Consolidation of the European World-Economy, 1600–1750*. New York: Academic Press.

Wood, C. H. (1982). Equilibrium and Historical-Structural Perspectives on Migration. *International Migration Review, 16*(2), 298–319.

Zlotnik, H. (1992). Empirical Identification of International Migration Systems. In M. M. Kritz, L. L. Lim, & H. Zlotnik (Eds.), *International Migration Systems: A Global Approach* (pp. 19–40). Oxford: Clarendon Press.

CHAPTER 4

# Theorizing Asian Canada

*Rose Ann Torres*

## 1   Introduction

There are many ways of theorizing Asian Canada. In this chapter, I am using post-colonial theory and Indigenous feminism to imagine the lives of Asian Canadians in Canada. Theorizing is not only about using theory to understand our experiences but also using experience to understand the theory. It is a back-and-forth process. It is also about knowing the in-between and taken for granted practices. Theorizing is about understanding the self, others, institution, and the whole structural system. I believe all of these informs theorizing Asian Canada. In this chapter, I will be using the work of Said, Bhabha, and Spivak and Indigenous feminism to demonstrate how to theorize Asian Canada and Filipino Canadian. My hope is to see more work on how to theorize Asian Canada, in this way we can understand the deeper meanings of the experiences of Asian Canadians.

## 2   Said, Bhabha and Spivak

The work of postcolonial theorists, such as Said, Bhabha and Spivak, is central to in theorizing Asian Canada. In his book, *Orientalism*, Said (1978) provides a detailed explanation of the relationship between the Occident and the Orient. This relationship is one of power, of domination and, of varying degrees, a complex hegemony (Said 1978, p. 133). Said is able to encapsulate the treatment of the Orientals by the West. The West asserts that they have the power to represent the Orientals. The West ensures that the Oriental is totally and completely as inferior in terms of representation. Said (1978) further explains how the Oriental culture is being portrayed:

> Along with all other peoples variously designated as backward, degenerated, uncivilized, and retarded, the Orientals were viewed in a framework constructed out of biological determinism and moral-political admonishment. The Oriental was linked thus to elements in Western society (delinquents, the insane, women, the poor) having in common an identity best

described as lamentably alien. Orientals were rarely seen or looked at; they were seen through, analyzed not as citizens, or even people, but as problems to be solved or confined or-as the colonial powers openly coveted their territory-taken over ... Since the Oriental was a member of a subject race, he had to be subjected: it was that simple. (p. 207)

Said shows how the West demonized and criminalized the Orientals. He articulates here that the West perceives the Oriental as merely an animal and not worthy of recognition. Said employs historical texts in looking at how colonialism rules over the East. Subsequently, he states that the West's knowledge production in relation to the Oriental is racist, oppressive, ethnocentric, and manipulative, ideologically embedded, rationalized and portrays signs of imperial power (Childs & Williams 1997; Shahjahan 2005). He displays the Western way of treating other cultures in a fundamentally unacceptable manner. One of Said's very significant contributions is his warning about the need to be vigilant with respect to how the West produces knowledge related to the Orient. He points out how the West portrays universal knowledge as the knowledge that is from the West.

In addition, Said traces the discourse's discriminatory strategies across centuries and continents and into contemporary period (Childs & Williams 1997, p. 101). Said initiates energetic discussion on Colonial Discourse Analysis that is being theorized and argued over even today. However, according to Childs and Williams (1997), despite his contribution to colonial discourse, Said is being criticized on his analysis of Orientalism which is seen as —monolithic, totalizing, or just insufficiently nuanced, ignoring resistance within or outside the West, or the fact that the binary West/East divisions [project] outward, and thus [mask] splits within Western society (p. 115). Childs and Williams disagree with this criticism of Said and argue that —it is part of the persuasive power of Said's argument that it shows Orientalism marshalling texts which, while their form, content, aims, genre and disciplinary origins may be widely divergent, still work with negative, stereotyped or unexamined notions of cultural difference (p. 115). In fact, this study is in agreement with the assertion by Childs and Williams that Said lays a strong foundation of the analysis of the relationship between the West and the Orient, which could really help us understand the impact of colonization on the East. His profound colonial discourse analysis is a great tool to help us grasp the effect of colonization on the lives of the others.

The work of Said is relevant in theorizing Asian Canada because Asians in Canada have been represented in the text and perceived by (other occupied subjects). It explains where this perception comes from and also it teaches us that our analysis of how the Filipino Canadian women have been represented must be based on the historical imposition of colonial mentality among the subjugated. Yet still, it is easy to transpose blame onto the colonized subject, thereby playing a blame the victim game. We have to be aware that by doing this we are not really looking at the root of the issue. We are, instead, complying with the work of colonization. We end up becoming a conduit through which colonization and the independent ideational framework is sustained. We are no different from the colonizer and, as such, we end up becoming the handmaiden of oppression. It teaches us how the West creates the others to masquerade its political and economic agendas.

Bhabha and Said were apparently influenced by Foucault. In fact, they both employed Foucault as their starting points in exploring colonial relations. Evidently, Bhabha and Said are labeled as important proponents of post-colonial theory. However, they have different approaches to colonial discourse analysis. Said focuses his discussion on the relationship between the West and the East, colonizer and colonized, latent and manifest as Orientalism looks at the differences between them and resistance they faced. Bhabha centres his colonial discourse analysis on exploring the similarities of the colonizer and the colonized and points out, for example, that stereotypes are the fundamental point of colonial subjectification for both sides (Childs & Williams 1997, p. 122). He employs psychoanalysis and deconstruction in analyzing colonial relations.

Bhabha (1994 argues that the objective of colonial discourse is to construe the colonized as a population of degenerate types on the basis of racial origin, in order to justify conquest and establish systems of administration and instructions (p. 70). In looking at Bhabha's work, one cannot fail to see how he explores the process of subjectification. He examines the notion of ambivalence, which means to be in —two places at once, such as to be colonizer and colonized (Childs & William 1997).

The result of ambivalence to the colonizer is anxiety. Colonial identity is not only for the colonizer but also for the colonized. For Bhabha, the notion of colonial identity that arises between the colonizer and the colonized is problematic. It is problematic in the sense that it is of a violent nature. The colonizer is not ready to recognize the existence of the colonized, yet the colonizer has the desire of being colonized. This, the ambivalent identification outcome to the colonizer, is both a terrifying and a craving feeling. In this context, we can see that Bhabha balances his analysis of colonial discourse with both subjectivity and consciousness. Indeed, Bhabha's concern is to problematize the authority of colonial discourse (ibid).

We can see that Bhabha's work is focused on postcolonial identity. In looking at the postcolonial identity, he highlights the notion of hybridity. He states that:

> Hybridity is the revaluation of the assumption of colonial identity through the repetition of discriminatory identity effects ... It unsettles the mimetic or narcissistic demands of colonial power but reimplicates its identification in strategies of subversion that turn the gaze of the discriminated back upon the eye of power. For the colonial hybrid is the articulation of the ambivalent space where the rite power is enacted on the site of desire, making its objects at once disciplinary and disseminatory or, in my mixed metaphor a negative transparency. (pp. 34–35)

Using the notion of hybridity in the analysis of colonial discourse, Bhabha argues that hybridity serves as a form of resistance to the colonized in both the postcolonial arena as well and the colonial. For Bhabha, hybridity is an introduction of cultural relativism or a synthesized position resolving the dialectic of two cultures but a return of the content and form of colonial authority that (Childs & Williams 1997, p. 134) terrorize authority with the use of recognition, its mimicry, its mockery (Childs & Williams 1997, p. 134, qtd. Bhabha 1993, p. 115). The result of hybridity to the colonizer is a feeling of paranoia and persecution (Childs & Williams 1997). Consequently, this notion of hybridity and mimicry in the representation of culture presents a form of resistance.

Bhabha explains that when we discuss cultural engagement, it is important to look at it in the context of a migration home and away. He further explains that it is not static, and that in the discussion of race, class and gender, we must be resituated in terms of borderlines, crossings, in between spaces, interstices, splits, and joins (ibid). Through this we can see that this shift in subject-positions constructs cultural differences. In Bhabha's view, cultural differences resulting from subsequent moving culminates into the Third Space. Cultural differences thus replace knowledge from the standpoint of the minority. Bhabha perceives this Third Space as a location where the agency belongs because cultural meaning can be constructed with no original meaning, hence there are only cultural differences (ibid).

The narrative by Spivak is one of the most important works to consider in terms of exploring Asian Canada. Spivak focuses on postcolonial studies by interrogating feminist, Marxist, deconstructive and psychoanalytic ideas through debate. Spivak's main objective is to broaden the analysis of colonial discourse from reappraisals of the nineteenth-century European territorial expansion into debates over neocolonial relations. She speaks of racism in the

West, and the international division of labour. She employs the term imperialism rather than colonialism (ibid). She looks at the ways in which imperialism has constructed narratives of history, geography, gender and identity (ibid). Her main concern is the location of the subject. That is why one of her objectives is to dislodge the notion of essentialism, because, for her, essentialism is a trap. Essentialism in postcolonial theory, according to Childs and Williams (1997), is a concrete, specific, unchanging meaning for a term such as British or West Indian: as opposed to a belief that words take on their meanings through usage and discursive power (p.159). The consequences of essentialism can be oppressive, exclusionary, exploitative and dehumanizing. However, Spivak also discusses strategic essentialism. Spivak (1990) explains strategic essentialism as you pick up the universal that will give the power to fight against the other side, and what you are throwing away by doing that is your theoretical purity (p. 12). In other words, we use strategic essentialism not just to theorize, but to change the world. Spivak is focused on who is representing whom and how.

According to Shahjahan (2005), Spivak struggles with the question whether or not it is possible to represent the Subaltern voice or oppressed voice without falling under the rubric of essentialism (p. 221). She warns not to romanticize and homogenize the subaltern subject. Spivak urges us to engage in imperial history and its aftermath. She describes imperial history as epistemic violence. Epistemic violence, as explained by Childs and Williams (1997), is a term used by Spivak to refer to the way in which colonial and other historiographical writings forcefully manipulate representations while usually purporting to be disinterested commentaries (p. 231). According to Spivak (1994), epistemic violence is the remotely orchestrated, far-flung, and heterogeneous project to constitute the colonial subject as Other (p.76). In other words, epistemic violence is an establishment of imperialism as the normative explanation and narrative reality (Childs & Williams 1997). Shahjahan (2005) refers to Parry, who explains that Spivak believes that imperialism's epistemic violence annihilated the old culture and left the colonized without the ground from which they could reply and confront the other (p. 222). Consequently, postcolonial theory and its political practices seek to build on the rich inheritance, (and) the radical legacy of its political determination, (as well as) its refusal to accept the status quo, its transformation of epistemologies, its establishment of new forms of discursive and political power (Young 2001, p. 427). It does not mean that postcolonial theory forgets colonization. Its focus is instead to look at the impact of colonialism at the present time by considering the past. Said, Bhabha and Spivak employ different ways of explaining the influence colonization to colonizers and the colonized. They use different categories to analyze colonialism. In other words, postcolonial theory designates a new critical discourse that thematizes issues emerging from colonial relations and their aftermath (Shohat 1992).

## 3   Indigenous Feminism

When we talk about feminism, we assume the empowerment of women and we consider how women are portrayed in society. The Filipino Canadian women phenomenological incision and formulation is different, the word feminism does not exist. What exists as their orienting compass is the directing coordinate that women are the cohesive elements of their community and that they have a role in acting as the social molecular bond of the society. It is understood that without these adhesive properties, their culture is at risk of extinction. Their work is to weave, knot, bond and add colour and pattern to the social cloth. The Filipino Canadian women's role in their social order is as significant; each gender plays instrumental roles which are fundamental to the community's social, political, economic, cultural and spiritual survival.

The Filipino Canadian women and men do not see each other as different, although each uniquely holds a different social role. The Filipino Canadian men (like all men) are incapable of childbirth, but this does not connote the inferiority of the men. Men and women comprehend that they are both instruments of the Supreme Being, who has preordained joint procreation. Child rearing is hence understood as conjoint coalescence to ensure that their child grows healthily and learns culture and traditions. Both women and men understand that it is imperative to be instrumental in instilling their community's cultural values in their children (Torres 2012 as this process actualizes both the character and the well-being of their children. Parents are meant to give guidelines to their children as agents of cultural transmission on social norms including traditional healing practices. This is done by both the men and the women since unity of the sexes is pivotal in the maintenance and sustenance of their beliefs. This kind of practice existed prior to the advent of settler immigration (Martin & Sunseri 2011; Agoncillo 1960; Oyewumi 1995). Smith (1999) explains how colonization had a tremendous impact on gender relations:

> Colonization is recognized as having had a destructive effect on Indigenous gender relations which reached out across all spheres of Indigenous society. Family organization, child rearing, political and spiritual life, work and social activities were all disordered by a colonial system which positioned its own women as the property of men with roles

> which were primarily domestic ... indigenous women hold an analysis of colonialism as a central tenet of an indigenous feminism ... colonialism has influenced indigenous men and had a detrimental effect on indigenous gender relations. (pp. 151–152)

The Filipino Canadian women must incessantly remind their people, that their culture affirms the equality of women and men. Subsequently, women emerge as agents of decolonization detaching their men from patriarchal beliefs that have been codified as part of the hidden curriculum through modeled experience of colonial subordination. They are diligent in refreshing the Filipino Canadian men's consciousness; going beyond the underlying colonial dynamics of occupation of mental space to remind their kin that such luminal division is a divisive practice meant to control all the Filipino Canadian women through gender polarization. Hence countering this would be a fundamental part of the resistance work against oppression.

The Filipino Canadian women "feminist" posit that abandoning this culture is a form of enslavement. The Filipino Canadian women are aware that if they start to agree on the notion of gender differences, then it would be too easy for them to assimilate into the dominant culture that is based on colonialist ideology. They also form the vanguard community defense response through continuous cultural education. This kind of activism is done not only by Filipino Canadian women in their community but also by other Indigenous communities around the world, such as the First Nations Peoples in Canada, the Maori Peoples in New Zealand and Aboriginals in Australia, and the Maasai Peoples in Kenya, among others.

This kind of work has been theorized by Aboriginal/Indigenous Women in the West. While this study does not claim that Filipino Canadian women have exactly the same issues and challenges, it underlines that there are common issues facing these communities. For example, colonization, imperialism, racism, land expropriation/swindling, assimilation, sexism, and classism, among others, have been major impediments to their survival. These are some of the issues that the Filipino Canadian women face, which are different from those faced by the non-Asian. They know how to strategically fight and apply precise tactical instruments in specific combat situations as feminist activists. They want to be seen as distinct from others and, as such, to be treated based on their unique lived experiences (Torres 1996). It is in this context that the Aboriginal/Indigenous feminism framework was used in this study to theorize the thematic guiding issues of the Filipino Canadian women. It is argued in this study that feminism does not exist as a concept in their community, rather the nature of their activism conforms to the definition of Aboriginal/

Indigenous feminism described by Green (2007), in which it is stated that Aboriginal/Indigenous feminism:

> ... seeks an Aboriginal liberation that includes women, and not just the conforming woman, but also the marginal and excluded, and especially the woman who has been excluded from her community by virtue of colonial legislation and socio-historical forces. Thus, Aboriginal feminism is a theoretical engagement with history and politics, as well as a practical engagement with contemporary social, economic, cultural and political issues. It is an ideological framework not only of intellectuals but also of activists. It is an authentic expression of political analysis and political will by those who express it, who are self-consciously aware of their identities as Aboriginal women - with emphasis on the unity of both words. Aboriginal feminism interrogates power structures and practices between and among Aboriginal and dominant institutions. It leads to praxis theoretically informed, politically self-conscious activism. (p. 25)

Aboriginal/Indigenous feminism is important in framing the Filipino Canadian women's lives because they are marginalized women as a consequence of colonial policies and historical forces. The voices and representational forms have been silenced, slandered and misrepresented. They also face very real economic issues (which one may conjecture, using a materialist frame, may be the root of their other issues of colonial marginalization). This concept of land ownership has acted as the legal basis for expropriation; territorial claims by colonization continue and pose multiple menaces for the Filipino Canadian women integrity, land and continuity. Illustrating a typical such scenario may assist comprehension: an official property owner lays claim to an ancestral land and dispossesses people. The result is that the non-propertied population regards each other with a mutual suspicion. This patronizing doctrine governed the Filipino Canadian women community. By driving a wedge between settlers and natives, suspicion is established against those seeking to appropriate land and extract surplus value from land, and labor. Oppressive policies are often implemented in this process. Again, this tactic is hardly unique. In the British historian John Keay's insightful work, *The Great Arc: The Dramatic Story of How India Was Mapped and How Everest Was Named* (Keay, 2000), he lays out how, under the nominal pretext of determining the precise arch and curvature of earth for science, British survey teams would impinge on varying and subsequent jurisdictions of what would become India. When the officials and officers of these lands attempted to assert territorial claims, the British army (conveniently) was waiting to save the poor scholars from the terrorists. The result was a patchwork system of accommodations which (were later) integrated into the colonial State of India. Besides expiated wealth proprietary in markets, the English colonial administration was able to extract considerable taxes on lands and then export, and resell (and re-tax) the extractive capital, agricultural products and goods in England, around her Empire and the rest of the world. Britain was surpassed in 1865 as the leading industrial power by the United States owing to industrialization of the mills and ordinance factories of the Northern US States bolstered in order to execute and support the US Civil War. Britain remained the title of world's richest country until it lost it to the United States in another war which changed colonial and other boundaries as well as national power dynamics: The First World War in 1917.

The basis by which Britain retained its advantage in wealth was the extractive wealth from her Empire, most especially India and the lands which were expropriated through de facto land swindling fronted by scientific work (of mapping the arc). Rhodes did much the same in the well-documented Anglo-American operations in Africa through the establishment of Anglo-American and British control of Southern Africa. Look globally and the pattern is the same through the forms vary slightly based on the corresponding successes of resistances. The Filipino Canadian women skirmish in this global warfare and gamesmanship of group power was, and is, spear-headed on the resistance side by unifying efforts among the Filipino Canadian women community. Their women inoculate their men and children against the maladies brought by this colonial mentality which has become engrained through schooling media misrepresentation. To eliminate this media misrepresentation is a primary objective of this wellbeing campaign. Aboriginal/Indigenous feminism is focused on the emancipation of women, and Filipino Canadian women can be a part of this liberation.

## 4   Conclusion

This chapter demonstrates how to theorize Asian Canada. This is not a form of prescription rather a way of imagining Asian Canadian experiences. Asian Canadian has multiple histories, experiences, realities, cultures, belies, traditions, ethnicities and forms of differences. Having this in mind, there is no way we can theorize Asian Canada in a linear way. And for me, I leave this theorizing to every Asian Canadian. All forms of theorizing need to be recognized.

## References

Agoncillo, T. (1960). *History of the Filipino People.* Quezon City, Philippines: Garotech.
Bhabha, H. (1994). *The Location of Culture.* London: Routledge.
Cannon, M., Suneri, L. (2011). *Racism, Colonialism, and Indigeneity in Canada: A Reader.* England: Oxford University Press.
Childs, P., & Williams, P. (1997). *An Introduction to Post-colonial Theory.* London: Prentice Hall.
Green, J. (Ed.). (2007). *Making Space for Indigenous Feminism.* Halifax: Fernwood.
Keay, J. (2000). *The Great Arc: The Dramatic Tale of How India Was Mapped and Everest Was Named.* Toronto: Harper Collins.
Oyewumi, O. (1995). Colonizing bodies and minds. In Ashcroft, B., Griffiths, G. & Tiffin, H. (Eds.), *The Post-colonial Studies Reader,* (pp. 256–260). New York, NY: Routledge.
Said, E. (1978). *Orientalism.* New York, NY: Vintage Books.
Shajahan, R. (2005). Mapping the field of anti-colonial discourse to understand issues of Indigenous knowledges: Decolonizing praxis. *McGill Journal of Education,* 40 (2), 213–240.
Shohat, E. (1992). Notes on the post-colonial. *Social Text,* 31–32.
Smith, L. (1999). *Decolonizing Methodologies: Research and Indigenous Peoples.* London: Zed Books Ltd. University Press.
Spivak, G. (1994). Responsibility. *Boundary 2, 21(3),* 19–64. doi: 10.2307/303600.
Spivak, G. C. (1990). *The Post-colonial Critic: Interviews, Strategies, Dialogue.* London: Routledge.
Torres, R. (2012). "Exploring Indigenous Spirituality, Activism and Feminism in the Life of my Mother". Canadian Women Studies Journal, vol. 29, nos. 1 & 2, 135-140
Torres, R. (1996). The assessment on the role of the national alliance of advocates of Indigenous peoples in the Philippines on the popularization of the rights of the Indigenous Peoples to their ancestral land in Camachiles, Floridablanca, Philippines. Unpublished Thesis. Quezon City: University of the Philippines.
Young, R. (2001). *Post-colonialism: A Historical Introduction.* Oxford: Blackwell Publishers.

PART 2

*Race, Gender, Multiculturalism, Work*

∴

CHAPTER 5

# South Asian Women Migrants Living in Canada

*Prospects and Challenges in the Labor Market*

Sarah Alam

## 1  Introduction

The chapter draws on the cross-sectional analysis of gender and migration. It discusses post-immigration experiences of first and second-generation South Asian women living in Canada and its impact on labor. The study focuses on Canada as a recipient country of women migrants from South Asian countries such as India, Pakistan, Bangladesh, and Sri Lanka. The perspectives shared by the author in the chapter are critical ethnographic lessons to learn from for future South Asian women migrants aspiring to migrate to Canada. It will not just assist South Asian women migrants in their adaptability to settle in but also enable the Canadian system to be more equitable and inclusive. The chapter is divided into different sections; the first section discusses the migration theories, historical perspective, and migration of South Asian women to Canada. The second section discusses South Asian transnationalism, the diaspora, women's role within the diaspora, and acceptability in Canadian society based on existing scholarly literature. The chapter's final section reflects on social inequality, which leads to challenges and opportunities experienced by the South Asian women migrants in the Canadian capitalist labor market.

## 2  Context

The movement of people from one place to the other is called migration. The migrating people are referred to as migrants and become immigrants when they settle in the host country (Rahim, 2014). The last two decades have seen a rise in the number of women migrating from developing countries to developed countries such as Canada to pursue economic opportunities. According to a Statistics Canada report, the 2006 census estimated that nearly 3.2 million women from 220 countries migrated to Canada. Out of this total female population, around 18% of migrant women hailed from Asia (Chui, 2015, November 30). Like other Asian women, South Asian women have also been migrating to the Middle East and other developed countries such as Canada to pursue labor. In 2007 Statistics Canada reported that the number of people of South Asian origin increased considerably than the overall Canadian population. Statistics suggest that South Asian migrant people make up one of the largest non-European ethnic groups in Canada. However, in this one of the largest ethnic migrant groups, men are slightly more in numbers than women. In Canada, the South Asian population has diverse ethnic, cultural, and religious orientations. As per the 2001 Census, 74% South Asians shared they were East Indians, while 8% were Pakistani, 6% were Sri Lankan, 5% were Punjabi, and 4% were Tamil, as reported by Statistics Canada (2007, July 16).

South Asians hail from Asia's southern region, which comprises of eight countries, including India and Pakistan. Along with Bangladesh, these two countries were called the sub-continent before the partition in 1947 and 1971. Pakistan and India emerged as the two most powerful and populous countries in South Asia. Both these countries are nuclear powers, but most people are impoverished and fall below the poverty line (Panchal 2020, June 03). Several ILO reports suggest that the three most populous South Asian countries are recipients and migrant laborers' senders to other countries. In the global context, people from India, Pakistan, Banglades, and Sri Lanka are usually referred to as South Asians (Sivaramamurti, et al. n.d.). To comprehend South Asian women, migrants living in Canada, and analyze their participation in the Canadian job market, it is crucial to discuss South Asian transnationalism and women's role within their diaspora. Since it will enable us to determine whether patriarchy is prevalent in South Asian culture and if so, does it give men preferential access to the resources available in society while affecting women's ability to acquire a job in the Canadian labor market?

## 3   Methodology

The chapter is a cross-section and ethnographic study based on existing data, literature, and the author's lived experiences, encounters, and informal conversations with other South Asian migrant women living in Canada. The existing literature reviewed for the chapter includes several scholarly articles, books, recently published newspapers, blogs, and survey reports published by Statistics Canada and the International Labor Organization. Based on the ethnographic observations and literature review, the student researcher provides a critical lens on gender migration and theorizes the experiences of South Asian women migrants living in Canada.

## 4 About the Author

A student researcher and a racialized migrant woman of color living in Canada, hailing from a developing country within the South Asian region in the Asian Continent. The author identifies herself as a Muslim by birth having lived the majority of her life in Pakistan. For several years, she has worked as a public diplomacy specialist, social activist, and a staunch advocate for women and children's rights in South Asia.

## 5 Theoretical Framework

The movement of the majority of laborers, especially women, to serve the interest of a capitalist society is widely witnessed only in the 21st century (Willis & Yeoh 2000). The continuously growing worldwide free trade in domestic and sex laborers intensifies old capitalist-patriarchal forms of utilizing women's emotional, physical, and sexual labor (Hart 2005), which results in gender-based divisions defining of roles within the labor market. The international migration theories are not very relevant to women as they turn a blind eye towards gender (Truong 1996). The social reproduction theories put forward by feminist theorists classify the gender divisions and indicate how patriarchy and social construction impact the migrant labor force. The arguments to support feminist theorists view gender as a "social construction" point toward patriarchy's role, or the hierarchies of power, domination, and control men use over women. The way patriarchy leverages men's preferential access to the resources available in society affects women's ability to migrate; it also leads to obstacles women experience before and after migration. More recent research by the feminist framework highlights the importance of interconnecting coercion systems, such as gender, and race, that shape diasporic experiences. Therefore, I have analyzed some of the leading work on gender and racial identities in migrant contexts, and to do so, I have looked explicitly at George and Ramkissoon (1998). Since they overtly provide a discourse on the experiences of oppression faced by women of color in the Canadian context. The discussion enables us to understand the complexities of gender migration within the South Asian diaspora since family plays a vital role within the South Asian community; therefore, it is pertinent to examine the role of family and its implications on women migration. According to Barbara Cottrell, Madine Vanderplaat"Cottrell and Vanderplaat (2011, p.268), "It is increasingly recognized that the family, rather than the individual, is the integral unit of analysis within the immigration experience ... the experience of immigration is profoundly affected by familial ties and relationships" Rajiva, M. (2013, January). \"Better lives\": the transgenerational positioning of social mobility in the South Asian Canadian diaspora. In Women's Studies International Forum (Vol. 36, pp. 16-26). Pergamon"Rajiva, M. (2013, January). Although patriarchy overshadows women's role within a family unit, recent migration trends suggest an increased number of women migrate to provide financial support to their families.

Nevertheless, in contrast to males in the labor market, women migrants are more vulnerable and considered a weaker segment of the capitalist society Aguilar, D. D., & Lacsamana, A. E. (Eds.). (2004). Women and globalization. Humanities Press International"(Delia Aguilar 2004). Women workers in a neoliberal world are subjected to continuous exploitation at the helms of their capitalist employer. In capitalism, patriarchy serves as its byproduct, as it directly leverages its rooting in the family or individual, therefore impacting women's lives. Since the South Asian women, migrant workers from India and Pakistan working in Canada, consider themselves socially, politically, and geographically outside their homeland, some of these women feel they are part of the social group displaced and excluded from the mainstream socio-economic institutions of society (Das Gupta 1994). Therefore, systemic racism, transnationalism, and patriarchy are suitable frameworks for studying South Asian women's postimmigration experiences who confront Canada's status quo.

## 6 Factors for Migration

The factors that led to the migration of women is a complicated and broad topic. It cannot be generalized easily; however, in the context of Indian, Pakistani, Bangladeshi, and Sri Lankan women from South Asia, it can be narrowed based on extreme poverty, low literacy rate, lack of job opportunities, and large families to support. Women laborers from these South Asian countries are skilled workers serving in domestic, care, and entertainment industries or factory workers. The most prominent cause of labor migration is higher income, which compels women to leave their homes and even their countries.

In most cases, inflation and unemployment in their country of origin force them to look for jobs abroad. Notably, in countries where the exchange value of money is high, and the minimum wage per hour is greater than the salary they could earn in their home country. Another primary reason for immigration is state-supported migration to make a foreign remittance. Since South Asian countries such as India, Pakistan, Bangladesh, Nepal, Sri Lanka have huge populations, they face significant unemployment and poverty challenges.

The sending countries are, to some extent, dependent on the foreign revenue earned and sent back by their overseas nationals. Hence, they support the migration of women laborers to increase their foreign exchange earnings. Migrant workers send remittances to their home countries of nearly US$ 73 billion every year, usually from relatively modest incomes (Wickramasekara 2000). Migrant worker remittances represent the second-biggest international monetary trade flow, exceeded only by petroleum exports for many countries; remittances represent more significant foreign exchange sources than total foreign direct investment or foreign aid (Wickramasekara 2000). Thus, migrant workers add monetary value to their host country and their country of origin.

## 7  South Asian Race and Gender in Canada

Today, in Canada, South Asians are considered the largest visible minority (Islam, Khanlou & Tamim 2014). Although the South Asian population living in Canada was relatively small some years ago, the number of people increased drastically. In the early 1900, South Asians started migrating to Canada for an extended period; men dominated the migration flow since the South Asian women were not entitled to enter Canada till 1919, legally (Jamal 1998). The prime reason being speculated that the white population was concerned with creating foreign communities that may disrupt the white supremacy. Their existed wide cultural distinctions between the white mainstream population and non-white immigrant communities formed cultural conflict. The racial tensions directed towards South Asians can be tracked as early as 1906 onwards; over the years, their presence was resented by Caucasians since South Asian men were given preference over Caucasians due to their work ethics at lower pays. The resentment caused a great deal of racial chaos, the Canadian government started taking notice, and South Asians were laid off from work (Buchignani, Indra & Srivastava 1985). The early migration saw racial discrimination towards South Asians, resulting in them being evicted from their homes, barred from entering public facilities, physically abused by local community and police, and misrepresentation by the media and local press. There were exclusionary and racist groups formed to discriminate and mistreat the South Asian migrants; one such group was Asiatic Exclusion League. History is witness to the league's riots, which caused South Asians to lose their livelihoods (Buchignani, Indra & Srivastava 1985). In addition to discriminatory treatment based on race, the South Asian community also had to deal with a lack of family presence.

Since Canadian regulations barred women and children under eighteen from entering Canada, from 1904 to 1920, only nine South Asian women migrated to Canada. It resulted in intense anger and organizing among South Asian men who lived in bachelor societies, sharing households, cooking, shopping, and caring for the sick and unemployed Das Gupta, Tania 1986 Learning From Our History: Community Development By Immigrant Women in Ontario 1958 - 86. Toronto: Cross Cultural Communication Centre"(Das Gupta 1986). The resentment caused a stir in the Canadian government policies towards women migrants over time. With the changes in Canadian immigration policies from time to time, South Asian women's migration trends also changed. In the 1980s, as the policies relaxed, and the number of women migrants increased, Canada's overall immigrant women population grew as reported by Statistics Canada. South Asian women historically and even today find it quite challenging to land in Canada as independent immigrants and continue to come as wives, daughters, and mothers. The South Asian women's dependency has dominated immigration policy and the community's responses to it. The former point system or present express entry, which indiscriminately accords different values to education levels, income, etc., is believed to be sexist and racist because it sets criteria that are hard to meet by most South Asian women, especially those from the working classes (Jamal 1998). Regardless of the discriminatory immigration policies towards independent working-class women from South Asia in 1991, statistics indicated 245,000 South Asian women living in Canada, comprising approximately 15% of Canada's total immigrant women. Currently, Ontario has the most massive number of South Asian women migrants, according to Statistics Canada Report, 2007.

Despite the growing number of South Asian women migrants living in Canada, race and gender intersectionality historically is perceived to have played a crucial role in the preferential treatment towards South Asian men in the labor market compared to women migrants making race the entry point leading to gender discrimination.

## 8  Transnationalism and Women within South Asian Diaspora

In South Asian culture, the primary importance is given to family well-being. Women tend to play the most crucial role in the family's welfare, and men are generally regarded as the primary bread earner in a South Asian family. The general South Asian culture promotes collectivism where sacrifices are made in the family; women tend to make more significant sacrifices to ensure family well-being where individual and family goals conflict (Rahim 2014). Cultural retention among South Asians is quite common and makes the basis of the diasporic experience. South Asians, although originating from different countries, more or less have quite a lot of similarities within Indian, Pakistani, Bangladeshi, and Sri Lankan culture; the differences between them are mostly faith-based. Therefore, the values, norms, and traditions also overlap among the South Asian population. Due to several cultural similarities among South Asia people from different countries, the diaspora is usually examined collectively. For this chapter, I have mostly looked at studies relating to first and second-generation South Asian women living in Canada. Statistics Canada defines the generations as follows: the first generation is considered anyone born in Canada. A second generation is a person born in Canada having one or more parents born outside Canada, the third generation, as having both parents born in Canada. The Canadian culture of individualism is quite contrasting compared to the South Asian culture of collectivism. The differences between the two cultures make the South Asian generation acceptability of Canadian culture more challenging (Rahim 2014).

However, scholars suggest that South Asians are more than willing to adapt and integrate Canadian values in their lifestyle while retaining their belief system. The South Asian culture is stereotyped, where women are regarded generally as dependent on South Asian male workers. Some sociologists have blamed the South Asian women stereotyping into wives, dependents, and mothers on various methodological and conceptual factors such as the sex bias in immigration policies and the data collection procedures of employment and immigration commissions (Jamal 1998). Here, I will specifically share an acquaintance narrative who explicitly expressed interest in sharing her workplace encounter of racism. She was subjected to differential treatment by her colleagues on her first working day in a Canadian clinic for being a Pakistani female wearing the "Hijab" (Islamic head covering), regardless of her being a specialized orthodontist having a degree from Canada's most prestigious university. Although South Asian women are quite competent and capable of being at par with any male worker, it is the Canadian history of colonialism, patriarchy, racism, and capitalist exploitation that undermine South Asian women's labor power. Generally, women from South Asia are looked upon to provide labor for the family and cheap work for the capitalist economy; they occupy specific social and cultural places allotted to them in Canadian society due to race and gender interaction (Jamal 1998). In my perspective, capitalist economies not only flourishes labor power manipulation by creating gender divides, it also further makes subdivisions of exploitation for women, primarily as migrant laborers based on race, color, socio-economic conditions, religion, ethnicity, sexuality, LGBTQ + communities, etc. Due to these differences, most women migrants, laborers from South Asian countries are more oppressed and become a victim of exploitation. Since most of the women migrant workers from India, Pakistan, and Bangladesh migrate with family, the male patriarchal norms make it quite difficult for individual women to migrate independently. In a patriarchal society such as India and Pakistan, most women are considered objects of desire, sensual, voiceless by their male counterparts. They are used according to the desire of the party in power.

Women within the South Asian diaspora are considered the epitome of contention since, on the one hand, they have to retain their cultural identity to contain modernity and to safeguard their cultural values for the future generation from Canadian surroundings. On the other hand, they have to be protected from the vulnerabilities forced upon cultural authenticity by living in the diaspora, away from their country of origin. However, while upholding their transnationalism, the first-generation South Asian women appear to the Canadian population as a repository of backwardness, not just through their thought process but also in their preference of attire. In contrast, the second-generation South Asian women in Canada are mainly seen as troubling because their presence points to the contradictions between modernity and traditionalism. The racialization of differences is a prominent factor in positioning South Asian women of color compared to white women. Therefore, race and gender-based discrimination is a significant hindrance to the fair and equitable treatment of South Asian women in the job market.

## 9 Prospects and Challenges for South Asian Women in the Canadian Labor Market

The South Asian women's labor power is organized into three categories, which often overlap: the wage economy (paid labor), the household (unpaid work), and in "ethnic enclaves" (as paid or unpaid labor) (Jamal 1998). Based on the discussed three categories, women from most South Asian countries living in Canada are either not working or are in precarious jobs that include working in factories, domestic care, service, and entertainment industry or are working from home in food catering despite having some or a higher level of education. This observation evaluates various social media groups for women exclusive to multiple South Asian women communities. According to the Statistics Canada report published in 2007, South Asians are twice more likely to have higher education than the general migrant population. In 2001, 25% of South Asian Canadians had either a bachelor's or post-graduate degree, compared with 15% in the overall adult population. The same year, 9% of

South Asian adults had either a Master's degree or a Doctorate, compared to 5% of all Canadian adults. However, due to the deep rootedness of systemic racism embedded in Canada, South Asian women who are experienced professionals are compelled to realign their aspirations and lower their ambitions to seek employment. It will be fair to state that the Point based immigration program (Federal Skilled Workers Program/Express Entry Program) to induct new immigrants supports class as a global phenomenon combined with race and gender. The research, conducted by Mythili Rajiva, Institute of Women's Studies, University of Ottawa, has shown that highly paid professionals experience numerous challenges while settling in Canada. Class and social capital play a pivotal role in acquiring jobs in the Canadian capitalist economy. The concepts of class permeate Canadian immigration policy; indeed, this policy's defining feature for several years has been considering potential immigrants as class assets. To be successful candidates, they must hold social and cultural capital, which is deemed necessary to acquire success in the Canadian labor market. The induction of migrant workers through the point system supports all aspects of Canada's prevailing class system. It will not be wrong to state that those who qualify and migrate to Canada through the point system already possess the Canadian labor market's resources.

Therefore, class, race, and gender are all systematically embedded in Canada's immigration policy to support the capitalist labor market. Due to systematic racialization, the highly skilled migrants are forced to look for precarious jobs to survive. However, in the second-generation South Asian women, there is a level of awareness, and they are found to be acquiring education and aiming for professional jobs. According to Statistics Canada, South Asian men are more likely than their female counterparts to be employed outside the home. In 2001, 70% of adult men of South Asian origin aged 15 and over were part of the paid workforce, compared to 54% of adult women of South Asian origin. Men of South Asian origin are also more likely to be employed than men in the overall population, whereas the opposite is true for women. In my encounters with South Asian women in different spheres such as education and the labor market often share their experiences of discrimination based on skin color. Most of this discrimination is due to degrading images of South Asian women permeating the media, social policy, and western civil society. Apart from differential treatment at work and challenges in acquiring jobs, South Asian women are also subjected to patriarchal norms deep-rooted in South Asian culture, which means looking after kids, home chores, and cooking are considered the ultimate responsibility of a woman. Nevertheless, women from India, Pakistan, and Bangladesh often find themselves with limitations to work in the absence of aid to shoulder family responsibilities

As a result, many women migrants from these three South Asian countries experience a lack of employment, low income, and poverty. After several engagements with the women migrant workers from the South Asian diaspora living in neighborhoods such as Thorncliffe, Scarborough, Mississauga, Brampton, in Greater Toronto Area, it will not be wrong to state that most migrant laborers are juggling between their professional and family lives. Due to overall employment and family conditions, many migrant workers from the South Asian countries are compelled to seek employment as domestic laborers and join the caregiving or service industry where these women migrant workers are often provided with minimum wage and experience exploitation in terms of the number of hours of service and fair treatment by employers.

## 10   Conclusion

The intersectionality of race and gender experienced by women migrant workers from South Asian countries supports the feminist and capitalist theories which highlight immigrant women as a particular category of worker that is important for capital not solely as surplus labor but for the fact that their race and gender constitute them ideologically and politically as the lowest paid and most exploited worker. The discourse provided in the chapter makes it evident that patriarchy and capitalism is the leading cause of exploitation for women migrant workers. It is evident from the above discussion that the employers' interest in a capitalist country comes first, and the patriarchal norms of South Asian culture suit the Canadian capitalist economy. In contrast, the well-being of labor is not a consideration under capitalism. Respectively, the state also regulates exploitation in employment through supporting racism, class system, and gender discrimination through its immigration policies.

### References

Aguilar, D. D., & Lacsamana, A. E. (Eds.). (2004). *Women and globalization*. Humanities Press International.

Barbara Cottrell, Madine Vanderplaat *"My kids want to eat pork": Parent–teen conflicts in immigrant families* Evangelia Tastsoglou, Peruvemba Jaya (Eds.), Immigrant women in Atlantic Canada: Challenges, negotiations, re-constructions, Canadian Scholars' Press Inc, Toronto (2011), pp. 267-296

Buchignani, N., Indra, D. M., & Srivastava, R. (1985). *Continuous Journey: A Social History of South Asians in Canada*. Toronto: McClelland.

Chui, T. (2015, November 30). Immigrant Women. Statistics Canada. Retrieved from: https://www150.statcan.gc.ca/n1/pub/89-503-x/2010001/article/11528-eng.htm

Das Gupta, T. 1994. Political economy of gender, race, and class: Looking at South Asian immigrant women in Canada. *Canadian Ethnic Studies*, 26(1): 59–73.

Das Gupta, Tania 1986 Learning From Our History: Community Development By Immigrant Women in Ontario I958 - 86. Toronto: Cross Cultural Communication Centre.

George, U., & Ramkissoon, S. (1998). Race, gender, and class: Interlocking oppressions in the lives of South Asian women in Canada. *Affilia*, 13(1), 102–119.

Gould, L. L. (1991). *The Great Migration in Historical Perspective: New Dimensions of Race, class, and gender* (Vol. 669). Indiana: University Press.

Gupta, Vineeta, Johnstone, Lucy, & Gleeson, Kate (2007). Explaining the meaning of separation in second-generation young South Asian women in Britain. *Psychology and Psychotherapy*, 80, 481–495.

Hart, M. (2005). Women, migration, and the body-less spirit of capitalist patriarchy. *Journal of International Women's Studies*, 7(2), 1–16.

Islam, F., Khanlou, N. & Tamim, H. South Asian populations in Canada: migration and mental health. BMC Psychiatry 14, 154 (2014). https://doi.org/10.1186/1471-244X-14-154

Jamal, A. (1998). Situating South Asian immigrant women in the Canadian/global economy. *Canadian Woman Studies*, 18(1), 26.

Panchal, K. (2020, June 03). Poverty in India and Pakistan. https://borgenproject.org/india-and-pakistan/

Rahim, A. (2014). Canadian immigration and South Asian immigrants. Xlibris Corporation.

Rajiva, M. (2013, January). "Better lives": the transgenerational positioning of social mobility in the South Asian Canadian diaspora. In Women's Studies International Forum (Vol. 36, pp. 16-26). Pergamon.

Sivaramamurti, C. et al. (n.d.). South Asia. Britannica. https://www.britannica.com/place/South-Asia.

Statistics Canada. (2007, July 16). The South Asian Community in Canada. Retrieved from: https://www150.statcan.gc.ca/n1/pub/89-621-x/89-621-x2007006-eng.htm.

Truong, T. D. (1996). Gender, international migration, and social reproduction: implications for theory, policy, research, and networking. *Asian and Pacific Migration Journal*, 5(1), 27–52.

Wickramasekara, Piyasiri (2000). "Asian Labour Migration: Issues and Challenges in an Era of Globalization." In: Report and Conclusions: ILO Asia-Pacific Regional Symposium for Trade Union Organizations on Migrant Workers, 6–8, December 1999, Kuala Lumpur, Malaysia, ILO. Bangkok, International Labour Office: Bureau of Workers Activities.

Willis, K., & Yeoh, B. (2000). *Gender and Migration*. Edward Elgar Publishing.

CHAPTER 6

# Unmapping Diasporic Pilipina Geographies

*Rose Ann Torres and Dionisio Nyaga*

1    Introduction

> By what sort of interconnections, sidesteps, and lines of escape can one produce feminist knowledge without fixing it into a new normativity?
> 
> MOHANRAM, 1999, p. 81

> So, it is not that mourning is the goal of politics, but that without the capacity to mourn, we lose that keener sense of life we need in order to oppose violence
> 
> BUTLER, 2006, p. xviii

This chapter comes at a disjunctive moment of retheorizing and reimagining the representation of Pilipina bodies in diaspora. While writing this chapter, we struggled with the complicated place of representation of women of colour in the beyond merely as objects of exploitation whose presence is frozen as an object of analysis, which fails to recognize their subtle points of resistance and desires. We are at a point where the academics look at development as the linear movement of an immigrant Pilipina as toilet cleaner becoming a university researcher and don. We ask whether this trajectory speaks to what we would refer to as development, and where is the place of the recent immigrant in this developmental trajectory? In this White linear trajectory, we grapple with the politics of margin and centre and how we are implicated in lateral violence. We look at the question of the toilet and university as mired in Whiteness, and that such a focus denies the very agency of the toilet. The toilet comes to be a point of degeneracy and those occupying such spaces as not fully developed and formed. The people who occupy such a space come to be constructed as irredeemably broken, and we educated immigrants as being White enough to save them from their degeneracy. To claim that our place of degeneracy was necessary for our evolution to the human speaking subject yet in the end collapse our original place as broken through disembodying ourselves from the frozen other speaks of the corrupted narrative of representation of the immigrant other, to which we are implicated. Though the movement would represent many stories told by immigrants to justify their place in the metropole and showcase resiliency and hard work as the only way to humanity, we trouble such narratives as being steeped in colonialism.

## 2    The Speaking Self

Much research has been undertaken on Filipina caregivers in Canada and other Western countries (e.g., Khan, 2009; Lindio-McGovern, 2003, 2004; Nyaga & Torres, 2017). These studies speak of different forms of social, economic, physical, and sexual abusive labour relationships that Filipino caregivers face in the West. A majority of these studies (most of which were undertaken by Filipino scholars) implicates the system and by extension policies (such as the Live-in Caregiver Program) in the oppression of Filipino women (Khan, 2009). Filipino caregivers are conceptualized as deportable bodies and yet they are part of reproducing the nation (Khan, 2009; Lindio-McGovern, 2003, 2004). They are placed at the intersection of the nation and White mythology in what has come to be defined as the outer limit of the state where violence is imminent; yet we fail to analyze and recognize how they negotiate violence. Mohanram (1999), in looking at women as place without place, says:

> Woman's body intersects place, race and gender, as indicated in Freud's description of woman as the "dark continent," or in Plato's *Timeaus*, where the woman is place, *chora*, "unnameable, improbable, hybrid, anterior to naming, to the One, to the father, and consequently maternally connoted." Luce Irigaray, too, suggests that woman functions as place for men: A doubling, sought after by man, of a female *placenessness*. She is assigned to be place without occupying a place. (p. xv)

The caregiving woman we speak of in this chapter occupies a very complicated space; that of unwanted yet wanted, deportable yet present. This woman functions not only to reproduce national boundaries but also to reproduce White women who come occupy the place of the rational being and consequently embody heterosexual citizenship. It is on their back that the nation comes to define itself as gender-sensitive in ways of including (White) women in public space.

While speaking of and acknowledging the narrative of oppressed women, this chapter takes a different turn and questions our place in the banishment (read deportation) of immigrant women to the very point we seek to emancipate them from. Could our focus on representing them as oppressed and our failure to identify their resilient self be a form of double consciousness where we return and fix them as irredeemable bodies, and is this our point of implication? While discussing the reading and representation of the other through Spivak, Mohanram (1999) says:

> In the mechanisms of reading a text there is a subject/object dichotomy between reader and the text, where the reader always has agency. The reader worlds the text according to her own meaning and subject production. In the reading of a Third world text, or Third world as text, by a first world reader, certain positions of privilege are assumed by the reader. Spivak argues that the insertion of a Third world reader might produce a different reading, but in reality it maintains the same structure and mechanisms if reading with privileged subject positions. In this way the production of knowledge is moved forward only through the dichotomy between subject/object. (p. 194)

In fact, Spivak implicates herself in the worlding of the colonial text in the reading of marginality. This speck of imagination speaks of our reading of the migrant bodies/text and reaffirming coloniality on their bodies. How has it become so easy for us to read ourselves as the extension of the colonial text? How is it that we continue to take the subject position when reading the caregiver as broken and in need of salvation for we who belong to the academic world order? We revisit the toilet/academy and the park/academy split to ask how we devalue the park and the toilet as spaces of degeneracy and waiting for civilization. Asked differently, is our now developed self-connected to their pain? Are we stealing (read harvesting) the pain of others (Razack, 2007)? Do we recognize their role in who we have become? We also seek to ask: Does our representation of their pain work towards sustaining our dreams in the academy and subsequently freezing them to the border? These questions are the ground through which this chapter is set as a reflexive piece of who we are in the representation of the Pilipina migrant other.

The question of the caregiver woman returns us to the work of Mohanram (1999) quoting Fanon on veil. To understand our role in the reproduction of Pilipina as broken and the implication to the same, this chapter juxtaposes the role of the veil to that of caregiving in ways that nuisance the place of the caregiver and the researcher. According to Mohanram (1999),

> Fanon traces the shifting discursivity of the veil on the woman through the Algerian war of liberation, wherein first it was a signifier of tradition and culture; the French desire to unveil woman revealed their intention to bring her into modernity. As the independence struggle intensified,

women joined up as revolutionaries and deliberately unveiled themselves so they could have more access to the French and be successful in the resistance movement. In yet another stage, when the French became suspicious of unveiled women, they donned their veil again so they could strap weapons secretly to their bodies. The veil underwent yet another marked shift in that it now read ambiguously, as both traditional and revolutionary, patriotic yet unfeminine. (p. 62)

There is an interesting focus of the women's veil in feminist discussion and the place of the woman in resistance. Western feminism looks at women of colour as broken and in need of salvation from their violent male. In fact, a lot has been discussed on the role of the White woman in saving the Islam women (Razack, 2008). While such discussion implicates feminism in the production of the other racialized woman as wrecked, this chapter takes this discussion further and presents an irritation to the discussion of the Pilipina as not only savable but also as political bodies that negotiate institutional and ideological terror directed at her personhood in very complicated ways. This negotiation of the state-sanctioned violence against the immigrant other reaffirms their place in nationhood in ways that are fluid. The question of veil is an important point at which we can recognize how Pilipina is not just an object/template of introspection and knowledge production (for which no one in the academy is safe) but also producers of knowledge. On the question of caregiving as veil, we want to ask: Why do we unveil the veil? How does unveiling of the Pilipina veil work towards social production of the academic Filipina? Does the unveiling the Pilipina help produce them for the market? Have we taken the role of the prison tower in the construction of the other as broken? How are we implicated in the technology of unveiling the pain of the other? How can unveiling work towards producing new Pilipina futurism?

We are informed by Butler (2006) to consider:

> A dimension of political life that has to do with our exposure to violence and our complicity in it, with our vulnerability to loss and the task of mourning that follows, and with finding a basis for community in these conditions. (p. 19)

Why is it important to unveil the trauma of the other? What place do we occupy while we unveil the other? What is the role of the veil in resistance? A majority of the time, we in the academy are quick to unveil the other and justify the act of unveiling as necessary for reparative justice. We embody our past pain as the ticket to imagining the pain of the other. We see other people's pain and replace it with ours. Their pain reminds us of what we went through and take our experience as reason enough to unveil the other. The process of unveiling the other become the same one that erases and replaces them with our own image. We need to ask: Is our anger and pain enough to uncap the other only to deport and fix them in their border as unable to progress? We need to ask ourselves as researchers and academics how our place of anger works toward affirming our place as fully developed humans while placing them as disabled. To extend this argument of anger born of mourning, we question our implication and the necessity for reflexive practice (read mourning). Which body is grievable and which one is not when we erase the pain of the other and replace it with our past pain? Butler (2006) says:

> If we believe that to think radically about the formation of the current situation is to exculpate those who committed acts of violence, we shall freeze our thinking in the name of questionable morality. But if we paralyse our thinking in this way, we shall fail morality in a different way. We shall fail to take collective responsibility for a thorough understanding of the history that brings us to this juncture. We shall thereby deprive ourselves of the very critical and historical resources we need to imagine and practice another future, one that will move beyond the current cycle of revenge. If we paralyse our thinking in the name of a questionable morality in a different way. (p. 10)

This conversation pushed the conversation on how we need to facilitate the process of unveiling in ways that caregivers come to represent both their desires while acknowledging their pain. It is the Pilipina who knows their own pains.

Our empathy towards the Pilipina is implicated and needs to be grilled. Could our very form of saving ourselves be a point at which we move from one prison into another, in what Mohanram (1999) phrases as "Instead of emphasizing her free choice as subject, the French unveiling of Algerian woman reinscribes her into another form of patriarchy" (p. 63). Why does our pain act as the formula through which we unveil the other? If Peminist development trajectory is linear, why then do we look back at their pain in ways that elicit our anger to save them? In the process of looking at them as pain and embodying our past pain as a point of imagining them, are we not also removing them from the act of performance, and is that not act of deportation?

Rose Ann Torres identifies ways in which a professor's comment in 2008 made her rethink her place in Peminist development. The professor would always tell her "how come that every time I see a White baby in a stroller, I see a Pilipina like you pushing it?" The comment is traumatic to her and sets the stage to reveal the place of Pilipina within the national memory. Trauma sets the stage to remind the wretched of their bordered self and their complicated place in the body politic. This statement takes the form of a reminder—a kind of returning the undesirable other to the violent border. To see the other and speak of them this way is to imagine the other as placed on the outer limits of the nation, where violence is imminent and expected. That the Pilipina is expected to provide caregiving is not only a normalizing statement but a construction of the Pilipina as a placeless place and whose presence is unimaginable, hybrid, and unwanted yet wanted (Mohanram, 1999).

That liminal point of self vis-a-vis the nation invites us to break boundaries of social construction and reimagine other forms and ways that the Pilipina negotiates national fantasies. We come to ask whether the fantasies of the Pilipina are represented in the national memories. It is at this point that we also challenge ourselves and reflexively question the place of anger in the representation of the other. Why would we be angry and for whose benefit? Could our anger be self-serving and a ground through which we could be implicated in the suppression of Pilipina, knowing well that we are academics who may not be intimately connected to the local spaces and experiences, where Foucault says the illegality of law meets the skin? Why would the pain of the other be represented by the academic other in ways that come to evict the represented from the national memory? As a member of the community, where does Rose position herself when such colonial encounters in the university corridor remind her of her borderline using the Pilipina caregiver. Why does the caregiver have to occupy the bridge from where Rose becomes the object of introspection? When representing such discursive constructions, how then do we construct the Pilipina as strong and capable of negotiating violence in ways that come to represent them as powerful? Could the bridge be their point of strength?

As a decolonial scholars who fosters a commitment to acknowledging racial and sexual violence against Pinays and is committed to undoing its persistent framing of them as nannies and caregivers who are naturally malignant and out of place, we would like to uncouple spaces as negotiable, alterable in ways that centre the desires of the oppressed other. Through such negotiation of geographies, we come to see ourselves as united and capable of presenting ourselves as part of space. It is this conception that marks us as nature—a case of us belonging to the family of fauna and flora. This Cartesian marking is used to imagine Pilipina as a necessary evil in White space. That is, they are deportable when not in need.

The marking of bodies as not belonging elicits securitization of White spaces in ways that expunged the dangerous other to the violent borderlines of gender, race, sexual orientation, nationhood, and disability. This perspective leads us to interrogate how the Pilipina unmaps colonial space in ways that frees them from social incarceration and internment as broken and subhuman. According to Smith (2007), unmapping

> refers to showing how the spaces and places are socially organized in ways that hide hierarchies of power. Just as mapping helped white European settlers to imagine and make claims that they discovered and therefore owned lands, unmapping reveals the ideologies and practices of domination that continue to shape the spaces in which we live and park today. (p. 276)

It is interesting how Pilipina caregivers convert Toronto parks and recreation centres as places not only of social engagement but also as places of community building. A majority of the time they bring their employers' children with them to the park. The park is not just an open space that contains slides, swings, sand, and toys. It is also a space where negotiations are made to happen. To the Pinay, the park is a place where the negotiation and maneuvering of racial, sexual, and gender violence is made real. It is in the park where they meet around lunch time to discuss their everyday challenges in ways that question their life chances while presenting their fantasies. It is in the park that they speak in their dialect, therefore questioning the place of colonial grammar in the beyond. It is in the park that they bring their cultural food delicacies in ways that re-presents national culture in the beyond; a case of representing the country in the city. While we have to be cautious of reducing culture to delicacies, it is equally important to acknowledge how food demystifies Whiteness in the park. We say re-represent as a point of national cultural negotiations of the park in ways that births and reimagines Canadian geographies through the Pilipina fantasies. The park collects their national intimacy in ways that restores and reimagines the Pilipina. The park occupies a place of reimagining the self in the perspective of their immigration challenges. It is in the park that counter discourse is represented and affirmed.

According to Razack (2007), "space comes to perform something in the social order, permitting certain actions and prohibiting others"; she argues that it is possible to "unmap" spaces—to 'denaturalize' them—in order to see the raced, gendered, and classed social hierarchies that are protected and hidden when we accept that such orderings occur naturally. The presence of the Pilipina in the park denaturalizes the space in ways that come to question Canadian mythology of Whiteness. Un-mapping is dis-identificatory or out-habiting strategies and tactics that challenge and trouble spatial White narrative. The park is a violent encounter of presentation that unravels the naturalization of spaces as White and pure. The park and the academic corridor occupy very strategic points of annunciation. They are a point of emerging negotiations between the totalizing and subjugated knowledges and experiences. The hierarchy of knowledge and its production juxtaposed these spaces as emotional and the other as rational. While both spaces are landscapes of knowledges, academic space is represented as rational while the park as out of order. Occupants of such spaces are collapsed and seen in that perspective such that the Pinay caregiver comes to be seen as irredeemably broken.

In fact, philosophical death is necessary to visualize the racist society and its everyday performances of expulsion of undesirable migrant others while also returning ourselves to our implication to this expulsion. For example, a majority of the time we present Pilipina caregivers as oppressed, consequently placing them as irredeemably weak and broken. While we need to acknowledge the presence of physical, emotional, and other forms of ills invested on Pilipina bodies, it is equally important to see their other forms of resiliency and resistance. We speak of resiliency not in the colonial sense of self management but grounded in the Indigenous praxis. We would ask therefore: How do Pilipina caregivers engage with their spirituality to denaturalize the park and the academy? Thinking of the ocean as full of monsters and spirits, could our place of annunciation be our very death bed? While in the sea, can the self-implicate itself in ways that complicates the narrative of decolonization of the park and the academy?

Within the capital greed, our role is complicated and complex and calls for critical imagination of social geographies of the Pilipina. We need to question Peminism in ways that centres spirituality as a point of self-emergence. A White feminism that perpetuates self-exaltation, and the notion of "the saviour" of racialized women needs to be questioned in ways that come to centre on other forms of feminisms. We argue that spirituality is the new geographies of Pinay representation in the beyond. Such a representation is a necessary point of Pilipina reflexivity in ways that we understand ourselves through other and acknowledge the pain of others. Rather than that feminism that treats racialized women as "welfare queens," this new form of representation is immersed in transnational spirituality that seeks to negotiate anger and reimagine the enemy.

We reimagine Peminist praxis as reflexive. What we mean by this is to critically look into our self, our beliefs, ideologies, values, and everyday practices. It is important to ask the self on implication to the racial and sexual violence of Pinays in Canada. To ask this question is not to forget the racial and sexual violence brought by the racist system but rather is an acknowledgement of our place in the removal of ourselves from the body politic. "Being reflexive involves a recognition of how we ourselves, as whole people, influence the situations and contexts in which we interact" (Fook 2002, p. 130). We are not also forgetting the institutions and its implication to this act of violence against Pinays. However, as we theorize, we cannot forget that Pinays who are nannies are also producers of theories and not just a subject of analysis.

## 3   Endogenous Framework

We envision Peminism as a theory, methodology, and pedagogy that can be utilized not only in the university setting but also especially in the community. The challenge is identifying how do we achieve this vision. Drawing from our research among Pinays in the Greater Toronto Area, we asked the participants about their ideas on feminism; some responses that I heard were, "we don't talk about Peminism in our group; we talk about our everyday experiences in Toronto." These are discussions of not only oppression but also strengths. These forms of negotiations are important tools of Peminism. According to Dei (1993),

> The integration of localized, empirical research with theoretical, generalized studies demands that researchers accord some importance not only to country-specific research, but also, to research studies that explore grassroot level of understanding, discourses on human problems and local strategies to problem solving. While community or locality studies by themselves are insufficient to offer a comprehensive understanding of society, they nevertheless, do provide relevant data needed to ground our theoretical discussions in the everyday lived experiences of people. Such studies provide opportunities for willing researchers to hear what people on the ground and at the grassroots have to say, what their everyday thoughts are, and how they make meaning of their social world. (p. 105)

Such an endogenous framework focuses on the knowledge, negotiations, and lived experiences of Pinay in the communities. The Pilipinos need to be included in developing and transforming Peminism. They have knowledge, forms of strategies, and ways of navigating Canadian White geographies in ways that invert and question it. They trouble the land through their presence in the park. They question the racist policies that govern and regulate the migrant other while marking them as coming from somewhere. They challenge policies in terms of immigration, education, labour, and health by participating in park gossips. They interrogate interlocking systems of oppression brought about by terrorization of spaces. This chapter therefore calls for a reimagining of Pilipina as ontologically (nature of being), epistemologically (theory of knowledge), and axiologically (deals with ethics and religion) grounded in and necessary for emancipation.

## 4  Differences

The notion of acknowledging differences within and without Pinays in Canada and beyond is a necessary part of Peminist emergence. We need to theorize within the understanding that Pinays are ontologically, axiologically, and epistemically (knowledge) complex in nature. Differences in terms of culture, traditions, spiritualities, sexualities, dialects, education, and lived experiences must be part of our theorizing. According to Lorde (1984),

> The literatures of all women of Color recreate the textures of our lives, and many white women are heavily invested in ignoring the real differences. For so long as any difference between us means one of us must be inferior, then the recognition of any difference must be fraught with guilt. To allow women of Color to step out of stereotypes is too guilt provoking, for it threatens the complacency of those women who view oppression only in terms of sex. Refusing to recognize difference makes it impossible to see the different problems and pitfalls facing us as women. (p. 118)

As women of colour we have the responsibility to acknowledge our different abilities, politics, positionality, power, and privileges to challenge the normative systems of power. We must understand that our struggles are connected to others' struggles. Wehbi (2017) cites Barnoff and Moffat in stating that "oppressions need to be seen as intersecting and ranking them on a scale of which is more or less harmful is misleading and counterproductive" (p. 149).

## 5  Conclusion

Our celebration of peminism reminds us of the complicated and multifaceted trajectories of theorizing and conceptualizing Pilipina-Canadians both at home and beyond. While we engage with these imaginary paths of conceptualizing the other, we cannot fail to connect failure to the success of peminist futurism. This terrain of thought grapples with the question of Asian geographies in the home and abroad. The queer art of failure intimates the necessity of rethinking success through failure. The successful self comes to be imagined as a reconfigured failure in ways that bring new understandings, rethinking, and a new beginning. Success is remodelled as a means to an endless end. This chapter focuses on reimagining peminist development reflexively by asking: Who gains out of peminism? Is peminism only for pinays? Drawing from an Indigenous, women of colour feminism and queer of colour critique, this chapter seeks to ask about peminist futurity and the place of Indigenousness, sexuality, and womanhood in a transnational movement of bodies. This chapter seeks to create and recreate peminism that speaks to the differences in terms of race, class, ethnicity, citizenship, nationhood, sexuality, and other identity politics. This is a poetic reconstitution of Asian imaginaries beyond a provincial conception of a normal pinay. The chapter complicates politics of negotiating boundaries in ways that come to imagine Asian bodies as being capable of circumventing a Western conceptualization of broken bodies.

We therefore should focus on working with and not working for the Pilipina communities. To understand that the "centre" we know is not the "centre" for others. Instead of trying to bring ourselves to the centre of theorizing, we need to reimagine our marginality (death bed/the sea) as our point of emergence.

## References

Butler, J. (2006). *Precarious life: The powers of mourning and violence*. Verso.
Dei, G. (1993). "The Challenge of Anti-Racist Education in Canada" in Canadian Ethnic Studies. 1993. Volume 25. Issue 2.
Fook, J. (2002). *Social Work: Critical Theory and Practice*. LA: SAGE.
Khan, S. A. (2009). From labour of love to decent work: Protecting the human rights of migrant caregivers in Canada. *Canadian Journal of Law and Society/La Revue Canadienne Droit et Société, 24*(1), 23–45. https://doi.org/10.1017/S0829320100009753
Lindio-McGovern, L. (2003). Labour export in the context of globalization: The experience of Filipino domestic workers in Rome. *International Sociology, 18*(3), 513–534. https://doi.org/10.1177%2F02685809030183004
Lindio-McGovern, L. (2004). Alienation and labor export in the context of globalization. Filipino migrant domestic workers in Taiwan and Hong Kong. *Critical Asian Studies, 36*(2), 217–238. https://doi.org/10.1080/1467271041000167604 3.
Lorde, A. (1984). *Sister outsider: Essays and speeches*. Crossing Press.
Mohanram, R. (1999). *Black body: Women, colonialism, and space*. University of Minnesota Press.

Nyaga, D., & Torres, R. A. (2017). Gendered citizenship: A case study of paid Filipino male live-in caregivers in Toronto. *International Journal of Asia Pacific Studies, 13*(1), 51–71. http://dx.doi.org/10.21315/ijaps2017.13.1.3

Razack, S. H. (2007). Stealing the pain of others: Reflections on Canadian humanitarian responses. *Review of Education, Pedagogy, and Cultural Studies, 29*(4), 375–394. https://doi.org/10.1080/10714410701454198

Razack, S. H. (2008). *Casting out: The eviction of Muslims from Western law and politics.* University of Toronto Press.

Smith, A. (2007). Native American feminism, sovereignty and social change. In Green J. (Ed.), *Making space for Indigenous feminism* (pp. 93–106). Halifax, Nova Scotia: Fernwood Publishing.

Whebi, S. (2017). The Use of Photography in Anti-Oppressive Research. In Reimagining Anti-Oppression Social Work Research, Whebi, S., Parada, H. (eds.). Toronto/Vancoouver: Canadian Scholars.

CHAPTER 7

# Reciprocity Policies and Institutional Practices as Exclusionary Exceptions

*Filipino Nurses as Recruited and Excluded Subjects*

Valerie G. Damasco

## 1  Introduction

In this chapter, I discuss the research I conducted for my doctoral thesis, which examined the international labour migration of Filipino nurses who immigrated to Canada from the Philippines and via the United States between 1957 and 1969. As an efficient and short-term solution to combat nursing shortages, Canadian hospitals, in coordination with immigration officials, recruited nurses from the Philippines (Bejar, 2006; Boschma et al., 2012; Damasco, 2012; Ronquillo, 2010, 2012; Ronquillo et al., 2011) and the United States (see Bustamante, 1984; Chen, 1998a; Chen 1998b).

Although they were initially appointed as staff nurses, after securing licensure with the nursing regulatory institution in the province in which they were hired, they were re-classified as registered nurses. Among those who participated in the study, half were appointed to supervisory positions (i.e., head nurse, nurse coordinator, nurse supervisor, or director of nursing) or nurse educator positions (i.e., nursing instructor, clinical instructor, professor of nursing) shortly after their tenure as registered nurses. They were enlisted to prominent teaching and municipal hospitals in Saskatchewan, Ontario, and Quebec and worked in various specializations. Moreover, these nurses were trained in first tier and second tier private nursing schools in the Philippines which were founded according to an American model of nursing curriculum and clinical practice.

Although the nurses attained occupational mobility prior to the liberalization of Canadian immigration policy in 1962, and before the enactment of the Canadian Points System in 1967, their successful career trajectories do not suggest that Canadian immigration or labour policies were post-racial. Rather, the findings confirm that the practice of identifying and hiring 'ideal immigrants' for labour market shortages and demands followed a racialized manner. Although the nurses I interviewed achieved occupational mobility in

Canada during the 1950s and 1960s, this was temporary and was impacted by their year of arrival.

## 2 Methods

As a methodological framework, I employed institutional ethnography (Campbell & Gregor, 2002; Smith, 1987, 2005a, 2005b. 2006, 2014) in combination with historical methods (Ginzburg, 2013; Gottschalk, 1969; Howell & Prevenier, 2001) to investigate how the migration of my participants was organized. By employing this method of inquiry, what contributed to their attainment of labour mobility in an international arena despite the enforcement of state securitization, strict border control, and restrictive immigration policies became apparent. As Smith (2005) explains, "in every case what is being explicated is how people's work is coordinated in a given institutional process or course of action" (p. 159).

I conducted oral history interviews (Anderson et al., 1987; Boyd, 2013; Gluck & Patai, 2013; Layman, 2009; Smith, 2003; Summerfield, 2004; Thompson & Bornat, 2017) with two cohorts of retired Filipino nurses who immigrated to Canada from the Philippines or via the United States. Nurses who were hired from the Philippines were licensed under the Philippine Board of Nursing (PBN) and had worked at prominent teaching hospitals in the Philippines. Those who arrived from the United States were former exchange visitor nurses who worked at notable teaching hospitals for a maximum of two years through the Exchange Visitor Program (EVP). In addition to conducting oral history and life history interviews, I analyzed historical documents obtained from provincial and federal archival repositories in Canada and the United States, including Archives of Ontario, Library and Archives Canada (LAC), and United States National Archives and Records Administration (NARA).

## 3 Restructuring of Canadian Healthcare System, Immigration Policies and Recruitment of Foreign-Trained Nurses for Labour Market Needs

During the mid-twentieth century, the nursing profession in Canada drastically changed. The Canadian federal government became more involved in health and bestowed capital grants for the expansion of hospitals and their corresponding services. In 1948, the Federal Hospital Grant Program funded healthcare institutions for education and capital costs (McPherson, 1996). Moreover, a combination of government funding, economic growth, and new medical technologies lead to the expansion of hospitals and the growth of nursing positions following the second world war (McPherson, 1996; Toman, 2005).

Many of the new medical interventions, however, required the assistance of skilled nurses (McPherson, 1996), and medical advances were becoming increasingly "contingent on the availability of reliable skilled nurses" (Toman, 2005, p. 101). At the same time, the nursing curriculum and clinical program became more scientific and specialized. As a result, staff nurse positions began to increase, while racial and ethnic barriers to admission into nursing schools became more prominent.

These changes resulted from the establishment and expansion of the Canadian national healthcare system and the introduction of Medicare in the 1960s (see Hicks, 2011; Twohig, 2011, 2018). In 1957, the federal government enacted the Hospital Insurance and Diagnostic Services Act (HIDS), which established a cost-sharing arrangement with the provinces for medical expenses. Nationalized public healthcare, formerly the Hospital Insurance Program, was initially limited to the province of Saskatchewan and Alberta. In 1959, all provinces had been in the process of espousing nationalized public healthcare, which was expanded to universal healthcare in 1966 under the Medical Care Act, a nationalized a program of public insurance which covered the cost of all physician services (Fierlbeck, 2011). Its support of hospital-based care reinforced the technology-based expansion of hospitals and the growth of nursing positions.

In addition to changes in the national healthcare system, the growth of the Canadian population also necessitated the development, operation, and management of additional hospital units. The domestic labour pool, however, was not able to provide for the demand in the proliferating hospitals, which resulted in a shortage of nurses (see Bustamante, 1984). Canadian hospitals thus resorted to hiring foreign-trained nurses from the United States, Europe, India, Philippines, and the Caribbean (see Calliste, 1993; Ronquillo, 2012; Ronquillo et al., 2011; Shkimba et al., 2005; Statsiulis and Bakan, 2005).

During the early period of immigration in Canada, the Canadian government balanced competing interests with immigration and focused on the economic needs of the country (see Fleras, 2010). Moreover, the government and associated industries filled labour shortages which 'white' Canadians had refused, which continued until 1962 (see Li, 2017; Pon et al., 2017). In 1962, Canadian immigration policy shifted away from a focus on race, ethnicity, and country of origin to a presumably de-racialized emphasis on skill, education, and experience (Corbett, 1963; Finkel, 1986; Green and Green, 1995, 1999, 2004). Turning to 1967, under the Canadian Points System, applicants were assessed based on occupation, education, and English-language skills (Reitz, 2004, 2005, 2013). Although these immigration policies were supposedly colour-blind and exempt of racial bias, Fleras (2010) argues that it continued to favour applicants with class advantage and access to educational credentials.

Despite the shift in the 1960s toward the point system, the economic performance of immigrants significantly declined (Galabuzi, 2006). This is reflected in the income disparity between racialized immigrant groups and the remainder of the Canadian population, which is caused by barriers to employment and concentration in low-paying jobs. Gender discrimination among racialized immigrant groups is also widespread. For instance, racialized immigrant women have continuously been channelled into lower ranks, particularly in the healthcare and domestic work sector, (Bakan & Stasiulis, 1994, 1995; 1997; Stasiulis & Bakan, 1997, 2005), garment industry (Ng, 1998, 1999, 2002, 2007), and service sector. Additionally, they are disproportionately subjected to precarious forms of employment (Cranford, 2005; Cranford & Vosko, 2006; Cranford, Vosko, & Zukewich, 2003; Mirchandani et al., 2005, 2008, 2018; Vosko, 2000, 2006; Vosko, Preston, & Latham, 2014).

Majority of Filipinos who immigrated to Canada during the 1950s and 1960s had class advantage and comprised of professionals who filled labour shortages in various sectors (see Aranas, 1983; Bustamante, 1984; Cusipag & Buenafe, 1993; Damasco, 2012; Kelly, 2006; Laquian, 1973; McElhinny et al., 2012). During the 1980s, many Filipino women entered Canada through the Foreign Domestic Movement (FDM) program, which was succeed by the Live-In Caregiver (LCP) program in 1992. Between the 1980s to the present, a significant number of Filipino women had continued to arrive through the Live-In Caregiver Program (LCP) (de Leon, 2009; Tungohan et al., 2015).

Although the nurses I interviewed were admitted prior to the liberalization of immigration policy and had attained occupational mobility, those who had entered the decades following faced structural discrimination. Despite their training in nursing in the Philippines, they are hired as domestic workers and subjected to deskilling, unfair wages and lack of benefits, and denied citizenship (Bakan & Stasiulis, 1994, 1997; Stasiulis & Bakan, 1997, 2005).

## 4 Filipino Nurse Labour Migration to Canada from the Philippines

Interviews I conducted with nurses who were hired from private nursing schools and teaching hospitals in the Philippines revealed the economic factors in Canada that led to their recruitment and how they achieved labour mobility. Furthermore, what prompted Canadian immigration officials to provide them admission during a period when 'white' immigrants (i.e., British, French, and American citizens) were being prioritized manifested. The historical data I reviewed confirm that Canadian authorities admitted Filipino nurses prior to the liberalization of immigration policy in 1962. It is crucial to emphasize, however, that although immigration policy had ostensibly been 'liberalized,' Asian migrants were still being discriminated from entering the country.

Notably, the admission of Filipino nurses in Canada prior to the legislative amendments of 1962 is documented in federal government communication I retrieved from Library and Archives Canada. I reviewed correspondence, dated September 21, 1962, which T.G. Major, Consul General of Canada at Canadian Consulate General in Manila, Philippines had addressed to Mr. W.R. Baskerville, Director of the Immigration Branch, Department of Citizenship and Immigration (Library and Archives Canada. RG 76, volume 826, file 552-1-611). The communication, as well as preceding negotiations which had ensued between the Philippine and Canadian state governments since the late 1950s, confirm that Canadian immigration authorities admitted Filipino nurses as permanent immigrants beginning in 1958.

Importantly, the correspondence reveals that the first wave of Filipino nurse arrivals in Canada was enabled by a reciprocity policy that had evolved from a lengthy process of negotiations between the Philippine and Canadian governments since the late 1950s. The bilateral agreement, which the Philippine government imposed on Canadian immigration officials, was known as the *Filipino First Policy*. In point seven of the correspondence, it states,

> [T]he large number of aliens in the Philippines has forced the [Philippine] government into a "Filipino First" policy, and [Philippine] officials are extremely sensitive about visa refusals to Filipino citizens. They tend to take an "individual" approach to visa questions and it is becoming increasingly difficult to obtain visas or renewals for the Canadian (business and religious) community in the country. Anything that you can do to help us avoid representations to the local authorities by disappointed visa applicants would be greatly appreciated.

On August 21, 1958, under the administration of former President Carlos P. Garcia, the National Economic Council (NEC) of the Philippines, the highest consulting body to the president on matters related to economic policy making, had approved Resolution 204 and proclaimed the *Filipino First Policy*. The purpose of the policy was to encourage the growth of businesses in the Philippines though favourable foreign exchange allocation. Moreover, it encouraged Filipinos to engage in enterprises and industries that were vital to the economic growth, stability, and security of the Philippines. The National Economic Council (NEC) recognized that the allocation of foreign exchange was the most effective means by which this objective could be realized (see Abinales & Amoroso, 2005; Takagi, 2014).

Other communication I reviewed illuminates that since the late 1950s, the Philippine government rigidly applied the *Filipino First Policy* to foreign nationals who sought permanent residence in the Philippines (Library and Archives Canada. RG 76, volume 826, file 552-1-611). The ruling was largely imposed upon Canadians who had entered the Philippines on a non-immigrant basis with pre-arranged employment in mining, petroleum, manufacturing, and trading. Interestingly, in exchange, nurses from the Philippines were admitted in Canada. In correspondence dated November 16, 1960, which R.M. Dawson, Acting Consul General of Canada in Manila, Philippines had addressed to the Under-Secretary of State for External Affairs in Ottawa, Canada, they discussed the policy of reciprocity and pre-arranged employment of Canadians in the Philippines.

> [S]ince Canada does not permit Filipinos to enter as pre-arranged employees, the Philippines, under their reciprocity policy, will deny access to Canadians.

In the correspondence, they addressed the denial of applications of Canadians who had worked in the manufacturing industry in the Philippines by extending their requests under a pre-arranged employment basis. Paradoxically, in the same communication, it confirmed that, to reciprocate, Canada had agreed to the entry of Filipinos, particularly trained nurses, as non-immigrants based on confirmation of pre-arranged employment. As it states,

> Canada does, in fact, permit non-immigrant entry to Filipinos on the basis of pre-arranged employment. However, each case is individually judged on its merits. A clear indication of this is the fact that up to the present time, approximately 20 nurses have gone to Canada this year on a pre-arranged employment basis.

Furthermore, in the communication it states that as early as early as 1960, Canadian immigration officials had ensured that nurses, specifically those who were admitted on a non-immigrant visa, would eventually be granted permanent admission. While nurses were permitted non-immigrant entry based on pre-arranged employment, after several years, they were admitted as immigrants. Importantly, although Canadian immigration policy had remained conservative, applications were evaluated on an individual basis. The passage illustrates the fluidity of the admissions process for nurses who came from the Philippines.

Although nurses were admitted based on pre-arranged employment, several were given student visas and, ironically, a full salary. Later they were permitted on an immigrant visa or non-immigrant visa. According to R.M. Dawson, Acting Consul General of Canada in Manila, Philippines,

> This brings me to the question of our Immigration Department's policy with regard to pre-arranged employment for Filipino nurses. We have received a number of enquiries from Philippine nurses who are anxious to practice their profession in Canada and have received letters of acceptance from Canadian hospitals. The general practice once these nurses have been screened by our Immigration Branch is to send them to Canada on a student visa, even though they will be working in hospitals earning a full nurse's salary. The Director of Immigration has informed us that they are, at present, reviewing the situation. Meanwhile, the most recent Filipino nurse that has gone to Canada [...] travelled to Canada on an immigrant visa. Now this week we received instructions for a nurse who will shortly go to Canada to issue a non-immigrant visa under Sec. 7 (1) (h) of the Immigration Act. Once she is in Canada, the Immigration Branch will seek authority for her permanent admission.

The inconsistencies in the admission process, as noted in the passage above, reveals the discrepancies in how Canadian immigration officials evaluated the credentials, skills, and experience of Filipino nurses. Furthermore, it demonstrates that Canadian immigration officials maintained flexibility in their practices, when needed, to uphold economic exchanges with the Philippine government in mining, petroleum, manufacturing, and trading. Practices in the immigration system can be altered during a period of economic and labour need.

Although the nurses attained occupational mobility prior to the liberalization of Canadian immigration policy in 1962, and before the enactment of the Canadian Points System in 1967, their successful career trajectories do not suggest that Canadian immigration or labour policies were post-racial. Rather, the findings confirm that the practice of identifying and hiring 'ideal immigrants' for labour market shortages and demands followed a racialized manner.

Through the immigration regulations of 1962, candidates were assessed according to their probable capacity to integrate into Canadian society. Filipino nurses were deemed to be the most likely to meet occupational and language qualifications. During the early 1960s, although the Department of Citizenship and Immigration Canada refused entry to those who had desired to remain in the country permanently and instead favoured applicants from 'white' nations, an exception was made for nurses from the Philippines. These nurses were considered the 'desirable types' who were hired permanently, as immigrants or permanent residents, provided however they met immigration requirements.

## 5  Paradoxes of Identifying Nursing Professionals as 'Exempted Cases' and 'Cases of Exceptional Merit' in a Racialized Immigration System

Although the data from this study reveals the exemptions that Canadian immigration officials provided on behalf of Filipino nurses, and the flexibility they employed in their assessment practices for these workers, the admissions process remained a racialized system. Characterizing Filipino nurses as 'exempted cases' as opposed to 'cases of exceptional merit', which Caribbean nurses have been portrayed, illustrates how Canadian authorities privileged particular ethnic groups. Although Canadian immigration officials made concessions on behalf of Filipino nurses and eventually granted them permanent admission, in contrast, Caribbean women were required to present nursing qualifications that exceeded those of white nurses to be admitted as permanent residents. Although this condition was not explicitly communicated to Filipino nurses, it applied to them as well. Thus, the exemptions were not simply benevolence but a provision that perpetuated racialization and marked the exclusion that Asian workers faced in the Canadian labour market.

Pon et al. (2017) emphasize that racialized immigrants are sought for their labour in Canada. However, once the demand for their employment diminishes, the admission of subsequent waves becomes restricted and constraints are placed on the civil liberties of those who are already in the country. For instance, those who attempt to settle are often denied citizenship (Stasiulis & Bakan, 2005), refused entry into regulated professions (e.g., nursing, medicine, law) (Boyd, 2013; Kelly, 2007, 2012, 2014; Kelly, Astorga-Garcia, Esguerra, 2009), and prevented access to social welfare programs and services (Thobani, 2007, 2017).

Although Canadian immigration officials prioritized Filipino nurses and made necessary concessions on their behalf, racism still existed in immigration practices and in the country at large. The exceptions, however, illuminated the urgent need of Canadian hospitals to hire exceptionally qualified nursing professionals who not only were capable of assuming the role of registered nurses, but who were also qualified for supervisory or administrative positions and educator roles, the ranks which my participants were appointed to.

Nurses who were trained in Philippine private nursing schools who acquired American training and experience, in the Philippines and in the United States via the Exchange Visitor Program (EVP), fit the criteria Canadian hospitals deemed suitable in candidates during the 1950s and 1960s. Moreover, they were exempted from entry examinations and specialization requirements. Nurses who were recruited from Europe, however, required additional training in the English language and in various specialization. Although Filipino nurses were characterized as 'special cases' or 'exceptional cases' and achieved mobility, not all Filipino immigrants who were considered skilled or professional workers achieved mobility.

Historical documents I reviewed reveal that in January 1967, nine months prior to the enactment of the Canadian Points System, the Ontario Human Rights Commission had been in the planning stage of a small-scale study to investigate the growing Filipino community in Toronto (Archives of Ontario, RG 76-3-0-593, B270203). The following month, the Ontario Department of Labour, Human Rights Commission Branch, conducted research on the community after the Ontario Human Rights Commission learned that many Filipinos, considered highly educated, had not been receiving recognition for their skills and scholarship. As it states,

> The purpose of the Ontario Human Rights Commission is to administer the Human Rights Code through a three-fold program of conciliation, education and research.
>
> The Commission consults with community groups who are interested in knowing more about the Code and the Commission's work, and who wish to acquaint their members with the provisions of the code and the steps to be taken when discrimination is encountered.

To determine whether Filipinos had been experiencing discrimination, in March 1967, Mr. A.M. De Swaaf, Information and Referral Officer at the Ontario Human Rights Commission, and field placement at School of Social Work of the University of Toronto, met with the Filipino community in Toronto. As indicated in the report, the Ontario Human Rights Commission had sought *'to learn of the experience of the various ethnic, racial and religious groups as to what extent they may experience discrimination and what suggestions they may have for the Commission in the development of its work.'*

An interview conducted by Mr. A.M. de Swaaf with Dr. Teodoro, who was President of the Filipino Association in Toronto and a physician trained in the Philippines, importantly reveals that only Filipinos who were considered skilled and professionals were accepted in Canada, majority of whom were nurses, physicians, and engineers. As Mr. de Swaaf confirmed, 'Nurses have no problem finding jobs and accommodations.'

## 6   Racialization and the Limitations on the Mobility of Filipino Nurses in Canada

Although the nurses I interviewed achieved occupational mobility in Canada during the 1950s and 1960s, this was short-lived and was impacted by their year of arrival. Another report reveals that the Ontario Human Rights Commission continued their investigation in the Filipino community in Toronto into the 1970s (Archives of Ontario, RG 76-3-0-593, B270203). In November 1970, Mr. Mark Nakamura, former Human Rights Officer for the Ontario Human Rights Commission, met with various individuals in the Filipino community in Toronto. The employment situation of Filipino nurses and physicians during this period was revealed through his interview with Mr. Andy Felix, who was President of the Filipino Association in Toronto.

The report reveals that professional associations or licensing institutions in Canada, specifically the Registered Nursing Association, Canadian Medical Association, and Canadian Dentistry Association, were rigid in their assessment of prospective professionals. In the report, the Registered Nursing Association was emphasized. As it states,

> He [Mr. Felix] told me that previous to this year [1970] Registered Nurses from the Philippines were given Graduate Nurse status and that they had to pass only one or two exams (pediatrics being one) to attain Registered Nurse status. He said that at present an immigrant nurse must pass four exams, for it is much harder now for a Filipino nurse to get full recognition as a Registered Nurse in Ontario.
>
> Centenery Hospital came under special criticism from Mr. Felix. He had heard from certain nurses that this hospital (one of several) screens immigrant nurses as to language capability. Some Registered Nurses from the Philippines are hired as Registered Nursing Assistants and others as Graduate Nurses. The standard of judgement set for this decision is an interview with the Personnel Director who decides as to their language

ability. (This appears unusual to the officer because most Filipinos in Canada are extremely well educated and articulate).

In the area of medicine he told me that a Doctor from the Philippines could practice medicine in the United States. However, in Canada he would have to intern and make up certain courses. Mr. Felix could not comprehend the duality of the approach by the different Medical Associations.

Importantly, the report points to the chronology of the economic, political, and labour precursors which manifested during the late 1960s and beyond, which further racialized Filipino nursing and healthcare professionals in Canada. It also confirms that the period of the 1970s marked the beginning of their de-professionalization and deskilling. That is, those who were hired in nursing during the late 1960s and the years thereafter faced labour immobility, which is beyond the scope of this study but nonetheless merits investigation.

The data in this study illustrate that in order for Filipinos to achieve mobility in Canada during the 1950s and 1960s, one had to be a nurse. However, this predicated upon several factors, including: (i) class position; (ii) completion of training at private nursing schools in the Philippines; (iii) economic, social, human, and cultural capital; and (iv) appropriate networks. This was complicated further, however, by the amendments that were made to immigration policy in Canada, healthcare policy, and changes to the nursing program in Canada from the 1950s to 1970s. Notably, 1975 marked the beginning of when schools of nursing in hospitals moved into universities.

### References

Abinales, P. N., & Amoroso, D. J. (2005). *State and Society in the Philippines*. Lanham: Rowman & Littlefield Publishers.

Anderson, K., Armitage, S., Jack, D., & Wittner, J. (1987). Beginning Where We Are: Feminist Methodology in Oral History. *The Oral History Review, 15*(1), 103–127.

Aranas, M. Q. (1983). *The Dynamics of Filipino Immigrants in Canada*. Alberta: Coles Printing Co. Ltd.

Archives of Ontario. RG 76-3-0-593. Filipino association (Toronto, Ontario). Summary of interview with Mr. Barry F. Cunnings, March 14, 1967. Report by A.M. de Swaaf.

Bakan, A. B., & Stasiulis, D. (1994). Foreign Domestic Worker Policy in Canada and the Social Boundaries of Modern Citizenship. *Science & Society, 58*(1), 7–33.

Bakan, A. B., & Stasiulis, D. (1995). Making the Match: Domestic Placement Agencies and the Racialization of Women's Household Work. *Signs, 20*(2), 303–336.

Bakan, A. B., & Stasiulis, D. (1997). *Not One of the Family: Foreign Domestic Workers in Canada*. Toronto: University of Toronto Press.

Bejar, J. (2006). *Transnational Communities: Filipina Nurses in Rural Manitoba, 1965–1970*. Unpublished Master's Thesis. Immigration and Settlement Studies. Ryerson University. Toronto.

Boschma, G., Santiago, M. L., Choy, C. C., & Ronquillo, C. (2012). Health Worker Migration in Canada: Histories, Geographies, and Ethics. 1–30. http://mbc.metropolis.net/assets/uploads/files/wp/2012/WP12-02.pdf.

Boyd, M. (2013). Accreditation and the Labor Market Integration of Internationally Trained Engineers and Physicians in Canada. In T. Triadafilopoulos (Ed.), *Wanted and Welcome? Policies for Highly Skilled Immigrants in Comparative Perspective* (pp. 165–197). New York: Springer.

Bustamante, R. E. (1984). Filipino Canadians: A Growing Community. *Polyphony, 6*, 168–171.

Calliste, A. (1993). Women of 'Exceptional Merit': Immigration of Caribbean Nurses to Canada. *Canadian Journal of Women and the Law, 6*, 85–102.

Campbell, M. L., & Gregor, F. M. (2002). *Mapping Social Relations: A Primer in Doing Institutional Ethnography*. Toronto: University of Toronto Press.

Chen, A. B. (1998a). *From Sunbelt to Snowbelt: Filipinos in Canada*. Calgary: Canadian Ethnic Studies Association.

Chen, A. B. (1998b). Filipinos. In *Encyclopedia of Canada's Peoples*. Toronto: Ontario.

Corbett, D. (1963). Canada's Immigration Policy, 1957-1962. *International Journal, 18*(2), 166-180.

Cranford, C. J. (2005). From Precarious Workers to Unionized Employees and Back Again? The Challenges of Organizing Personal-Care Workers in Ontario. In C. Cranford, J. Fudge, & E. Tucker (Eds.), *Self-employed Workers Organize: Law, Policy, and Unions* (pp. 96–135). Montreal: McGill-Queen's University Press.

Cranford, C. J., & Vosko, L. F. (2006). *Precarious Employment: Understanding Labour Market Insecurity in Canada*. Montreal: McGill-Queen's University Press.

Cranford, C. J., Vosko, L. F., & Zukewich, N. (2003). The Gender of Precarious Employment in Canada. *Relations Industrielles/Industrial Relations, 58*, 454–482.

Cusipag, R. J., & Buenafe, M. C. (1993). *Portrait of Filipino Canadians in Ontario (1960–1990)*. Etobicoke, Ontario: Kalayaan Media Ltd.

Damasco, V. (2012). The Recruitment of Filipino Healthcare Professionals to Canada in the 1960s. In R. S. Coloma, B. McElhinny, E. Tungohan, J. P. C. Catungal, & L. M. Davidson (Eds.), *Filipinos in Canada: Disturbing Invisibility*. Toronto: University of Toronto Press.

de Leon, C. (2009). Post-reunification reconciliation among PINAY domestic workers and adult daughters in Canada. *Canadian Woman Studies, 27*(2), 68-72.

Fierlbeck, Katherine (2011). *Health Care in Canada: A Citizen's Guide to Policy and Politics*. University of Toronto Press.

Finkel, A. (1986). Canadian Immigration Policy and the Cold War, 1945-1980. *Journal of Canadian Studies/Revue d'Études Canadiennes, 21*(3), 53.

Fleras, A. (2010). *Unequal Relations: An Introduction to Race, Ethnic, and Aboriginal Dynamics in Canada.* Toronto: Pearson Education Canada.

Galabuzi, G. E. (2006). *Canada's Economic Apartheid: The Social Exclusion of Racialized Groups in the New Century.* Toronto: Canadian Scholars's Press.

Ginzburg, C. (2013). *Clues, Myths, and the Historical Method.* Baltimore: Johns Hopkins University Press.

Gluck, S. B., & Patai, D. (Eds.). (2013). *Women's Words: The Feminist Practice of Oral History.* New York: Routledge.

Gottschalk, L. R. (1969). *Understanding History: A Primer of Historical Method.* New York: Random House Inc.

Green, A. G., & Green, D. A. (1995). Canadian Immigration Policy: The Effectiveness of the Point System and Other Instruments. *Canadian Journal of Economics, 28*(4b), 1006–1041.

Green, A. G., & Green, D. A. (1999). The Economic Goals of Canada's Immigration Policy: Past and Present. *Canadian Public Policy / Analyse de Politiques, 25*(4), 425–451.

Green, A. G., & Green, D. A. (2004). The Goals of Canada's Immigration Policy: A Historical Perspective. *Canadian Journal of Urban Research, 13*(1), 102–139.

Hicks, B. (2011). Gender, Politics, and Regionalism: Factors in the Evolution of Registered Psychiatric Nursing in Manitoba, 1920-1960. *Nursing History Review, 19*, 103-126.

Howell, M., & Prevenier, W. (2001). *From Reliable Sources: An Introduction to Historical Methods.* Ithaca: Cornell University Press.

Kelly, P. F. (2006). Filipinos in Canada: Economic Dimensions of Immigration and Settlement. *CERIS Working Paper No. 48*, 1–43. http://www.ceris.metropolis.net/wp-content/uploads/pdf/research_publication/working_papers/wp48.pdf.

Kelly, P. F. (2007). Filipino Migration, Transnationalism and Class Identity. *Asia Research Institute Working Paper No. 90.* Available at SSRN: https://ssrn.com/abstract=1317153 or http://dx.doi.org/10.2139/ssrn.1317153.

Kelly, P. F. (2012). Migration, Transnationalism, and the Spaces of Class Identity. *Philippine Studies: Historical and Ethnographic Viewpoints, 60*(2), 153–185.

Kelly, P. F. (2014). *Understanding Intergenerational Social Mobility: Filipino Youth in Canada.* Montreal: Institute for Research on Public Policy.

Kelly, P. F., Astorga-Garcia, M., Esguerra, E. F., & Community Alliance for Social Justice. (2009). *Explaining the Deprofessionalized Filipino: Why Filipino Immigrants Get Low-Paying Jobs in Toronto.*

Laquian, E. R. (1973). *A Study of Filipino Immigration to Canada, 1962–1972* (Vol. Publication 2). Ottawa: United Council of Filipino Associations in Canada.

Layman, L. (2009). Reticence in Oral History Interviews. *Oral History Review, 36*(2), 207–230.

Li, P. S. (2017). The Racial Subtext in Canada's Immigration Discourse. In R. S. Coloma & G. Pon (Eds.), *Asian Canadian Studies Reader* (pp. 49–63). Toronto: University of Toronto Press.

Library and Archives Canada. RG 76-1270-227. Selection and Processing. General Series. Occupational Selection Nurses Philippines.

Library and Archives Canada. RG 76-826-231. Immigration from the Philippine Islands.

Library and Archives Canada. RG 76-868-152. Philippine Islands Immigration to – Laws and Regulations.

McElhinny, B., Davidson, L., Catungal, J. P., Tungohan, E., & Coloma, R. S. (2012). Spectres of Invisibility: Filipina/o Labour, Culture, and Youth in Canada. In R. S. Coloma, B. McElhinny, E. Tungohan, J. P. C. Catungal, & L. M. Davidson (Eds.), *Filipinos in Canada: Disturbing Invisibility* (pp. 5–45). Toronto: University of Toronto Press.

McPherson, C., Ndumbe-Eyoh, S., Betker, C., Oickle, D., & Peroff-Johnston, N. (2016). Swimming against the tide: A Canadian qualitative study examining the implementation of a province-wide public health initiative to address health equity. *Int J Equity Health, 15*(1), 129.

McPherson, K. (1996). *Bedside Matters: The Transformation of Canadian Nursing, 1900–1990*. Oxford: Oxford University Press.

Mirchandani, K., Ng, R., Sangha, J., Rawlings, T., & Coloma-Moya, N. (2005). Ambivalent Learning: Gendered and Racialized Barriers to Computer Access for Immigrant Garment Workers. *Canadian Journal for the Study of Adult Education, 19*(2), 14–32.

Mirchandani, K., Ng, R., Coloma-Moya, N., Maitra, S., Rawlings, T., Siddiqui, K., Shan, H. and Slade, B. (2008). The paradox of training and learning in a culture of contingency. In D. Livingstone, Sawchuk, P. and Mirchandani, K (Ed.), *The Future of Lifelong Learning and Work: Critical Perspectives* (pp. 171-185). Rotterdam: Sense Publishers.

Mirchandani, K., Vosko, L. F., Soni-Sinha, U., Perry, J. A., Noack, A. M., Hall, R. J., & Gellatly, M. (2018). Methodological K/nots: Designing Research on the Enforcement of Labor Standards. *Journal of Mixed Methods Research, 12*(2), 133-147.

Ng, R. (1998). Work Restructuring and Recolonizing Third World Women: An Example from the Garment Industry in Toronto. *Canadian Woman Studies, 18*(1), 21.

Ng, R. (1999). Homeworking: Dream Realized or Freedom Constrained? The Globalized Reality of Immigrant Garment Workers. *Canadian Woman Studies, 19*, 110–114.

Ng, R. (2002). Freedom for Whom? Globalization and Trade from the Standpoint of Garment Workers. *Canadian Woman Studies, 21*, 74.

Ng, R. (2007). Garment Production in Canada: Social and Political Implications. *Studies in Political Economy, 79*.

Pon, G., Coloma, R. S., Kwak, L., & Kenneth, H. (2017). Asian Canadian Studies Now: Directions and Challenges. In R. S. Coloma & G. Pon (Eds.), *Asian Canadian Studies Reader* (pp. 3–28). Toronto: University of Toronto Press.

Reitz, J. G. (2004). Canada: Immigration and Nation-Building in the Transition to a Knowledge Economy. In W. A. Cornelius (Ed.), *Controlling Immigration: A Global Perspective* (pp. 97–140). Stanford: Stanford University Press.

Reitz, J. G. (2005). Tapping Immigrants' Skills: New Directions for Canadian Immigration Policy in the Knowledge Economy. *Law and Business Review of the Americas, 11*(3/4), 409–432.

Reitz, J. G. (2013). Closing the Gaps Between Skilled Immigration and Canadian Labor Markets: Emerging Policy Issues and Priorities. In T. Triadafilopoulos (Ed.), *Wanted and Welcome? Policies for Highly Skilled Immigrants in Comparative Perspective* (pp. 147–163). New York: Springer.

Ronquillo, C. (2010). *Immigrant Filipino Nurses in Western Canada: An Exploration of Motivations and Migration Experiences Through Oral History.* (Unpublished Masters Thesis), University of British Columbia, Vancouver.

Ronquillo, C. (2012). Leaving the Philippines: Oral Histories of Nurses' Transition to Canadian Nursing Practice. *CJNR (Canadian Journal of Nursing Research), 44*(4), 96–115.

Ronquillo, C., Boschma, G., Wong, S. T., & Quiney, L. (2011). Beyond Greener Pastures: Exploring Contexts Surrounding Filipino Nurse Migration in Canada through Oral History. *Nursing Inquiry, 18*(3), 262–275.

Shkimba, M., Flynn, K., Mortimer, B., & McGann, S. (2005). In England We Did Nursing: Caribbean and British Nurses in Great Britain and Canada 1950–1970. In B. Mortimer & S. McGann (Eds.), *New Directions in the History of Nursing: International Perspectives* (pp. 144–157). London: Routledge Taylor & Francis.

Smith, D. E. (1987). *The Everyday World as Problematic: A Feminist Sociology.* Athens: Northeastern University Press.

Smith, D. E. (2005a). *Institutional Ethnography: A Sociology for People.* Lanham, Maryland: AltaMira Press.

Smith, D. E. (2005b). Where We've Got To and Where We Can Go. In *Institutional Ethnography: A Sociology for People* (pp. 205–222). Lanham, Maryland: AltaMira Press.

Smith, D. E. (Ed.) (2006). *Institutional Ethnography as Practice.* Lanham, Maryland: Rowman & Littlefield Publishers, Inc.

Smith, D. E. (2014). Discourse as social relations: Sociological theory and the dialogic of sociology. In D. E. Smith & S. M. Turner (Eds.), *Incorporating texts into institutional ethnographies.* Toronto: University of Toronto Press.

Smith, R. C. (2003). Analytic Strategies for Oral History Interviews. In J. F. Gubrium & J. A. Holstein (Eds.), *Postmodern Interviewing* (pp. 203–224). Thousand Oaks, CA: SAGE Publications.

Stasiulis, D. K., & Bakan, A. B. (1997). Regulation and Resistance: Strategies of Migrant Domestic Workers in Canada and Internationally. *Asian and Pacific Migration Journal, 6*(1), 31–57.

Stasiulis, D. K., & Bakan, A. B. (2005). *Negotiating Citizenship: Migrant Women in Canada and the Global System.* Toronto: University of Toronto Press.

Summerfield, P. (2004). Culture and Composure: Creating Narratives of the Gendered Self in Oral History Interviews. *Cultural and Social History, 1*(1), 65–93.

Takagi, Y. (2014). The "Filipino First" Policy and the Central Bank, 1958–1961: Island of State Strength and Economic Decolonization. *Philippine Studies: Historical and Ethnographic Viewpoints, 62*(2), 233–261.

Thobani, S. (2007). *Exalted Subjects: Studies in the Making of Race and Nation in Canada.* Toronto: University of Toronto Press.

Thobani, S. (2017). Nationals, Citizens, and Others. In R. S. Coloma & G. Pon (Eds.), *Asian Canadian Studies Reader* (pp. 29-48). Toronto: University of Toronto Press.

Thompson, P., & Bornat, J. (2017). *The Voice of the Past: Oral History* (4th ed.). New York: Oxford University Press.

Toman, C. (2005). Body work, medical technology, and hospital nursing practice. In C. Bates, D. Dodd, & N. Rousseau (Eds.), On all frontiers: Four centuries of Canadian nursing (pp. 89-106). Ottawa, ON: University of Ottawa Press.

Tungohan, E., Banerjee, R., Chu, W., Cleto, P., de Leon, C., Garcia, M., ... Sorio, C. (2015). After the live-in caregiver program: Filipina caregivers' experiences of graduated and uneven citizenship. *Canadian Ethnic Studies Journal, 47,* 87-105.

Twohig, P. L. (2011). "An immediate solution to our nurse shortage": The reorganization of nursing work in Nova Scotia, 1940-1970. *Journal of the Royal Nova Scotia Historical Society, 14,* 138.

Twohig, P. L. (2018). The Second "Great Transformation": Renegotiating Nursing Practice in Ontario, 1945–70. *Canadian Historical Review, 99*(2), 169-195.

Vosko, L. F. (2000). *Temporary Work: The Gendered Rise of a Precarious Employment Relationship.* Toronto: University of Toronto Press.

Vosko, L. F. (2006). *Precarious Employment: Understanding Labour Market Insecurity in Canada.* Montreal: MQUP.

Vosko, L. F., Preston, V., & Latham, R. (2014). *Liberating Temporariness?: Migration, Work, and Citizenship in an Age of Insecurity.* Montreal: MQUP.

CHAPTER 8

# OutsourcEd

*International Practicums as Responses to Internationalization in Canadian Teacher Education*

Kailan Leung

## 1   Introduction

Much has been written on the subject of internationalization in the past twenty years, particularly in relation to education. However, descriptions and definitions of the term itself remain amorphous. Internationalization has been described as "an approach, a set of activities, a movement, a framework, [and] a process" (Begeny 2018). It is often paired—or used interchangeably—with the equally nebulous 'globalization' (Garson 2016). Knight (2004) suggests the term carries different meaning for different people, but when it comes to education generally involves "the inclusion of an international, intercultural, and/or global dimension into the curriculum and teaching [and] learning process" (p. 6). For the purposes of this chapter, I adhere to this last description, while at the same time recognizing the complex, shifting nature of the term.

In keeping with other institutions of higher education around the world, Canadian universities have made internationalization a top priority. International student recruitment is not only essential to innovation and research; it is equally vital to university financial strategies. Increasingly, Canadian institutions are reliant on the high tuition fees paid by international students to offset deficits in public funding (King 2019). In 2019–2020, international undergraduates paid nearly five times more in annual tuition than their Canadian counterparts (Statistics Canada, 2020, July 25). At the University of Toronto—Canada's largest university by enrollment—international tuition was the single greatest source of revenue in 2019, at thirty percent of the total incoming funds (Takagi 2019).

While significant research has focused on the impact of internationalization on higher education, Yemini (2014) offers the important reminder that "internationalization cannot suddenly occur in tertiary education without direct continuation from the earlier stages of high school" (p. 68). Teacher education programs straddle this divide between higher education and the secondary school system. Research into the innovations surrounding internationalization in Canadian teacher education is therefore highly relevant, with important policy implications in both K-12 and higher education.

This chapter considers the growth of international practicum (IP) experiences as part of an ongoing effort to internationalize faculties of education across the country. While the existing literature on Canadian IPs is overwhelmingly positive, I suggest these experiences are problematic on a number of fronts, particularly with regard to the unidirectional flow of knowledge, resources, and long-term benefits. Despite their imperfections, however, I believe IPs still hold innovative potential if program organizers and participants can recommit themselves to centering equity and reciprocity.

## 2 Scope and Sequence of Inquiry

I examine IPs primarily in light of two recent documents published by the federal government and the Association of Canadian Deans of Education (ACDE), respectively. The former, *Building on Success: International Education Strategy 2019–2024* (Government of Canada 2019), highlights the economic importance of internationalization to Canada. The latter, an *Accord on the Internationalization of Education* (Association of Canadian Deans of Education 2014), represents a commitment on the part of almost every Canadian tertiary education program "to stimulate discussion of critical issues and institutional responsibilities in the internationalization of education, and to give careful consideration to representations of marginalized individuals, groups, and communities" (p. 3).

Together, these documents provide a useful framework through which to understand the role of internationalization in driving innovation within Canadian teacher education programs. Following an overview of internationalization in Canadian education and a brief review of the relevant literature, I consider possible implications of IPs along the lines of equity and inclusion and offer some recommendations for the future.

## 3 Internationalization in the Context of Canadian Education

Canadian society is becoming increasingly heterogeneous in terms of race, language, and cultural backgrounds, especially in major metropolitan areas (Larsen 2016). Recent government reports on immigration and diversity predict that international migration will be "the main growth component of Canada's population until 2036" (Statistics Canada, 2020, July 27). Links between transnational movement, economic success, and educational outcomes are implied in a plethora of ministerial proclamations from across the country: British Columbia's *Policy for Student Success* highlights "a greater need to enable all students to have essential skills, adaptability, global competencies and citizenship" (BC Ministry of Education 2018) while Ontario's *Strategy for K-12 International Education* is premised on the need for students to "appreciate and understand the global perspectives they will need to succeed in our diverse and interconnected world" (Ontario Ministry of Education 2015). At the school level, one result of internationalization has been a growing demand for teachers who possess the knowledge and dispositions associated with critical global citizenship (Larsen 2016; Larsen and Searle 2017).

The ACDE's *Accord* (2014) highlights the need for a "reconsideration of the curriculum in Canadian [teacher education]" in response to "increasing levels of complexity, uncertainty, diversity, and inequality in Canada and internationally" (p. 4). The *Accord* (2014) prioritizes partnership, interdependence, and reciprocity in its conception of internationalization, while also highlighting the risk of unintended complicity in exploitative neocolonial projects. By contrast, the government's *Building on Success* (2019) is explicitly conceived along economic lines. While not directly concerned with teacher education programs in Canada, *Building on Success* (2019) offers an important glimpse into the underlying logic for internationalization at the federal level.

*Building on Success* (2019) lists the acquisition of "new skills" and "opportunities in key global markets" (p. 7) as priority objectives for Canadians studying abroad, and advocates for the recruitment of international students from "target countries [...] based on the needs of Canadian provinces and territories" (p. 9). It also outlines a new era of global competition as "more countries recognize that international students represent an important source of revenue and human capital" (p. 3). Read in conjunction with the *Accord*, the government's unidirectional conception of international education as a means to Canadian prosperity becomes more pronounced, highlighting a significant tension between the social, political, and economic dimensions of internationalization. Teacher education programs in Canada are thus faced with the difficult task of developing practices and experiences that promote "economic, social, and global justice" (*Accord*, p. 10) while also producing teacher candidates equipped with sufficient "global competencies" (*Building on Success*, p. 3) to compete for employment within a broader neoliberal framework.

## 4 International Practicums: A Canadian Review

More than half of Canadian education faculties now offer IPs as part of their Bachelor of Education programs, and teacher candidates have shown consistent eagerness to participate (Larsen 2016; Larsen and Searle 2017). Typically, candidates apply toward the end of their degrees after acquiring previous field experience in a local Canadian school. Home faculties may coordinate the logistical aspects of the IP, but teacher candidates often need to take on some financial responsibility for their experience. Placements are usually quite short—between three and six weeks—and unlikely to be repeated in the teacher candidate's degree.

Diverse practicum experiences, which include international placements, have generally been shown to benefit pre-service teachers: through contact with new cultures and societies, IPs encourage multiperspectivity, tolerance, and global-mindedness (Cantalini-Williams et al. 2014). Research into IP outcomes suggests a range of personal and professional benefits to candidates, including "expanded worldviews, deeper and more critical understanding of global interdependence, and awareness of different educational systems" (Larsen 2016, p. 5). Maynes et al. (2012) write that international teaching experiences "create both personal and professional paradigm shifts for those who engage in them" (p. 72). This potential for personal and professional change—if not outright transformation—is implied in much of the marketing for IPs found on university websites.

While the characterization of IPs in the academic literature has been highly favorable, some studies have raised questions regarding the extent to which teacher candidates experience any lasting shifts in their perspectives or practices upon returning home. In their cross-case study on international service-learning practicums, Larsen and Searle (2017) found that while teacher candidates demonstrated increased awareness of systemic relationships between privilege and power, this did not catalyze major behavioral changes upon returning to Canada. This was not, the authors suggest, indicative of any particular failures in the practicum or the participants, but rather the fact that "two weeks [was] far too short a time to engage in this deep learning through confronting [...] 'difficult knowledge'" (Larsen and Searle 2017, p. 203).

Black and Bernardes (2014) offer more optimistic conclusions regarding the transformative power of IPs in their study of Canadian teacher candidates in Kenya. The authors, who also facilitated the experience, note significant differences in teacher candidate responses to Hett's (1993) Global-Mindedness Survey before and after practicum:

> "[The teacher candidates'] improved self-confidence was evidenced in their statements about overcoming adversity and challenges. They expressed a deeply felt personal concern for other people and thought in terms of what was good for the global community. Finally, they recognized the interrelatedness of all peoples and the need to build community."
>
> BLACK and BERNARDES 2014, p. 13

It is worth noting that the existing literature on IPs relies almost exclusively on qualitative methods such as interviews, surveys, and focus group responses. Without an extensive database or shared metric by which to assess the outcomes of IPs, there are limitations as to how generalizable individual studies can be. Still, it is possible to theorize the current state of IPs in relation to what has been established as most important when it comes to successful student teaching experiences.

## 5 Analysis and Implications

Beck and Kosnik (2002) found that associate teacher mentorship had a significant impact on teacher candidates' perceptions of good practicum experiences. Interview data from teacher candidates highlighted the need for emotional support, consistent feedback, and professional collaboration with their mentors. The importance of trained, capable, and willing mentors has been highlighted elsewhere in the world: Ulvik and Smith (2011) point out "a difference in the views of the mentors with and without a mentor education", and the need for mentor teachers to undergo formal preparation for what is "a complex and demanding process" (p. 531).

Explicit and extended discussion of the role—and sometimes even the presence—of associate teachers from host countries is conspicuously absent in much of the IP literature. This is noteworthy given the philosophy of collaboration traditionally espoused in Canadian teacher education, but it is also unsurprising when situated within the larger Eurocentric framework of inquiry that has historically guided academic research (Stanton 2014). The exclusion of host teacher and student perspectives is one aspect of IPs and the resultant research that suggests the difficulty in avoiding the perpetuation of neocolonial power imbalances, especially when practicums take place—as they so often do—in postcolonial contexts. In its subsection on the risks of internationalization, the *Accord* specifically highlights the following:

"[Attempts] to export educational practices and norms may have an impact similar to enforced social and economic colonization: the subjugation of one group to the power and control of another, and the elevation of a predominantly imported mode of thinking above all other forms of knowing." (p. 6)

Black and Bernardes (2014) admit to this tension in the introduction to their study, citing "the politicized (multicultural) analysis of Western ways of being and thinking imposed on indigenous students and communities" (p. 4) as a theme they struggled with as both facilitators and researchers. This sort of reflexivity is a positive step but must extend to all stakeholders—from program organizers to teacher candidates—in order to move beyond mere rhetoric.

Larsen (2016) draws explicit connections between internationalization, cultural and economic globalization, and an increase in IPs being offered by education faculties worldwide. In her comparative case study of internationalization in Chinese and Canadian teacher education, Larsen (2016) suggests "opportunities to engage in (practice) teaching and study abroad through teacher education can be viewed as manifestations of economic globalization", while also pointing out that "increasing numbers of Canadian student teachers are choosing to participate in IP placements in order to enhance their career options and teaching abroad opportunities" (p. 7–8).

Studies on the motivations of students from the Global North choosing to study abroad suggest participants in IPs are clearly aware of the personal benefits associated with their experiences. Tiessen (2012) finds that international experiences (specifically in the Global South) "are perceived (by the volunteers and the hosts alike) to improve their CVs and to give them a 'leg up' when applying for jobs" (p. 74). Current IPs may be seen as emblematic of these tensions between individualism and a more altruistic collectivism. The brief duration and singular nature of each practicum certainly presents challenges in building the sort of lasting, respectful, and reciprocal relationships envisioned in the language of the *Accord*. In the existing literature, the beneficiaries of Canadian IPs are clear: teacher candidates, followed by facilitators-cum-researchers. As Tiessen (2012) claims, "systemic (perhaps neo-colonial) challenges prevent the host country participants from some of these same rewards" (p. 74).

As a means of engendering small shifts in attitudes and behaviors toward difference, however, IPs do offer some value. While Larsen and Searle (2017) find the brevity of most international experiences fails to catalyze long-term changes within a conceptual framework of Critical Global Citizenship (Larsen 2014), some exposure to difference is clearly better than none. Writing on the subject of diversity training, McCauley (2002) advocates for an experiential "feet-first" approach grounded in dissonance and reciprocity; this, in theory, is what IPs attempt to accomplish. McCauley (2002) suggests that "head-first" learning (no matter how persuasive) is unlikely to compel changes in belief or behavior in the same way as on-the-ground learning, and if "past behavior can become a reason for and a cause of future behavior" (p. 254), IPs still hold innovative value in preparing teacher candidates for increasingly diverse educational settings.

In the context of internationalization, providing IP opportunities is important for Canadian education faculties to remain competitive and relevant. International education is becoming an increasingly attractive option for current and prospective Canadian educators as many provinces continue to deal with teacher surpluses, making globally focused innovation a priority in teacher education. The *Accord* provides a valuable and carefully considered guide to responsible internationalization and should be utilized as a philosophical roadmap for achieving innovations based on genuinely reciprocal relationships. Unfortunately, much of the marketing and academic literature surrounding IPs runs counter to many of the *Accord's* recommendations. In the claims of individual 'transformation' and newfound 'awareness' present in the conclusions of some studies, it is difficult not to hear echoes of the federal government's exhortation to "develop intercultural competencies, strong international networks and a deeper understanding of economic regions of importance to Canada" (*Building on Success* 2019, p. 5).

## 6    Recommendations

While imperfect, IPs still have the potential to realize many of the benefits associated with internationalization. To achieve this, all parties involved in the planning and participation of these experiences must (re)commit to centering equity, sustainability, and reciprocity. I offer the following three recommendations as a starting point for what should be a continual process of improving IPs in Canadian teacher education.

1. *Shared data collection and long-term tracking*: As an increasing number of education faculties begin to offer IPs to teacher candidates, the opportunity exists for interuniversity collaboration in creating a network and database for IPs. Currently, there is a lack of longitudinal research to help identify trends in IP experiences as well as the long-term effects on pedagogies in Canadian classrooms. Understanding the ways in which IPs can contribute to approaches to teaching and learning, catalyze engagement with equity issues, and encourage personal and professional reflexivity

are important in assessing their value as an innovation as well as highlighting specific areas for development.

2. *Principles of exchange*: In order to counter the historically unidirectional flow of pedagogical knowledge from the Global North to the Global South, IPs should be based on principles of exchange. When possible, the organization of IPs should involve offering internationally educated teachers or teacher candidates the opportunity to learn and participate in Canadian classrooms. While this would necessitate greater funding and increased coordination with Canadian immigration services, the concept is not unprecedented. Not-for-profit organizations such as the recently shuttered Canadian Education Exchange Foundation have demonstrated the feasibility and value of international teaching exchanges for decades.

3. *Longer practicum commitments*: While small changes in perspective and behavior are positive outcomes associated with current iterations of IPs, stories of paradigmatic shifts after three weeks abroad cannot help but ring hollow. Larsen and Searle (2017) point to the need for more time on the ground in order for teacher candidates to move toward a 'thicker' global citizenship based in criticality and engagement with social justice. Longer practicums would require greater commitment on the part of teacher candidates and would also allow for more attention to be given to "adequate cultural and language preparation prior to departure, support during [candidates'] time away, and opportunities to debrief and share their learning on their return" (*Accord*, p. 8). This would also help IPs avoid negative construal as a form of neocolonial 'edutourism'.

The recommendations above are in no way exhaustive or sufficiently nuanced. Rather, they are meant to initiate further discussion and reaffirm the innovative potential of IPs in Canadian teacher education. The *Accord* makes explicit both the risks and benefits of internationalization to education, and yet it is far easier in today's globalized world to be guided by the economic motives laid out in strategy documents such as *Building on Success* (2019).

## 7 Conclusion

In this chapter I have examined IPs as a response to internationalization in Canadian teacher education. While problematic in their current forms, IPs still hold innovative potential as one way for teacher candidates to exchange knowledge and skills in the pursuit of critical global citizenship. In order for this to occur, education faculties must recommit to the principles agreed upon by their deans in the *Accord* (2014). Federal strategies explicitly promote economic gain and Canadian prosperity at the expense of serious attention to social justice, reciprocity, and the sustainability of respectful transnational relationships; IPs must seek to counter this mindset of exclusivity.

The current literature on IPs in a Canadian context lacks generalizability and would benefit from further research involving longitudinal and cross-case studies to help determine the efficacy of IPs in relation to stated global competency goals. Much more attention needs to be paid to the host contexts—from local teachers and students to Indigenous epistemologies—in order to avoid the unidirectional flow of information and knowledge.

As trustees of the next generation of leaders, thinkers, and activists, teachers—and by extension, teacher education—must resist the individual and exclusionary pressures of internationalization and embrace the more difficult path leading toward collaboration, inclusion, and justice. IPs should not be abandoned, but they must be reconceptualized along these lines in order to fulfill their potential as innovations in teacher education.

## References

Association of Canadian Deans of Education. (2014). *Accord on the Internationalization of Education*. https://csse-scee.ca/acde/wp-content/uploads/sites/7/2017/08/Accord-on-the-Internationalization-of-Education.pdf

BC Ministry of Education. (2018, July 30). Vision for student success. Government of British Columbia. https://www2.gov.bc.ca/gov/content/education-training/k-12/administration/program-management/vision-for-student-success

Beck, C., & Kosnik, C. (2002). Components of a good practicum placement: Student teacher perceptions. *Teacher Education Quarterly, 29*(2), 81–98.

Begeny, J. C. (2018). A working definition and conceptual model of internationalization for school and educational psychology. *Psychology in the Schools, 55*(8), 924–940.

Black, G. L., & Bernardes, R. P. (2014). Developing global educators and intercultural competence through an international teaching practicum in Kenya. *Canadian and International Education, 43*(2), 1–15.

Cantalini-Williams, M., Wideman-Johnston, T., Tedesco, S., Brewer, Courtney Anne, Tessaro, M. L., Rich, S., Maynes, N. A., Grierson, A. L., Cooper, L., & Tedesco, S. (2014). *Innovative practicum models in teacher education: The benefits, challenges and omplementation omplications of peer mentorship, service learning and international practicum experiences*. Higher Education Quality Council of Ontario.

Garson, K. (2016). Reframing internationalization. *Canadian Journal of Higher Education, 46*(2), 19–39.

Government of Canada. Global Affairs. (2019). *Building on Success: International Education Strategy 2019–2024*. Global Affairs Canada.

Hett, E.J. (1993). The development of an instrument to measure global mindedness. Doctoral dissertation, University of San Diego, 1993.

King, C. (2019). Internationalisation of higher education in a Canadian context: responses to the Bologna Process from Canadian universities. *European Journal of Higher Education*, 9(1), 58–72.

Knight, J. (2004). Internationalization remodeled: definitions, approaches, and rationales. *Journal of Studies in International Education*, 8(1), 5–31.

Larsen, M. A., & Searle, M. J. (2017). International service learning and critical global citizenship: A cross-case study of a Canadian teacher education alternative practicum. *Teaching and Teacher Education*, 63(Complete), 196–205.

Larsen, M. A. (2016). Globalisation and internationalisation of teacher education: a comparative case study of Canada and Greater China. *Teaching Education*, 27(4), 396–409.

Larsen, M. A. (2014). Critical global citizenship and international service learning: A case study of the intensification effect. *Journal of Global Citizenship and Equity Education*, 4(1), 1–43.

Maynes, N., Allison, J., & Julien-Schultz, L. (2012). International practica experiences as events of influence in a teacher candidates' development. *McGill Journal of Education*, 47(1), 69–91.

McCauley, C. (2002). Head-first vs. feet-first in peace education. In G. Salomon & B. Nevo (Eds.), *Peace Education: The Concepts, Principles & Practices around the World* (247–258). Mahwah, NJ: Lawrence Erlbaum Associates.

Ontario Ministry of Education. (2015). Ontario's strategy for K-12 international education. Government of Ontario. http://www.edu.gov.on.ca/eng/policyfunding/strategyK12.pdf

Stanton, C. R. (2014). Crossing methodological borders: Decolonizing community-based participatory research. *Qualitative Inquiry*, 20(5), 573–583.

Statistics Canada. (2020, July 25). Canadian and international tuition fees by level of study. Retrieved from https://www150.statcan.gc.ca/t1/tbl1/en/tv.action?pid=3710004501

Statistics Canada. (2020, July 27). Immigration and diversity: population projections for Canada and its regions, 2011 to 2036. Retrieved from https://www150.statcan.gc.ca/n1/pub/91-551-x/91-551-x2017001-eng.htm

Takagi, A. (2019, February 24). *U of T receives more money from international students than from Ontario government*. The Varsity. https://thevarsity.ca/2019/02/24/u-of-t-receives-more-money-from-international-students-than-from-ontario-government/

Tiessen, R. (2012). Motivations for learning/volunteer abroad programs: Research with Canadian youth. *Global Citizenship and Equity Education Journal, 2*(1), 1–21.

Ulvik, M. & Smith, K. (2011) What characterises a good practicum in teacher education? *Education Inquiry, 2*(3), 517–536.

Yemini, M. (2014). Internationalisation discourse What remains to be said? *Perspectives: Policy and Practice in Higher Education, 18*(2), 66–71.

CHAPTER 9

# Why I Don't Talk about Being Filipino (I Think)

*Wallis Caldoza (in thought with Peyton Caldoza)*

This rather temperamental autoethnography captures a specific moment of conversations/non-conversations I find myself trapped in over and over again – sometimes by my own doing. I approach these conversations/non-conversations using autoethnography rooted in quotidian dramaturgy – that is, the study of the narrative structuring of everyday life – informed by the works of hampton, 2020; hooks, 1992; Lorde, 1984; Jordan, 2000; Butler, 2006; Bala, 2017; Fanon, 1968; Harney & Moten, 2013; and Nolan, 2015, in order to think about resisting identity claiming; the contentious relationship between the un-assumed racialized identity of a Filipino-Trinidadian-Canadian scholar and her field of study rooted in social justice education; the impossibility and instability of the inheritance of intergenerational identity under and within colonial neoliberalism and racial capitalism; the failure of belonging to the nation-state; and writing from spaces of negation.

...

*I'm on a walk with my mum.*

A friend and fellow dramaturg, calls to ask how I'm doing, how school's going, if anything new is happening, if we're good for tomorrow's meeting - the usual. I field his queries and then, before I can stop myself or figure out why, I find myself telling him why I'm out on a walk with my mum this evening. Firstly, to enjoy the new season; it's autumn, *finally*. Secondly, because I need to get rid of this migraine developing somewhere near the top of my skull. The words keep spilling out: the source of the migraine is my inability to write this seemingly impossible chapter.A friend and fellow doctoral student asked me to write something for this collection detailing the marginalization and exclusion of Asian folks in Canadian society.

I explained to my friend on the phone what I'd said to my mama in the kitchen earlier:I couldn't fathom submitting anything. I don't "do" or "study" Asian studies, per se; it's never been a field of study that I have found myself standing in despite my being half Filipino. I told the friend who'd offered me the chance to submit a piece that I, regrettably, had nothing to offer. They maneuvered asking, , "Hmm, what about theorizing something that your Filipino side of the family has to put up with in Canada?" I think, not wanting to give up the offer to offer something up to my brilliant friend, in tandem with how open the line of inquiry was, I decided I'd at least open the door to this prompt - I don't know if I'd be sticking my head out or in yet - and think a little at the very least. I didn't realize that I'd actually been leaning against it – this proverbial door – until I started having to think and then write.

I spent far too long trying to figure out the dramaturgy of the tale of exclusion that the Filipino side of my family experienced in Canada. But I had a glaring problem: my father, my sister, and I make up the extent of the "Filipino side of my family" in Canada. We've got family elsewhere in the world from the Philippines, but that's it for here. If you add that up, it's, like, two people in total? And that's being generous as, really, my father carries our Filipino identity in its entirety by himself due to the lack of my sister and I's immersion into his culture. So, we're down to one ... and a half people, maybe, maybe. There are huge warning signals in my head telling me that this is not a big enough research pool for this kind of work. What even is this kind of work?

I realized - or, rather, found myself re/turned to some*thing*, a truth, that I had been forgetting to remember: I never write about myself in my entirety. I usually cherry-pick what part of me gets to be churned through the critical paradigms recognized by the academe; it's often utilizing those parts to be a/ part of it all (awful, ain't it?).So, I think, speak, write, and frame myself and my work in a way that generalizes to the point ofover-accessibility. It doesn't feel good. I'm starting to stop replying with "I'm Brown" when asked about my racial and cultural identity because it makes the architecture of me a little too porous; the door's wide open But it's the closest thing to the truth that I've got at the moment. I don't feel I am Filipino, or Trinidadian, or whatever else I'm made of – even, and especially, "Canadian", for that matter!

I do not write about being Trinidadian or Filipino ever. I'll admit finding myself wanting to acknowledge and nod towards my Trinidadian heritage in my writing every now and then – or at points when it seems to be a method of building coalition with someone or provide me with a necessary buffer in white-dominated spaces. This is probably due to the literal proximity of my mum's Trinidadian family and their more direct presence in my life; however, I never, ever talk about being Filipino let alone study it, but now the door is open. So.

...

*I'm cracking 4 eggs into a bowl in the kitchen. My father is here, too, de-shelling shrimps. He's planning to make a soup of some sort. My stomach isn't really feeling too keen on eating shrimp– today, but maybe he'll forego adding any kind of dairy to it. It's always better when he cooks like a Filipino instead of a white man.*

*I'm tempted to ask him whilst I'm cracking the eggs and he's de-shelling the shrimp, "How do you say 'egg' in Tagalog?" I don't know why I'm asking since I won't remember what he says. That's how it's always been. Well, no. When I was younger, I asked – I asked a bunch - and I tried to remember. I did. But I grew out of that urge to remember long ago. Now, why would I ask? Because I'm writing this paper? Maybe I'll remember this time? Because it'll maybe do something of note? I don't ask him.*

*We continue in silence. I make the eggs. I go to wash the pan while it's still hot. He's at the kitchen sink, cleaning and preparing green beans with a plastic bag at the side where all the trash from the food prepping can be tossed. A little garbage bag. He's a chef. That's a chef-tip, I guess. I've picked up his and my mum's cooking habits. Not to brag but, besides being a perpetual student, cooking and baking are really the only other things I'm confident I'm good at.*

...

I don't have a great relationship with my father. It's deteriorated over the years and, currently, sits in a kind of space where I am obligated to make a choice about its longevity, its viability, and its potential. I do not bear confrontation well and, here, I am confronted with the reality of my father being my one stable tethering point to being Filipino and, given my relationship with him, my relationship with my identity as a half-Filipino feels ... not so great either.

Everything I've come to know about being Filipino has been taught to me consciously and inadvertently by my father. These teachings were epistemically ingrained thoroughly and immovably in me by the time I was about 10 years-old and now, in my 24th year, I am trying to figure out just how ossified this knowledge is and what the consequences are.

This narrative is probably not an uncommon one. From childhood, I've curated, collected, and archived the inheritance of my identity and heritage by bearing witness to my parents' own curatorial, collective, and archival tendencies with their respective heritages and identities - and, also, their combined identity as it exists in my sister and I. It's always been easier to say that I was Canadian when I was growing up because of the instability of the Trinidadian and Filipino aspects of my identity. My parents both immigrated to Canada from their home countries and then, once they were married, would move to a long list of other countries for work. This continued when my sister and I came into the picture as well; it's important to note that we never lived in either the Philippines or Trinidad. My sister and I have spent the majority of our lives in Bermuda and Canada. So, it was easier to be "Canadian". That ease, though, is always short-lived, because that claim to Canadian citizenship is always prodded at further with a "Yes, but where are you *really* from?" And there's a real seediness to this question because underneath it comes a command: *open the door; let me in*. There is no safety in these state-sanctioned identities. There is no stability in them. The process of running down the list of things under the heading of "Identity" becomes tedious. This ritual maintains my recognizability as an Other through colonial mimicry (hooks, 1992). I don't want to let anyone in. This place is falling apart!

Based purely on what I observed of my father and his proclivities, I had grown up believing that the following was what it meant to be Filipino:

- Being Filipino meant constantly moving wherever the work was and moving away from where the work wasn't, so my relationship with space and land was one that has always been, and remains, mostly semi-un-rooted.
- Being Filipino meant working all the time in order to be a good breadwinner, a good provider for your family, and someone who could bear the burden of what I now know the names for: neoliberalism and racial capitalism[1] - all with a very personable smile and an affability that doesn't display any noticeable thorns. You see, part of being Filipino is about being an excellent people-person, apparently. I don't have enough appendages to count all the times I've heard folks (mostly liberal and white) say, "I know a Filipino person! They're so nice!" as if "niceness" is the variable to be measured when determining a person's Filipino-ness. As someone who tries on "Canadian" every now and then, I've also heard that same phrase uttered about citizens of this nation-state; it's a double whammy of niceness over here! And it is oppressive; it can be a tool used to cause social death (Cacho, 2012). Niceness, for a racialized person, isn't an identity when its definition and parameters are curated, collected, and archived by the neoliberal state – whether the Philippines, Canada, or otherwise. Niceness, in this case, translates to my being doubly able to be policed by the state because it's supposed to be inherently part of my heritage and identity.
- Being Filipino also meant having access to the language, Tagalog, which my father never shared with me and my sister, despite my mother's constant asking for him to do so. He would use work and exhaustion as an

---

[1] See hampton (2020) for more on neoliberalism and racial capitalism within the academe.

excuse not to. I wonder about that justification now and whether there was any exclusionary intentionality from my father; maybe we did not really fit the Filipino identity enough for him. Or, perhaps, he felt he was doing my sister and I a solid by not allowing us access to the language. Or maybe he was just genuinely tired – I wish I'd asked. I should probably figure out why I haven't tried learning it myself.

- Being Filipino entailed having and maintaining *massive* transnational networks of connections and communities made of Kuyas, and Ates, and Tiyos, and Tiyas - related by blood and by choice and, most often, by work. Growing up in Bermuda, my sister and I were toted along by our father to Filipino gatherings and social events. The Filipino attendeesseemed to know my sister and I almost too wellwell, namely because my father was very well-known, well-liked, and he would find any opportunity to make sure we were seen. But these folks, kind as they were, were strangers to us because we were missing the ability to really be in conversation – not just in terms of the language but in terms of the missing cultural context(s). They'd switch from Tagalog to English after watching my sister and I fumble for words, staring sheepishly back, desperately wanting to be *something* to them that was mutually recognizable. I felt quite ashamed and embarrassed – and angry, too, at my father. I remember, being the eldest sibling, wanting to create bridges between my sister and other Filipino kids there in those spaces; it was easier for me to blend in, at least, given that I seemed to have inherited much of my father's face and my sister inherited my mum's. Those physical differences were pointed out, too, and often exoticized in those spaces, but I didn't have the words to describe what that felt like at the time especially because, in the end, it was not a currency that helped in this particular kind of social economy.
- Being Filipino meant embracing a kind of martyrdom. I witness my father engage frequently with other Filipinos in rhetoric that suggests that one must always be reaching out for that "greener grass on the other side" at whatever cost; reaching out for some kind of memorability, something that people will remember you for - but it wasn't exactly legacy-building in the same way that would be recognized in neoliberal, capitalist, white, Western culture. It felt a bit clandestine, this recognition by one's own people and I know it is not mine to try and claim.
- Being Filipino meant existing liminally and being able to move within as many spaces as possible to ensure social security, social stability, and social mobility (this can also read: being *really good* at bullshitting the system(s) but not too radically that they notice one's disruptive presence).

> One has to be everything, everytime, everywhere to everyone. At whatever cost.
> – Being Filipino also came with ramifications of being designated as having one's identity predicated and founded upon an assumed natural state of servitude from what I've witnessed of the countless Filipino babysitters, nannies, nurses, and other positions of caretaking. Thanks a lot, American imperialism. You just keep doing your thing, don't you?
> – Being Filipino also meant taking pride in one's autonomy so long as it directly benefitted the greater whole. In the case of my parents' intersection, with my mom being Trinidadian and my father being Filipino – and both and being Canadian – there was a kind of tension that arose about where to place this particular pride. They made education the locus of that pride; it was the economy of choice, for them, which explains why I am where I am today as a scholar who has gained access to institutions that guaranteed that I would be a recognizable Other (hooks, 1992) – how's that for legacy?
> – Being Filipino was also about music, and singing, and eating, eating, eating, and joy, and feeling a sense of longing for home and/but being able to make home wherever you were.
> – Being Filipino felt complicated because it felt like an identity tied to understandings of the fiscal; it felt like everything came at a cost and I felt the economic weight of that identity enmeshed with all the other sections of who I was.
> – Being Filipino meant being my father.

Is this what it means to be Filipino? I'm not sure, but that's not the question that I keep re/turning to: will I find out and what then?

I explained to my friend on the phone and my mum that I'm struggling to write this chapter because I am having to write from a space of negation, a space of absence, a space where nothing exists – at least, nothing I can confirm using the normal tools of the academic trade, I think. I usually write about what's there. Or at least from a space where there is at least the ghost of a theory for me to commune with. This feels like some*thing* that doesn't adhere to time, or space, or any of the Western academic structuring that I have been conditioned to utilize throughout my education which I have now come to recognize as, perhaps, my life. I am reminded byby Audre Lorde (1984) that there is no separation between the personal and the political.

My mum, privy to my turmoil over this chapter, asked outright why I was writing it at all. She tossed the hard-hitting questions my way: why do you have to like and be in good relations with all of your identity? Why defend, advocate for, and reconcile that with which you do not have a strong or good relationship with? Why do you need to do this right now when it's not had an impact on your life previously? My fellow dramaturg asks me the same questions over the phone, phrasing them in a way that appeals to our mutual dramaturgical practice which asks us to continuously find entry points: *why don't you write about why you don't want to write this paper?*

He's asking me to *let them in*. The knock on the door sounds different.

The question of my Filipino identity and its analogous manifestation as my father has always mattered, but it's always lived in a space of absence, so it's not always readily available to be scrutinized by my scholarship; it was out of sight. But how it came to be in that space of absence still confounds me. I am more than willing to accept that, given my age, the time, the circumstances, I may have created or, at least, continued to cultivate and uphold this particular relationality to my Filipino identity and, thus, my father *intentionally*. And that choice has specific consequences for me and they don't particularly feel good right now.

I'm supposed to "be" a PhD student in the field of social justice education. My research looks at how to prevent Othering in "Canadian" tertiary academic institutions using quotidian dramaturgy - that is critically analyzing and manipulating the narrative and stories of everyday life. My dramaturgical praxis is informed by and in coalition with Black Studies and Indigenous Studies pertaining to land sovereignty (Coulthard, 2017). I attribute my understanding of "Othering" to bell hooks (1992) and to an anonymous colleague of mine (2018) who described it as feeling "accused of something you don't understand or being accused of not being able to do something that you don't understand". Othering is universal; who is impervious to feeling excluded? I use Othering to welcome universal culpability in this work towards equity in education (hooks, 1992; Bala, 2017; Fanon, 1961; Said, 1978; Butler, 2006; Derrida, 2017 Salverson, 2008, 2011; Erevelles, 2016; Pateman & Mills, 2007).

Those are a lot of big, ol' lenses to pass these recent revelations through.

There is detritus. My institutionalization has affected me, my identity, and my relation to it. In order to achieve and abide by the tenets of my Filipino-Trinidadian identity, I have, inadvertently, marginalized and excluded those identities from myself and done so in a way that there's invokes a real fear in me that it might be too late.

We have been riding and crashing into, out of, and under various waves of pandemics and pandemonium globally. In Canada, COVID-19 is starting its second wave - we've had a record amount of cases reported in one day this past week in Ontario (Rodrigues, 2020). The renewed anti-Asian racism (Kang et al., 2020) that emerged with the virus is still very much attached to this pandemic and it has not yet been acknowledged in its entirety, or yet been pushed through the all of the necessary critical paradigms that the academe is known for subjecting histories, presences, and futurities to (Pearson Clarke, 2016). The Black Lives Matter movement continues to be in what Sefanit Habtom and Megan Scribe (2020) refer to as "co-conspiratorship" with the movement for Indigenous sovereignty in this country. Justice, in the form of abolition and liberatory politics and pedagogy, is being sought and summoned by marginalized folks who are targeted by the systemic, state-sanctioned violence of the supremacy of whiteness (hampton, 2020). There is a necessity to ensure that the fight towards justice is one that is sustainable.

I've been toying with a thought: does sustainability require those involved in these battles to be able to acknowledge the extent, power, and promise of their wholeness? There are a multitude of ways to determine what wholeness entails for the individual and the collective, and there are a multitude of ways in which wholeness can be handled. I think of all the activists, artists, teachers, students, friends, and family members I know who are grappling with keeping themselves whole, achieving wholeness, or perhaps culling away those parts of themselves that feel extraneous. I think, right now, I'd like to ascertain my wholeness, which requires an acknowledgement of *all* of me because I think all of me has something to offer for/to the fray. Even these bits that really make me uneasy.

I cannot possibly advocate for, ally with, work in coalition or solidarity with anybody - especially those who face marginalization and exclusion from society based on racist, homophobic, ageist, ableist, or classist premises, among others - when the internal geographies of my being are under a kind of colonial scrutiny that is tethered to frameworks rooted in capitalism, neo-liberalism, and white supremacy. I know now, for instance, that I ought to use Aguilar Jr.'s (2015) naming of the Filipino diaspora more explicitly. I know now that I ought to always name racial capitalism in relation to my understanding of diasporic Filipino identity. I know the impact of white patriarchy upon on the bodies of Filipino women. And I also know that tethered to all this knowledge is my father and my relationship with him. And the distinct lack of my connection to other scholars who are Filipino or who work in Asian Studies. That feels so very wrong, antithetical. I know better. So, what aren't I doing and why aren't I doing it?

I don't know how to write this chapter because I don't want to write this chapter. I don't know how to think, write, or talk about an part of my identity that has been archived in a particularly scary way within myself. What I have come to understand as being Filipino might be true and it might be the opposite, or something else entirely illegible to me. My father is Filipino. My father is the Philippines to me. And what else does it mean to be Filipino? Do I want to know what more there is? It's difficult to reconcile the desire to be whole with the knowledge of the risk and cost associated with that realization. This process sounds incredibly self-indulgent and self-righteous to me. Right now, becoming whole requires my acknowledgement of my identities – racialized and otherwise – and an acknowledgement of my proximity and willingness to engage with those identities. What it may mean is that I must fracture further my notions of identity, which is easier to talk about theoretically - I've been trained by the academe to do this in a way that is deemed "critical". It's easy to explain it to you who's reading, but... what do I do with my father once all that fracturing is over?

...

*Should I ask him how to say green beans? I count to ten.*

*I can count to ten in Tagalog out loud but I can't write it down. If I could, I'd have written that right here for dramatic and aesthetic effect/affect. I don't get to ten because I'm pretty grossed out - the same sick feeling in my stomach that the shrimp induced - at myself. I don't want to do whatever work this is on these kinds of contrived terms. But pushing it into this space - this one where I can start scholarizing it - might make it stick the way the rest of the shit I've scholarized has stuck.*

I hesitate to reach out. To confirm. To corroborate what my understanding of being Filipino was. To figure out why it doesn't feel good with others. With myself. I don't know how to want to subject this story to scrutiny. I feel a spacious melancholy when I think about how there are people who are feeling – or aren't feeling – good about this in the same way I am.

...

*We're standing at the sink. I don't know what green beans or eggs are called in Tagalog. I don't really know my father entirely and am worried about my only method of getting to know him might be through an academic lens. And I don't know myself and I know why on various levels. And it's not just me. My sister, too, might share this. That seems so sad.*

*There's nothing beautiful to write anymore.*

...

"Am I proud to be Filipino? Sure. Do I know what it means to be Filipino? No. So, what am I proud of?" I asked my sister right before this piece became written, when we were having our conversations/non-conversations. I'd opened the door to let her in, hoping she would be surprised to find it there, and instead found that she had actually been with me this entire time, leaning on it with me. It scares me to know that I hadn't seen her sooner. It thrills me to not be alone with this. You have my utmost gratitude for thinking with me.

We re/turn towards and away from conversation/non-conversation. We re/turnto the door, and it takes both of us pushing against it: keeping it out, keeping it in, keeping a look out.

...

*I'm assembling a bowl of the food: sautéed shrimp, green beans, carrots, bean sprouts, and Napa cabbage atop thick glass noodles. I ask: is this a Filipino dish? He says, no, he's just created this. I knew he'd say that. Funny how much you can know what something is not, and feel better about that, than hoping at what it could be. .*

...

I wrote this piece in thought with my sister, my mama, and my friends. My gratitude to you all.

As stated, this piece took shape whilst I was out walking with my mama,. We currently live, walk, work (remotely, for me), and are in the traditional territory of the Anishinaabe Peoples, neighboured by the communities of Alderville First Nation, Curve Lake First Nation, and Hiawatha First Nation. I offer my gratitude and wish to acknowledge the histories, the presents, and the futures of the land and its original and existing caretakers.

This gratitude, necessarily, is extended towards the Black communities of this land who have been and remain instrumental in the consistent unravelling of the colonial tapestry that is the identity of so-called "Canada"and the weaving of a different kind of futurity (hampton, 2020). We must continue to name and combat anti-Blackness; challenge and abolish the structures of racial capitalism, liberal hegemony, and the violence of the carceral state; and acknowledge and continue creating a justice that can actually contend with the continuing trauma of these particular diasporic histories.

I acknowledge my own history with this land and my people whose practices sit with me. I will work to make space for the land and those who have worked to provide me with the same accommodation time and time again.

I am humbled and indebted and working.

## References

Aguilar, F. V. (2015). Is the Filipino diaspora a diaspora? *Critical Asian Studies, 47*(3), 440–461. doi:10.1080/14672715.2015.1057392.

Bala, S. (2017). Decolonising theatre and performance studies. *Tijdschrift Voor Genderstudies, 20*(3), 333–345. doi:10.5117/tvgn2017.3.bala.

Butler, J. (2006). *Gender Trouble: Feminism and the Subversion of Identity.* Routledge. https://doi.org/10.4324/9780203824979

Cacho, L. M. (2012). *Social Death: Racialized Rightlessness and the Criminalization of the Unprotected.* New York, New York: New York University Press.

Caldoza, W. (2020, August 25). What's the best that happens if I think of schooling as my spirituality? Retrieved November 29, 2020, from https://medium.com/@walliscaldoza/whats-the-best-that-happens-if-i-making-schooling-my-spirituality-4e8eb73084d1

Coulthard, G. S. (2017). *Red Skin, White Masks: Rejecting the Colonial Politics of Recognition.* Vancouver, B.C.: Langara College.

Crenshaw, K. (2016). The urgency of intersectionality. Retrieved November 29, 2020, from https://www.ted.com/talks/kimberle_crenshaw_the_urgency_of_intersectionality?language=en

Derrida, J. (2017). *Gift Of Death.* Chicago: University of Chicago Press.

Erevelles, N. (2016). *Disability and Difference in Global Contexts: Enabling a Transformative Body Politic.* New York: Palgrave Macmillan.

Fanon, F. (1968). *The Wretched of the Earth: The Handbook for the Black Revolution That Is Changing the Shape of the World.* New York: Grove Press.

Habtom, S. & Megan Scribe (2020). To breathe together: Co-conspirators for decolonial futures. Yellowhead Institute. https://yellowheadinstitute.org/2020/06/02/to-breathe-together/

hampton, rosalind. (2020). *Black Racialization and Resistance at an Elite University.* Toronto: University of Toronto Press.

Harney, S., & Moten, F. (2013). *The Undercommons: Fugitive Planning and Black Study.* Wivenhoe: Minor Compositions.

hooks, b. (1992). *Black Looks: Race and Representation.* Boston: South End Press.

Jordan, J. (2000). Soldier : a poet's childhood (1st ed.). Basic Books.

Kang, P., et al. (2020). *June 18 Webinar: Addressing Anti-Asian Racism During the Pandemic* [Webinar]. Centre for Leadership and Diversity at the Ontario Institute for Studies in Education at OISE. https://m.facebook.com/UofTEastAsianLibrary/posts/2710523019272198?locale2=es_LA

Lorde, A. (1984). *Sister Outsider: Essays and Speeches.* USA: Crossing Press. Nolan, Y. (2015). *Medicine Shows: Indigenous Performance Culture.* Toronto: Playwrights Canada Press.

Pateman, C., & Mills, C. W. (2007). *Contract and Domination.* Cambridge, UK: Polity.

Pearson Clarke, M. (2016). Difficult histories: An interview with Deanna Bowen. *No More Potlucks* (*May-August*) 44, http://nomorepotlucks.org/site/difficult-histories-an-interview-withdeanna-bowen-michele-pearson-clarke/

Rodrigues, G. (2020, September 28). Ontario reports 700 new coronavirus cases, highest daily infections ever recorded. Retrieved October 02, 2020, from https://globalnews.ca/news/7363285/ontario-coronavirus-cases-september-28-covid19/

Salverson, J. (2008). Taking liberties: A theatre class of foolish witnesses. *Research in drama education*, 13(2), 245-255.

Salverson, J. (Ed.). (2011). *Community Engaged Theatre and Performance*. Playwrights Canada Press.

Said, E. (1978). Orientalism: Western concepts of the Orient. *New York: Pantheon.*

PART 3

*Citizenship, Multiculturalism, Culture, Identity*

CHAPTER 10

# The Multicultural Façade
*A Colonial Performance of Diversity in Canada and Indonesia*

Vania Soepriatna

## 1  Introduction

Multiculturalism has become a buzzword that has been generally accepted and expected in liberal democratic societies. Especially in communities where multiple ethnic and cultural backgrounds are present, multiculturalism has become the golden standard to address equality, diversity, and inclusion. As nations consider implementing multiculturalism into law, two countries that pride themselves on having accomplished this are Canada and Indonesia. As someone born in Indonesia and currently residing in Canada, I observe many similarities in how the two countries perform multiculturalism. These similarities are apparent despite the substantial difference in the history and experience of colonialism within the respective regions.

This chapter provides a comparative analysis of the historical reasons Canada and Indonesia adopted multiculturalism and how they implement it into policy. There are many definitions and interpretations of what multiculturalism entails. The Canadian Library of Parliament provides three different interpretations that comprehensively address the different facets of multiculturalism: 1) descriptive, 2) prescriptive, and 3) political (Brosseau & Dewing, 2018). For consistency, I am applying these interpretations to analyze multiculturalism in both Canada and Indonesia. I do not intend to use the Canadian interpretations of multiculturalism as a cookie-cutter definition to be applied to the Indonesian multicultural context. Instead, by applying these interpretations to both contexts, I want to highlight the similarities in how the two countries incorporate multiculturalism within their state policies despite them being on different sides of colonialism: Canada as a colonial power while Indonesia as a postcolonial nation.

Canada's Library of Parliament interprets multiculturalism as follows. First, the descriptive interpretation of multiculturalism refers to the sociological fact that people from diverse ethnic and cultural backgrounds are present within a society. Second, the prescriptive interpretation refers to the ideology that consists of a set of ideas and ideals on the celebration of multiculturalism. In the

Canadian context, this celebrates Canada's cultural mosaic. Finally, political interpretation refers to diversity management through formal initiatives in the federal, provincial, territorial, and municipal domains (Brosseau & Dewing, 2018). With these interpretations, I argue that the adoption of multiculturalism in Canadian and Indonesian legislature is an extension of colonialism that continues to reproduce colonial systems concealed by a façade of diversity and equality.

This chapter explores how multiculturalism policies affect the people within their respective geographic and symbolic borders. Geographic borders are the land or territorial boundaries of a nation as indicated on maps, and symbolic borders is the conceptual nationhood signified by citizenship status, along with the privileges that come with that status. The people within Canada's and Indonesia's geographic and symbolic borders experience multiculturalism policies differently, with some having more privileges and enjoying the benefits of such policies, while some continue to be marginalized and excluded.

In theme with the rest of this book, my focus in the Canadian context is on the Asian experience of exclusion and the complex positionality they experience as the "visible minority" group. As an Asian international student in Canada, my position here falls under this "visible minority" umbrella. Meanwhile, my focus in the Indonesian context is on the ethnic-Chinese minority experience of being excluded and having a complex positionality in Indonesia. As an ethnic-Chinese Indonesian woman residing in Canada, I find myself having to continuously negotiate, rationalize and justify my belonging as I am "othered" in both.

Systems like race, class, and citizenship have historically been the colonial dividing tools that continue to riddle communities within Canada and Indonesia. The coupling of multiculturalism and liberal democracy creates the illusion of equal individual power and autonomy. While it is undoubtedly empowering for individuals, for whom such power enables grass-roots organization and resistance, it also removes responsibility from the colonial power that created these systemic inequalities (Bannerji, 2000). Beneath the multicultural illusion of equality, diversity, and inclusion, the responsibility to dismantle oppressive systems lies on the very individuals that are oppressed by the system. Adopting multiculturalism as a policy to address inequalities caused by race, class, and citizenship is an oversimplified "solution" that cannot possibly reverse centuries of colonial division. Instead of addressing inequalities, Bannerji (2000) argues that multiculturalism reduces the struggles and differences caused by colonial systemic inequality down to mere ethnic differences, which are often conflated with differences in values, customs, and culture, where the problems are systemic.

Before divulging into the comparative analysis, there are a few distinctions that must be made clear. Canada is a settler-colonial nation led by the British and French (White) government that continues to occupy stolen indigenous lands, while Indonesia is a postcolonial country led by a native Indonesian government. As a settler colonial nation, Canada has accumulated much of its diversity through immigration, while Indonesia is an intrinsically diverse geographical area bound by a shared colonial history. In other words, Canada's diversity as we know today it is exogenous, whereas Indonesia's diversity is endogenous, with a few ethnic groups as an exception.

## 2   Multiculturalism in Canada

Canada is the first nation to adopt multiculturalism into state policy and it has been the centrepiece of Canadian pride (Jedwab, 2020). However, it is imperative, first of all, to acknowledge that Canada is a settler-colonial institution. It is built on stolen indigenous land, Turtle Island, which belongs and is home to the First Nations, Metis, and Inuit people. The region that is currently known as Canada consists of vastly different ethnic and cultural identities since time immemorial. However, with the arrival of White settlers followed by the establishment of Canada, new arrivants exponentially boosted the heterogeneity and diversity of what we now know as multicultural Canada (Bannerji, 2000).

Since the turn of the 20th century, there have been multiple waves of immigrants coming from other European countries, Asia, the Caribbean, and South and Central America (Brosseau & Dewing, 2009; Brosseau & Dewing, 2018). Prime Minister Pierre Trudeau officially implemented the Multiculturalism Act as a policy in 1971, intended to acknowledge that Canadians come from a wide variety of cultural backgrounds and that all of them have intrinsic value (Jedwab, 2020). However, for nearly 50 years since the adoption, Canada's multicultural policy has been contested with an ongoing debate over the confusing messages it conveys and how it applies to indigenous peoples and non-white immigrants, referred to as the "visible minority" (Bannerji, 2000). The "visible minority" category is designated for "persons, or other than Aboriginal peoples, who are non-Caucasian in race or non-white in colour" (Ontario Ministry of Finance, 2003).

Before 1971, the Canadian government was resistant to multiculturalism, and most aspects of the nation-building, including political, economic, and social institutions, were oriented toward replicating a British-like society (Brosseau & Dewing, 2018). However, the post-World War II influx of immigrants from non-British and non-French European countries, along with the influx of immigrants coming from Asia, the Caribbean, Central and South America, finally pushed the government to reconsider the role of "other ethnic groups" within the Canadian society (Brosseau & Dewing, 2018). The Royal Commission on Bilingualism and Biculturalism was appointed to investigate the contribution of non-Indigenous, non-French, and non-English ethnic groups in Canada. Opposed to the United States' model of the "melting pot" that push for assimilation, The Commission recommended the "integration" of ethnic groups in Canada (Brosseau & Dewing, 2018; Jedwab, 2020).

The recommendations made by The Commission led to the assembly of the Multiculturalism Policy in 1971 (Brosseau & Dewing, 2018). However, this policy was initially only made to address the tensions between British and French Canadians, as the report showed growing unrest among Quebecois who wanted protection over their language and culture (Jedwab, 2020). Prime Minister Pierre Trudeau announced the new Canadian policy opening with "a policy of multiculturalism within a bilingual framework … to break down discriminatory attitudes and cultural jealousies" and concluded with "I wish to emphasize the view of the government that a policy of multiculturalism within a bilingual framework is basically the conscious support of individual freedom of choice" (quoted in Driedger, 2011). In his speech, PM Trudeau was only speaking to the British and French Canadians.

Regardless, the institutionalization of the 1971 Multiculturalism Policy opened the doors for more non-European immigrants to come into Canada, adding to the "visible minority" population (Brosseau & Dewing 2018). Bannerji (2000) observes that along with the aspiration to create a more liberal democratic nation, Canada's capitalist industrial growth was also an underlying expectation. Non-European immigrants, mainly from former British colonies, provide cheap skilled and unskilled labour to fulfill the capitalist demand (Bannerji, 2000). The term "visible minority" was, thus, coined and prescribed to categorize this growing immigrant population, "stressing both features of being non-white and therefore visible in a way whites are not, and of being politically minor players" (Bannerji, 2000, p. 30).

The use of "visible minority" as an official terminology for non-white immigrants are not considered problematic by the immigrant population because they were content with having some political eligibility, better than none (Bannerji, 2000). Besides, the stereotype of Asians as the "model minority" conveniently supports the sentiment that they make contributions to the society. Although the stereotypes of Asians, particularly the Chinese, as model minority originated in the United States, the discourse has been implanted in Canada to support the neo-liberal ideology and fit together perfectly with the Canadian multicultural discourse (Pon, 2000).

The Asian image of being both "model minority" and "visible minority" reasserts the idea that Canada is a fair, tolerant society, despite the reality of systemic racism (Pon, 2000). Additionally, this image of Asian immigrants as the visible model minority, have repeatedly been used to show as proof that one could successfully overcome systemic barriers if they worked hard enough, which implicitly blamed the oppression of Black, Indigenous, and other racial minorities on their work ethics (Pon, 2000). This double-edged sword positions Asians as privileged enough to justify their exclusion from federal support while at the same time still subjected to the same discriminative, racist systems of oppression as other minorities.

In the 1980s, Canada improved its multicultural policies with an explicit focus on addressing racial relations (Brosseau & Dewing, 2018). The Canadian Charter of Rights and Freedoms institutionalize the recognition of Canada's multicultural heritage in the constitution and address the elimination of discrimination by guaranteeing equality and fairness to all under the law regardless of race or ethnicity (Brosseau & Dewing, 2018). The Department of Multiculturalism was created in 1987. The Canadian Multiculturalism Act was adopted in 1988 to help preserve culture and language and enhance cultural awareness by specifying everyone's right to identify with the cultural heritage of their choice yet still retain equitable participation in the Canadian society (Brosseau & Dewing, 2018). Under this act, all aspects of government agencies, including the Crown, are expected to promote Canada's multicultural mix.

In the same year, the government of Canada formally apologized for the wrongful incarceration, seizure of property and disenfranchisement of Japanese Canadian during World War II, which led to the Japanese Canadian Redress Agreement (Brosseau & Dewing, 2018). However, the redress and settlement prompted a collective forgetting of the horrendous acts targeted towards Japanese Canadians, along with the systems that allowed such history (Oikawa, 1999). This settlement serves as another example in which an Asian visible minority group is being displayed in Canada's performative multiculturalism to show the government's effort to close the gap on racial disparities. Meanwhile, the policies and systems used for the Japanese Canadian internment are the same strategies that have been and still are, the methods used to continue to segregate Indigenous communities in reservations (Oikawa, 1999).

In 2006, the Canadian government, again, performed a full apology to Chinese Canadians for the imposed head tax and refusal to accept Chinese immigrants in 1923 and 1947 (Brosseau & Dewing, 2018). However, again, the notion that perpetuates the foreignness of visible minority groups are still intact. Ideas about the dangerous internal foreigner continue to be salient, continue to reproduce racialized others, and continue to justify renationalization endeavours that deflect criticism of imperialist and colonialist agendas (Dhanmoon & Abu-Laban, 2009). Especially during crises, security concerns are deployed to legitimize laws and changes in laws that impose state powers in the name of security, further masking the state violence of perpetually producing foreignness towards non-white groups (Dhanmoon & Abu-Laban, 2009).

Currently, during the COVID-19 pandemic, frenzies over health and safety have caused the resurfacing and heightening of Asian visibility as perpetual foreigners. Growing anti-Chinese sentiments and hate crimes targeting Asian communities rose in correlation with the media's language and images that overrepresent Asian communities to associate the community with the virus (Patel & Bowden, 2020). The current rise in anti-Asian racism is not new, as history has repeatedly shown many occasions that blame Asian communities for diseases (Larsson, 2020; Madokoro, 2020). On the other side of this, however, most "visible minorities," including Asian communities, are also, in fact, at higher risk of infection due to the systemic racism that impacts living conditions that make social distancing impossible, perpetuates underlying health conditions from lower access to proper healthcare, and limits employment opportunities that generate the overrepresentation of minorities as essential workers (Bibbins-Domingo, 2020; CDC, 2020).

The current pandemic exposes how performative Canadian multiculturalism has always been and continues to be. The Canadian multicultural policies have always been intended to build on Canada's image as a multicultural, liberal, inclusive, and progressive nation that only benefits British and French (white) Canadians. The systemic oppression structures that marginalize non-white bodies—the "visible minorities," black, and indigenous populations—are still well intact.

## 3   Multiculturalism in Indonesia

Like Canada, Indonesia is considered a multicultural society. As a sociological fact, Indonesia is a diverse nation ethnically, culturally and religiously. The archipelago consists of about six thousand inhabited islands home to more than seven hundred ethnic groups and languages (Badan Pusat Statistik, 2011). The many ethnic groups and cultures existing within the Indonesian archipelago are united through Bhinneka Tunggal Ika, or Unity in Diversity as the national motto, the Pancasila, a set of five philosophical ideologies, as the national foundation, and Bahasa Indonesia as the national language. These are enshrined in the national constitution, Undang-Undang Dasar 1945, when Indonesia declared independence. Unity in Diversity and Pancasila is the prescriptive multicultural ideology and aspirational imaginary that Indonesia strives for as a developing nation.

Like Canada, Indonesia has become the multicultural nation that it is today due to colonization. Indonesia is home to such an immense diversity mainly because of the territorial borders that have been inherited from Dutch colonial rule. Before the Dutch colonization, these islands consisted of many different sovereignties, from dynasties to small tribes, all with their indigenous cultural values, traditions, and languages (Steenbrink, 1993). Additionally, the Srivijaya and Majapahit kingdoms in pre-colonial Sumatra and Java islands were great transit hubs for trade, which allowed entry to merchants from China, India, and the Arabian Gulf, and many of them settled (Anggraeni, 2011). Indonesia's geography had been previously established as the Dutch East Indies, and the hundreds of different ethnic groups in the Dutch East Indies are now united under the shared history of Dutch colonization.

Upon independence, the Republic of Indonesia is declared a democratic nation that strives for Unity in Diversity. However, the implementation of democracy and Unity in Diversity has not been easy. Foster (1982) contends that many colonized nations tend to fall into phases of denial and imagination as part of their attempt to reclaim a sense of nationalism after independence. The denial phase consists of a "break up with the past" mindset that rejects ideologies brought by their colonizers or any exogenous influence, and the imagination phase includes imaginaries of an ideal future of becoming an independent developed nation (Foster, 1982). However, it is also a common tendency for young independent nations to fall back into the structures established by colonial regimes due to the lack of time to build their infrastructures from scratch (Altbach, 1982)

As a young postcolonial nation, Indonesia has had many troubling eras and regimes. The pendulum swings back and forth in the tension between the progress towards Unity in Diversity that celebrates the cultural integrities that make up Indonesia and the dependence on colonial infrastructures that the country inherited. As stated in the introduction, Indonesia's multiculturalism is a by-product of colonial power mainly because of the territorial borders and the governmental bureaucratic structures that the nation inherited and continues to maintain. During the Dutch colonial era, the government was centralized on Java, where Batavia, now known as Jakarta, was built (Ricklefs, 1992). As a result, the Javanese are considerably more privileged in geography and political proximity to the Dutch (Steenbrink, 1993).

It is no surprise that all of Indonesia's political leaders and freedom fighters, including the founding fathers and Panitia Sembilan (The Nine Committee), are Javanese and Muslim (Brata & Wartha, 2017). Indonesia's plans for post-independence nation-building are based on and centralized around Javanese and Islamic philosophies that are not representative of Indonesia's population beyond Java (Soepriatna, 2019). In fact, Bhinneka Tunggal Ika is an old Javanese language from the pre-colonial Majapahit Kingdom in Java, and the Pancasila are based on the coupling of Islamic and Majapahit philosophies (Brata & Wartha, 2017). With the inheritance of Dutch colonial infrastructures, the newly independent Indonesian government maintains that structure with a new hegemony, the Muslim Javanese. This new hegemony continues to marginalize those who are non-Muslim and non-Javanese.

Most of Indonesia's ethnic groups are native to the archipelago, except for the Indians, Arabs and Chinese, who have started to settle in the area in waves starting from before the colonial period up to the early 20th century (Anggraeni, 2011). As part of the Dutch conquest, a system was introduced to categorize the area's inhabitants at that time (Steenbrink, 1993). The categories are 1) Europeans at the highest most privileged position, 2) Foreign Orientals at the middle position for non-Europeans and non-natives, and 3) Pribumi at the lowest position for the natives (Steenbrink, 1993). This system provides the base that evolved into systems of race, class and citizenship status in Indonesia today.

Although Foreign Orientals are technically placed above Pribumi, with more privileges in the form of job opportunities and closer contact with the European officials, both categories fell under the same legal footing in Dutch courts where both were subjects of the colonial rule (Lindsey, 2005). Over time, most Indian and Arab settlers come to be very well integrated with pribumi, presumably, because these ethnic groups brought huge religious influence to the area; Buddhism and Hinduism from the Indians and Islam from the Arabs (Anggraeni, 2011). However, until now, Chinese descents in Indonesia who have been in the area for generations have not been able to integrate with local pribumi (Ingketria, 2018a; Soebagjo, 2008; Suryadinata, 2008). Reasons for this phenomenon include the Chinese ghettoization during the colonial era that restricted them from travelling beyond their designated villages; and the Chinese being allocated a middle-management role to conduct the dirty work for Dutch officials, including agriculture management and tax collection (Anggraeni, 2011).

By the early 20th century, there was a new wave of Chinese immigrants who presumably escaped the communist regime, while at the same time, there was also a surge among ethnic Chinese in Indonesia to realign themselves with China due to the rise of Chinese nationalist and the precarious status that they were put in under the Dutch colonial rule (Lindsey, 2005). This precarity became the basis of mistrust among Pribumi against the ethnic

Chinese, and the stereotyping of ethnic Chinese as dual-faced, disloyal, and corrupt (Anggraeni, 2011; Ingketria, 2018a). As a result, the citizenship status for the ethnic Chinese, even those whose families have been in Indonesia for generations and never been to mainland China, has always been contested (Anggraeni, 2011). Ethnic Chinese Indonesians have repeatedly been forced to prove their citizenship and loyalty to Indonesia.

Although there is plenty of evidence showing ethnic Chinese involvement in Indonesia's fight for independence, this history has been collectively forgotten (Anggraeni, 2011). The leading cause for this collective amnesia is Soeharto's New Order regime. The regime began in the mid-1960s, and Soeharto came to power after he led a counterattack on an attempted communist coup, followed by a political genocide to completely eradicate any seeds of communism in Indonesia (Anderson, 1983). Soeharto then overturned the Indonesian government into an authoritarian rule that enforced unity through assimilation.

One major characteristic of the New Order Regime was the ban on SARA, short for suku, agama, ras dan antar-golongan, which translates to ethnicity, religion, race and intercultural relations. The ban on SARA prohibited any overt expression of differences between the four aspects of identities, especially in the socio-political realm, where it is considered a punishable crime (Dawis, 2009; Lembong, 2008; Lindsey, 2005; Purdey, 2006; Suryadinata, 2008). The only allowable expression of difference was traditional costumes, dances, culinary and architecture—trivial parts of ethnic identities—as part of his agenda to promote Indonesian tourism (Anggraeni, 2011). Even so, only native cultures are displayed.

The ethnic-Chinese in Indonesia were not granted citizenship despite their close involvement in the push for Indonesian independence (Anggraeni, 2011). In the 1960s, with the growing mainland-Chinese nationalism, the ethnic Chinese in Indonesia were faced with the choice to stay in Indonesia or "go back" to China (Anggraeni, 2011). For those who opted to stay, they must prove their loyalty to Indonesia in the following ways: they must change their Chinese names to Indonesian, give up their language, and must obtain the Certification of Indonesian Citizenship (SKBRI), a binding document to access governmental institutions like schools and banks (Lindsey & Pausacker, 2005). Simultaneously, Soeharto pushed to shut down any congregations and operations using the Chinese language, including schools, Confucian temples, and media (Lindsey & Pausacker, 2005). They must also adopt one of the five officially acknowledged religions in Indonesia: Islam, Christianity, Catholicism, Buddhism or Hinduism; any beliefs beyond these five are considered blasphemy—a punishable crime (Suryadinata, 2005).

As part of an affirmative action to bring Pribumi-owned businesses, rather than putting limits to big enterprises inherited from the Dutch colonies, the government instead banned ethnic-Chinese from operating businesses in smaller cities and villages (Anggraeni, 2011). Ethnic Chinese Indonesians were not allowed to gain political power because of their second-class citizenship status and the mistrust around their loyalty (Lembong, 2008). The only small window that ethnic-Chinese Indonesians could grow into was private businesses in big cities, where they flourished and became an integral part of Indonesia's economic growth (Soebagjo, 2008). The ethnic Chinese success in the economic sector became another stereotype: the Chinese are wealthy. This stereotype caused a bubbling resentment towards the Chinese when the Asian Financial Crisis hit Indonesia, which then blew up in May 1998 in the form of violent riots throughout big cities in Indonesia that targeted the ethnic Chinese (Purdey, 2006). The violence involved included the burning and looting of Chinese-owned homes and businesses as well as organized sexual violence towards ethnic-Chinese women (Anggraeni, 2011; Purdey, 2006).

The May 1998 riot put an end to Soeharto's dictatorship, which marked the end of the New Order era, and followed by the reformation era. The reformation era from 1998 to 2004 is also known as the era of massive democratization and decentralization as approaches to respond to and recover from Soeharto's authoritarian rule. The ban on SARA was lifted; government operations were decentralized from the capital, giving more autonomy for local leaders to cater to their own local needs in their respective areas; the education system was reformed to be adjustable by local standards, allowing the integration of local languages in the curriculum; the explicit use of the term pribumi was erased from federal laws, allowing equal legal footing for ethnic Chinese; Chinese New Year declared as a national holiday; and the eradication of the term "foreign descent" in Chinese Indonesian citizenships (Anggraeni, 2011; Chandra, 2012; Dawis, 2009; Ingketria, 2018a; Lembong, 2008; Lindsey & Pausacker, 2005)

Since the reformation era, Indonesia has made great strides to develop a more democratic and multicultural nation. The progress was especially promising when Joko Widodo, better known as Jokowi, entered the presidential race in 2014 as "man of the people" (Ingketria, 2018a). Jokowi gained popularity due to his populist bottom-up approach through up-to-date and straightforward outreach, innovative problem-solving infrastructures, and a firm stance on celebrating Indonesia as a multicultural society (Ingketria, 2018a). Because of his approach to politics, Jokowi gained the world's attention as the "Indonesian Obama" (Emont, 2014).

By this time, the ethnic Chinese Indonesians have started to be comfortable with their ethnic identity and agency in Indonesia, and while most keep their identities low-key, some have started to enter the political realm (Ingketria, 2018b). One notable ethnic Chinese politician is Basuki Tjahaja Purnama, better known as Ahok. Ahok has gained political power through his allyship with Jokowi as Jakarta's governor (Ingketria, 2018a). Despite his brash and short-tempered character, which clashed with Javanese mannerisms that value harmony and non-confrontation, Ahok gained popularity due to his substantial progress in solving Jakarta's flood and traffic problems (Ingketria, 2018a). His rise in politics was symbolic of Indonesia's progress in accepting the ethnic-Chinese minority as part of society, especially because he is a double minority, an ethnic-Chinese, and Christian.

However, this vision was soon shattered when Ahok got involved in a blasphemy case that resulted in a two-year prison sentence (Lamb, 2016). On his campaign trail during the Jakarta gubernatorial election period in 2016, a video of his speech where he quoted the Koran went viral and was interpreted as insulting to Islam (Lamb, 2016). During the uproar of the blasphemy case, most of the discourse was set on religious terms since his misconduct was based on him quoting the Koran, yet the anti-Ahok sentiments particularly stung to most ethnic-Chinese Indonesians as it reopened old wounds (Ingketria, 2018b). For many ethnic Chinese, his sentencing to prison seemed to weigh more on his double-minority identity rather than his message in the viral video (Ingketria, 2018b).

Ahok's imprisonment sparked momentum in the resurfacing of anti-Chinese sentiments that continue to haunt ethnic Chinese Indonesians. It also sparked the mainstreaming and legitimation of anti-pluralistic and conservative Islamic politics in Indonesia (Power, 2018). Power (2018) contends that, despite Jokowi's firm stance on multiculturalism during his first term, there are trends that point towards another authoritarian-like governance in the current second term of Jokowi's presidency, which has been supported by the mainstream society that is 80% Muslim. These trends show just how prominent and influential the Muslim Javanese hegemony is.

Additionally, beyond the racial divide between natives and Chinese, recent discriminatory violence against Papuans in Java highlights the power imbalances between the Javanese ethnic group and other indigenous ethnic groups in the archipelago (Guardian, 2019; Ghaliya & Fadli, 2019). Down's thesis elaborates further on central Indonesia's military presence in West Papua that he claims as Indonesia's colonial conquest of the territory (Down, 2015). A popular sentiment often used to justify the discrimination against ethnic-Chinese Indonesian is that the ethnic group has ancestry that is not indigenous to the archipelago. However, the marginalization of indigenous ethnic groups in Papua and many other regions in Indonesia shows how Indonesia's postcolonial struggle has become the colonial force that maintains systems of oppression under a new hegemony.

## 4 Conclusion

The diversity that qualifies Canada and Indonesia as "multicultural societies" is a product of colonization, and so are the policies that are part of the multicultural performance. Despite its pride in its cultural mosaic, Canada is still a settler-colonial nation. Meanwhile, Indonesia continues to maintain Dutch colonial structures despite the Unity in Diversity motto. Reiterating Bannerji (2000), multiculturalism is a way to both hide and enshrine power relations. Within multiculturalism comes the concept of diversity that "simultaneously allows for an emptying out of social relations and suggests concreteness of cultural descriptions, and through this process obscures any understanding of difference as a construction of power" (Bannerji, 2000, p. 36). As a result, the paradox obscures the ability to make a distinction between racist stereotypes and cultural differences; it erases the role of race, class, and patriarchy among the marginalized "others"; it reduces all political issues into a cultural one, implying them as a private matter; and it maintains the status quo of a capitalist, homogenous, and bourgeois society (Bannerji, 2000).

This chapter highlights the role of colonialism in the making, maintaining, and reproducing of systemic divisions in Canada and Indonesia, which have been obscured by performative multiculturalism. This comparative analysis shows how systems of oppression and segregation have been maintained by merely changing the façade of diversity and inclusivity, while the main structures that uphold these systems are still intact. Even with the jarring difference in which Canada is the colonizer and Indonesia the colonized, the two countries share the same system, performative multiculturalism, that preserves racial minority groups' perpetual foreignness. Without substantial dismantling of the systems of oppression, history is bound to repeat under a different façade that will continue to oppress those in the margins.

### References

Altbach, P. (1982). Servitude in mind? Education, dependency, and neo-colonialism. In P. Altbach, R.F. Arnove & G. Kelley, *Comparative Education* (pp. 469–484). New York: Macmillan.

Anderson, B. R. (1983). Old state, new society: Indonesia's new order in comparative historical perspectives. *The Journal of Asian Studies 42:3*, 477–496.

Anggraeni, D. (2011). Does multicultural Indonesia include its ethnic Chinese? *Wacana 12* (2), 256–278.

Badan Pusat Statistik. (2011). *Kewarganegaraan, Suku Bangsa, Agama, dan Bahasa Sehari-Hari Penduduk Indonesia: Hasil Sensus Penduduk 2010*. Jakarta: Badan Pusat Statistik.

Bannerji, H. (2000). *The Dark Side of the Nation*. Toronto: Canadian Scholars' Press Inc.

Bibbins-Domingo, K. (2020). This Time Must Be Different: Disparities During the COVID-19 Pandemic. *Ann Intern Med*. Retrieved from Ann Intern Med: https://doi.org/10.7326/M20-2247

Brata, I. B., & Wartha, I. B. (2017). Lahirnya Pancasila sebagai pemersatu bangsa Indonesia. *Jurbal Santiaji Pendidikan 7(1)*, 120–132.

Brosseau, L., & Dewing, M. (2018, January 3). *Canadian Multiculturalism*. Library of Parliament, Legal and Social Affairs Division. Ottawa: Library of Parliament. Retrieved from https://lop.parl.ca/staticfiles/PublicWebsite/Home/ResearchPublications/BackgroundPapers/PDF/2009-20-e.pdf.

CDC. (2020, April 20). *Racial and Ethnic Minority Groups*. Retrieved from Coronavirus Deseas 2019 (COVID-19) : https://www.cdc.gov/coronavirus/2019-ncov/need-extra-precautions/racial-ethnic-minorities.html

Chandra, E. (2012). "We the (Chinese) people": Revisiting the 1945 constitutional debate on citizenship. *Southeast Asia Program Publications at Cornell University*, 85–110.

Dawis, A. (2009). *Orang Indonesia Tionghoa Mencari Idenetitas*. Jakarta: Gramedia.

Dhamoon, R., & Abu-Laban, Y. (2009). Dangerous (internal) foreigners and nation-building: The case of Canada. *International political science review, 30*(2), 163-183.

Driedger, L. (2011). Multiculturalism: Sorting identities, rights, and conflicts. *Canadian Ethnic Studies, 43(1–2)*, 221–236.

Down, N. (2015). Indonesian Nationalism and Postcolonial Colonialism. *Dissertation: Macquire University*.

Emont, J. (2014, July 9). *Jokowi, the "Indonesian Obama," Is in a Presidential Nail-Biter*. Retrieved from The New Republic: https://newrepublic.com/article/118613/indonesia-election-results-2014-joko-jokowi-widodo-nail-biter.

Foster, P. (1982). The educational policies of postcolonial states. In L. Anderson & D.M. Wyndham (eds.), *Education and Development: Issues in the Analysis and Planning of Postcolonial Societies*. (pp. 3–25). Lexington, MA: Lexington Books.

Ghaliya, G., & Fadli. (2019, August 25). *The elephant in the room: Racism in Indonesia*. Retrieved from *The Jakarta Post*: https://www.thejakartapost.com/news/2019/08/25/the-elephant-in-the-room-racism-in-indonesia.html.

Guardian, T. (2019, August 31). *Racism, rage and rising calls for freedom in Indonesia's Papua*. Retrieved from *South China Morning Post*: https://www.scmp.com/print/news/asia/southeast-asia/article/3025191/racism-rage-and-rising-calls-freedom-indonesias-papua.

Ingketria, E. (2018a). Chinese Indonesians under Jokowi: Flourishing yet unsettling. *Open Journal of Social Sciences 6*, 94–121.

Ingketria, E. (2018b). Cultural pride in the era of pluralism: A closer look to Chinese Indonesians' ethnic identity under the reign of Jokowi. *Asian Journal of Social Sciences and Management Studies*, 114–122.

Jedwab, J. (2020, March 20). *Multiculturalism*. Retrieved from *The Canadian Encyclopedia*: https://www.thecanadianencyclopedia.ca/en/article/multiculturalism.

Lamb, K. (2016, December 12). *Jakarta governor Ahok's blasphemy trial: all you need to know*. Retrieved from *The Guardian*: https://amp.theguardian.com/world/2016/dec/12/jakarta-governor-ahoks-blasphemy-trial-all-you-need-to-know.

Larsson, P. (2020, March 17). *Anti-Asian racism during coronavirus: How the language of disease produces hate and violence*. Retrieved from The Conversation: https://theconversation.com/anti-asian-racism-during-coronavirus-how-the-language-of-disease-produces-hate-and-violence-134496

Lembong, E. (2008). Indonesian government policies and the Ethnic Chinese: Some recent developments. In L. Suryadinata, *Ethnic Chinese in Contamporary Indonesia* (pp. 48–56). Singapore: ISEAS Publications.

Lindsey, T., & Pausacker, H. (2005). *Chinese Indonesians: Remembering, Distorting, Forgetting*. Singapore: ISEAS.

Lindsey, T. (2005). Reconstituting the Ethnic Chinese in post-Soeharto Indonesia: Law, racial discrimination and reform. In T. Lindsey, & H. Pausacker, *Chinese Indonesians: Remembering, Distorting, Forgetting* (pp. 41–76). Singapore: ISEAS.

Madokoro, L. (2020, March 20). *Coronavirus: Racism and the long-term impacts of emergency measures in Canada*. Retrieved from The Conversation: https://theconversation.com/coronavirus-racism-and-the-long-term-impacts-of-emergency-measures-in-canada-134110

Oikawa, M. G. (1999). *The Known and UnknownL A community lost, a community remembered*. Toronto: University of Toronto.

OMF. (2003, February 5). *Census 2001 Highlights: Factsheet 6: Visible Minorities and Ethnicity in Ontario*. Retrieved from Ontarion Ministry of Finance: https://www.fin.gov.on.ca/en/economy/demographics/census/cenhi6.html.

Patel, A., & Bowden, O. (2020, March 16). *'A lot of fear': Asian community a target of racism amid coronavirus threat*. Retrieved from Global News: https://globalnews.ca/news/6467500/coronavirus-racism/

Pon, G. (2000). Importing the Asian model minority discourse into Canada: Implications for social work and education. *Canadian social work review/Revue canadienne de service social*, 277-291.

Power, T. P. (2018). Jokowi's authoritarian turn and Indonesia's democratic decline. *Bulletin of Indonesian Economic Studies, 54*; 3, 307–338.
Purdey, J. (2006). *Anti-Chinese Violence in Indonesia, 1996–1999*. Honolulu: Singapore University Press.
Ricklefs, M. C. (1992). Unity and disunity in Javanese political and religious thought of the eighteenth century. *Modern Asian Studies 26(4)*, 663–678.
Soebagjo, N. (2008). Ethnic-Chinese and Ethnic-Indonesians: A love-hate relationship. In L. Suryadinata, *Ethnic Chinese in Contemporary Indonesia* (pp. 137–153). Singapore: ISEAS.
Soepriatna, V. (2019). The pancasila as a racial contract. *(unpublished)*.
Steenbrink, K. (1993). *Dutch Colonialism and Indonesian Islam: Contacts and Conflicts 1596–1950*. Amsterdam.
Suryadinata, L. (2005). Buddhism and Confucianism in contemporary Indonesia. In T. Lindsey, & H. Pausacker, *Chinese Indonesians: Remembering, Distorting, Forgetting* (pp. 77–94). Singapore: ISEAS.
Suryadinata, L. (2008). *Ethnic Chinese in Contemporary Indonesia*. Singapore: ISEAS.

CHAPTER 11

# Impact and Implications of Rap and Hip-Hop Music as a Form of Resistance

*Juanna Nguyen*

## 1  Introduction

Originating in the 1970s in New York with African-American youth, rap and hip-hop music as a form of resistance can have a positive impact for South and Southeast Asian populations, as struggles and challenges are subverted through rap and hip-hop music. An empowerment theoretical framework can conceptualize this impact of resistance as an empowering process with empowering outcomes, which in turn has implications within the fields of music therapy and psychotherapy. In other words, the use of rap and hip-hop music as a way for these Asian populations to empower themselves is itself an intervention to counteract the adverse impact that marginalization or social exclusion has had or potentially has on individuals. Rap and hip-hop music as empowerment can also promote self-assurance, self-confidence, and self-expression. In this chapter, the author first narrows the focus to South and Southeast Asian and Asian-American/-Canadian communities, introduces the concept of empowerment theory, defines music therapy and psychotherapy, and provides an overview of a history, background, and literature review of rap and hip-hop in America and in Asian communities as well as Asian exclusion, stereotypes and racial trauma. There will be discussion about the ways in which rap and hip-hop music are empowering processes with empowering outcomes, empowerment theory in the context of resistance music in the field of music therapy and psychotherapy, and the future directions that research could take.

## 2  Situating the Self

I identify as an Asian-Canadian woman, as I was born and raised in Canada while also having a Chinese-Vietnamese ethnic background. I am also a Certified Music Therapist (MTA) and a Registered Psychotherapist (Qualifying), and I recently graduated from a Counselling Psychology program in the field of psychotherapy. While I have faced my own challenges growing up among some pressures to either live up to or resist particular stereotypes, I recognize that I cannot personally speak for those individuals who have faced instances of oppression and marginalization that I have not myself experienced nor do I intend to represent these persons in writing this chapter. But I do wish to discuss exclusionary events in a historical and theoretical sense, and how struggles and challenges are subverted through rap and hip-hop music.

## 3 Background

Asian individuals have been historically excluded in both the U.S. as well as in Canada, such as in the U.S. Immigration Act of 1917 which prohibited all immigration from most of the Asian continent including the Middle East, Central Asia, South Asia (then-British India), and Southeast Asia, or the Chinese Immigration Act in Canada in 1923 that restricted Chinese immigration to Canada. Another example of exclusion includes the 1914 incident when the Komagata Maru sailed from Hong Kong, proceeding via Shanghai and the Japanese ports of Moji and Yokohama, and arrived in Vancouver, British Columbia, and was denied docking because the majority of its passengers, mostly Sikhs from Punjab, India, and all British subjects, did not meet the criteria of the continuous journey regulation. Stereotypes of Asian individuals have continued racism, discrimination, and exclusion, or have been used to continually exclude other individuals of minority. To subvert these challenges from an empowerment theoretical framework, rap and hip-hop music can operate as a form of anti-racist resistance and can have a positive impact among Asian-Canadian communities. Further, music therapy and psychotherapy can play a role in allowing Asian-Canadian youth to fight back against systemic oppression.

## 4 South and Southeast Asian Populations

I will be focusing on the available literature on rap and hip-hop with South Asian populations, which include the nations of India, Afghanistan, Pakistan, Bangladesh, Nepal, Bhutan, Maldives, and Sri Lanka, as well as Southeast Asian populations comprising of Indonesia, Malaysia, Singapore, Philippines, East Timor, Brunei, Cambodia, Laos, Myanmar (Burma), Thailand and Vietnam. This will also include the Asian and Pacific Islander population, individuals with origins in any of the original peoples of the Far East, Southeast Asia, South Asia, or the Pacific Islands. Those with the above-mentioned ethnic backgrounds who were born in America or Canada, or who have emigrated from Asia to these countries, often identify as Asian Americans or Asian Canadians respectively.

## 5 Empowerment Theory

Empowerment, a value orientation, has been posited as a theoretical model that suggests actions, activities, or structures may be empowering, and that the outcomes of these processes result in a level of being empowered while taking on different forms for different people in different contexts (Zimmerman, 2000, p. 45). Carr (2003) suggests that empowerment is an interpersonal process in which individuals collectively define and activate strategies to gain access to knowledge and power, is a cyclical process of collective dialogue and social action effecting positive change and is premised on the individual's desire for and assessment of the possibility for change and on the possibilities for social transformation (p. 16, 18). Rolvsjord (2006) proposes that empowerment practises involve a distribution and promotion of power that does not imply the oppression or powerlessness of others.

Empowerment theory, according to Zimmerman (2000), differentiates between empowering processes and empowering outcomes; empowering processes attempt to gain control, obtain needed resources, understand one's social environment, and help people develop skills so they can become independent problem-solvers and decision-makers, while empowering outcomes are the consequences of peoples' attempts to gain more control in their community or the effects of interventions designed to empower participants. Empowerment theory also examines empowerment at the individual, organizational, and community levels, along with their interdependence. Psychological empowerment at the individual level includes beliefs about one's competence, efforts to exert control, and an understanding of the sociopolitical environment; empowerment at the organizational level develops and influences policy decisions, or offer alternatives for service provision, and provide opportunities for people to gain control over their lives or at least to develop skills and a sense of control; and empowerment at the community level makes efforts to improve the community, responds to threats to quality of life, and provides opportunities for participation (Zimmerman, 2000, p. 46, 51, 54).

## 6    Music Therapy versus Psychotherapy

According to the Canadian Association of Music Therapists (CAMT), music therapy is "a discipline in which credentialed professionals use music purposefully within therapeutic relationships to support development, health, and well-being" and "use music safely and ethically to address human needs within cognitive, communicative, emotional, musical, physical, social, and spiritual domains" (CAMT, 2016). The World Federation for Music Therapy (WFMT) also provides the definition of music therapy as "the professional use of music and its elements as an intervention in medical, educational, and everyday environments with individuals, groups, families, or communities who seek to optimize their quality of life and improve their physical, social, communicative, emotional, intellectual, and spiritual health and wellbeing" (WFMT 2011). Thus, music therapy treats many non-musical goals and domains, such as those mentioned above, in various populations and settings through the use of music-based interventions. Meanwhile psychotherapy is primarily a talk-based therapy intended to help people improve and maintain their mental health and well-being in a psychotherapeutic relationship where both the client and the therapist work together to bring about positive change in the client's thinking, feeling, behaviour and social functioning (CRPO, 2020). Music therapy, while can also be of a collaborative nature, uses music-based interventions including singing, playing instruments, rhythmic-based activities, improvising, composing and song-writing, imagery-based experiences, and music listening as a means of reaching one's goals. I personally have a desire to practice some form of music psychotherapy (for example, music-based interventions followed by verbal processing) to utilize the strengths from both disciplines and treatments and envision being able to incorporate rap and hip-hop into music-based interventions where it may be appropriate.

## 7    History, Background and Literature Review

### 7.1    *Anti-Asian Exclusion, Racism, Discrimination, Stereotypes and Racial Trauma*

Two stereotypes that have been used to discriminate against minority populations are the "model minority" and the "perpetual foreigner." The model minority myth arose in the 1960s during the Civil Rights Movement, and it was used to differentiate Asian Americans from other ethnic groups, and to create an opposition to or delegitimize the claims of African-Americans (Dennis, 2018,

p. 39, 44). Viewed to be the "model" of good citizenship that other minorities should achieve, other minorities were negatively compared to them blamed for failing to achieve model minority success, thus enforcing the stereotype of the lazy, complaining, and unintelligent Black or Brown other (Kim, 1999; Wang, 2008; as cited in Dennis, 2018, p. 39, 44; Li and Wang, 2008). Despite the model minority myth being immediately challenged for pitting minority groups against one another to divert attention away from Asian Americans' problems and the disparities between these minority groups and the major group, the stereotype still "gained steam" through the 1980s and 1990s (Chin and Chan, 1971; Osajima, 1988; Suzuki, 1977; as cited in Li and Wang, 2008; Dennis, 2018, p. 44). From this status, Asian Americans, or Asian Canadians, are also sometimes even considered "white adjacent," or "white enough." According to Bonilla-Silva (2004) and Okihiro (1994), while Asian Americans are stereotyped as closer to whites than blacks in a racial hierarchy due to this model minority status, they are also being pressured to "claim a bond with either black or white", in turn reflecting both Asian Americans' otherness and rejection by both racial groups (Bonilla-Silva, 2004; Okihiro, 1994; as cited in McTaggart and O'Brien, p. 651). Reyes (2005) however suggests that another stereotype has emerged that positions some Southeast Asian refugee youth as problem minorities who have fallen prey to stereotypes traditionally assigned to African Americans, and that low-income Southeast Asian American teenagers are often positioned more closely to the African American experience based on a shared socio-economic and minority status (p. 510).

Concurrent with the model minority stereotype, Asian Americans are homogeneously viewed as "other" or "perpetual foreigners", permanent outsiders to the norms of North American culture and the dominant inner circle, despite their citizenship (Dennis, 2018, p. 40, 41). This foreignness is presumed by the question "where are you from?" which assumes that Asian-ness and American-ness are mutually exclusive (Lee, 2015, p. 5, as cited in Dennis, 2018, p. 40). As observed by Dennis (2018) in a situation that occurred to one of her Asian American peers, the "perpetual foreigner" stereotype has not only applied to recent immigrant groups, but also to fourth-generation Asian immigrant groups who have gained a certain level of economic success in Canada, thus presenting an ethnic absolutist view of the Asian category (p. 40). Not only must Asian youth endure the stress of expectations and the shame of unmet expectations, these youth become stuck between being simultaneously wanted as the model minority that perpetuates stereotypes of other races that benefits white supremacy, and unwanted perpetual foreigners or outsiders of North American society.

Among racial stereotypes, many Asians Americans suffer from racial trauma, or race-based stress, which are events of danger related to real or perceived experience of racial discrimination, carrying psychological and physiological effects, and can cumulatively leave scars for those who are dehumanized (Comas-Diaz, et al., 2019, p. 1–2). Southeast Asian American (SEAA) youth find it difficult to fit into the identity of the White dominant culture, the Asian identity of their home culture and/or the Asian American identity (Lee and Zhou, 2004), and struggle to find cultural identity amongst 1) parental (gendered) beliefs and expectations (Xiong et al., 2005), 2) the "model minority" and "perpetual foreigner" stereotypes (Poon et al., 2016; Said, 1979), and 3) definitions of "Asian immigrant, Asian American, and mainstream U.S. cultures" (Crane, 2016; Mistry et al., 2016; as cited in Nguyen and Ferguson, 2019, p. 101). Healing racial trauma is even more challenging as racial wounds occur within a sociopolitical context and on a continuing basis, and microaggressions have become widely acknowledged as a form of racial trauma in the past decades (Comas-Diaz, et al., 2019, p. 2, 4). While I will be primarily focusing on the psychological aspect of race-based stress, this could also include physical acts of violence toward Asian individuals, which in turn affects psychological functioning.

## 7.2  Rap and Hip-Hop toward Asian Appropriation

Hip-hop originated as a music genre and culture among African-American youth in the urban neighbourhoods of the Bronx, Harlem and Brooklyn in New York City during the 1970s, building on Jamaican sound system culture and traditionally involving deejaying (DJing), rapping, break dancing, and elements of graffiti (Kitwana, 2003; Bradley, 2000; as cited in Warren and Evitt, 2010, p. 142). The term "rap music" was later used, shifting the focus in hip-hop from the deejays (DJs) to the emcees (MCs). When hip-hop was highly politicized in the late-1980s, it became a medium for a broader awakening of black political consciousness, leading to rappers utilizing their music as a communicative tool through which they could speak to the African American community and convey political, agenda-driven messages acting as coordinated attacks on the institutions of power within the United States (U.S.) (Nielson, 2012, p. 357). While critics often call hip-hop materialistic, misogynistic, homophobic, racist, vulgar, and violent, and dwell on the sexism and misogyny in some rap lyrics and violent incidents at rap concerts, mainstream media infrequently mention aspects such as personal empowerment, anti-drug rhetoric, and a celebration of Black community building, or how hip-hop across cultures has remained a vital progressive agenda that challenges the status quo (Beighey and Unnithan, 2006, p. 141; Chang, 2007, p. 60).

Since its origins, hip-hop has spread to become a global movement in Asia, primarily led by the South Korean K-Pop industry. While hip-hop and African-American culture influence trends in East Asia, there is little understanding of hip-hop's identity and culture or its history (Tai, 2018) such as the organizers from Cape Town to Paris using hip-hop in their communities to address environmental justice, policing and prisons, media justice, and education, and the rap made by the sons of disenfranchised African and Arab immigrants to serve as the soundtrack to riots in the French banlieues in 2005 and in post-election riots (Chang, 2007, p. 59–60, 64). Further, there are many English rap songs that directly address a sense of being watched by a hostile police presence and reference surveillance technologies that have complicated the ways in which opposition is often expressed and undermine resistance in an intolerant environment (Nielson, 2012, p. 351, 354). Political rap in particular questions hegemonic forces, and resists domination by producing alternative knowledge while presenting a uniquely Afro-American view of society (Kuwahara, 1992, as cited in Beighey and Unnithan, 2006, p. 135), and translates individual experiences into calls for attention and resistance against oppressive forces and existential oppression, while also offering opportunities to establish an empowering identity (Beighey and Unnithan, 2006, p. 134, 141). In addition, hip-hop is a source of empowerment and resistance against the societal mainstream that perpetuates discrimination and racism of ethnic minority population (Nguyen and Ferguson, 2019, p. 108), and also plays a role within marginalized youth subcultures in strengthening community, making sense of lived realities, and exercising said resistance (Dei 2008; James 2012, as cited in Gosine and Tabi, 2016, p. 447). There would be a benefit for Asian hip-hop to acknowledge the history and heritage of rap and hip-hop and its usage, as well as to use rap and hip-hop music as a way to subvert struggles and challenges that Asian individuals may encounter.

There is limited literature regarding the history of how Asian and Asian-American/-Canadian communities may have adopted or appropriated rap and hip-hop music as resistance or empowerment, although Bodden (2005) speaks to rap appropriation in Indonesian youth music. He proposes that one of the reasons rap music has been appropriated by Indonesian youth is because of its history as a protest genre for a racial minority against structural discrimination, yet the appropriation of rap and other genres also served a medium for populist expression and protest for a segment of a much more privileged social group that is increasingly dissatisfied with authoritarian rule and complicity with it. Asian American Pacific Islander participants in McTaggart's and O'Brien's (2017) study, however, shared that they often confronted cliques as youth and struggled to fit into both "Asian" and "white" expectations of them, thus seeking out and viewing hip-hop as 1) a liberating space where they can more easily counter or evade gender and racial oppression based on limiting stereotypes than in mainstream culture, 2) a way to take out our frustrations of limiting expectations placed on people due to their race, and 3) a place they can be true to themselves as they reject both these racist expectations as well as their own families' and communities' expectations for them (p. 635, 643–644). As a source of comfort in parent-child conflicts and a source of empowerment and identity resistance against the societal mainstream that perpetuates discrimination and racism, hip-hop is a fluid hybrid identity transcending race and ethnicity that allows SEAA youth to engage in multiple cultural worlds simultaneously, and aids in relational and identity harmony (Nguyen and Ferguson, 2019, p. 105–110). Through aligning with an identity associated with Black culture, SEAA youth resist stereotypes, including the model minority stereotype that is used to sustain racism and White supremacy (Poon et al., 2015, as cited in Nguyen and Ferguson, 2019, p. 110). Through rap and hip-hop, Asian youth are able to resist existing assumptions and Asian American stereotypes including the model minority, and therefore assert a level of agency over their identities. Rap and hip-hop can provide the opportunity for Asian individuals to represent their stories and showcase their resiliency.

How have or can rap and hip-hop operated as forms of anti-racist resistance among Asian-Canadian communities? Looking at the use of hip-hop by the SEAA population, anti-racist resistance can be seen from three perspectives: contact, assimilation, and marginalization. From a contact perspective, SEAA youth living in areas with high concentrations of African American and Latinx peers have familiarity with hip-hop and share their engagement with hip-hop with their peers in their communities, while from an assimilation perspective, SEAA youth engage with this popular form of music to prove their American-ness for societal acceptance and to demonstrate their willingness to adapt to U.S. culture, which can be seen as appropriation of Black culture where hip-hop originated and strain relationships between Asian and African American populations (Nguyen and Ferguson, 2019, p. 102). From a marginalization perspective, Asian youth face the challenge of invisibility in a sociocultural environment that views race as Black and White (Wu, 2002, as cited in Nguyen and Ferguson, 2019, p. 102), and turn to hip-hop to "find space on the margins of U.S. society and sometimes, of their home ethnic culture" (Nguyen and Ferguson, p. 103). They may develop a local identity while connecting to and joining a broader global community resistance against personal and institutional racism, discrimination, and stereotypes that impact the lives of ethnic minority people globally (Nguyen and Ferguson, 2019, p. 101–103, 110). Although Asian Americans may feel some sense of exclusion from hip-hop culture due to racialized gender norms, hip-hop can still offer an opportunity for empowerment and liberation for rebelling against the limited acceptable standards in white, mainstream, or parental expectations (McTaggart and O'Brien, 2017, p. 653).

## 7.3 Discussion

This history of exclusion, racism, discrimination, and stereotypes has created an atmosphere not conducive to fostering beliefs of competence or a felt sense of control. Asian individuals in North America, regardless of where they were born, are in a difficult position of assimilating into white culture as a "model minority" while never fully belonging as the "perpetual foreigner", and in this sense having no control over how they are seen and treated by others. Some perspectives of them may also be overburdening in the case of contributing to feelings of incompetency or incapability of living up to parental and societal expectations. This can, however, be countered to some degree through the development of an understanding of the socio-political environment and the many external factors that contribute to the systemic oppression embedded in the structures of societies that is typically routine and seen as natural, in addition to critically looking into one's self, beliefs, ideologies, values, and everyday practices.

Raising one's awareness that one's suffering arises from the ways in which one has been systemically invalidated, excluded, and silenced because of one's status as a member of a non-dominant group in the culture (Lerner, 1993, p. 14) helps the individual empower oneself through placing one's experience into their social context (Brown, 2004, p. 468), thus externalizing these problems from oneself by viewing them as symptoms of an institutional issue, and reducing shame and self-blame. Once this understanding is developed and fostered, the next step then would be to take a course of action in order to reassert the control in a society where that control was taken.

Those who are resisting against oppression are demonstrating their understanding of and at the very least develop a sense of control in the environment, and therefore are participating in empowering processes that potentially also become empowering results. On a more individual level of empowerment, Asian youth have the opportunity to exert control and articulate their understandings and insights through rap lyrics and hip-hop music in order to challenge one's "invisibility" in a sociocultural environment and resist the racial stereotypes against them. Possible empowering outcomes at the community level include being connected to the broader global community of hip-hop, educating the community of the existing oppression and marginalization, and joining a communal resistance against limited standards and expectations, racism, discrimination, and stereotypes, which consequently increases their base of support.

## 8  The Role of Music Therapy and Psychotherapy

What role can music therapy play in allowing Asian-Canadian youth to fight back against systemic oppression? In music therapy, we have the opportunity to help people to have access to the appropriation of music as a resource in their life (Rolvsjord, 2006). Identifying and understanding how the empowerment process unfolds is critical in operationalizing an empowerment-oriented practice (Carr, 2003, p. 18). When considering empowerment theory, therapists can offer rap and hip-hop music as empowerment tools for clients on the individual psychological level as they move toward the community level. Offering rap and hip-hop music in a therapy setting is a chance to "practice" the exertion of control in an environment and self-empowerment where an individual feels safe before moving toward taking action in the "real world." Herman (1992) also notes that for some individuals, "the ultimate path toward personal empowerment will occur through engagement with the world and the empowerment of others" (as cited in Brown, 2004, p. 469).

From a more counselling or psychotherapy perspective, Washington (2018) proposes that hip-hop culture and rap music can be integrated into individual counselling to discuss the social injustices they face, presenting a vignette of a Black male client who reports being stereotyped and prejudicially hypersurveilled on campus, and using Elligan's (2000) rap therapy model to incorporate rap music to broach conversation and action in response to this injustice (as cited in p. 99, 102). This rap model can also be used with Asian individuals in the therapy session to respond to injustices in a safe environment within the therapeutic relationship, and promote self-assurance, self-confidence, and self-expression. In addition, Carr (2003) suggests from a social work perspective that long-term, intensive, small-group work is a efficacious means of empowerment practice as it allows people to reflect on and interpret the social dimensions of their personal problems, to work to choose new strategic identities as they plan for social change, and to have the opportunity to find power in unison (p. 19). These counselling and social work viewpoints continue to be relevant, as these help to emphasize how rap and hip-hop music can help to initiate the conversation with a client, and how bringing this into a safe group therapy setting can further contribute to empowerment at the community level before engaging with the world outside of therapy.

Lightstone (2012) further posits that in clinical music therapy practice as well, rap can be used to express any form of alienation, and hip-hop is a natural way to confront, express, and begin working through those frustrations as it has always served that purpose for its creators. Some clients are willing and able to write down their original rap songs and better engage musically when working with this pre-composed material, while alternatively the use of familiar songs can be a non-threatening way to express emotions, as it offers participants an opportunity to channel their emotions through lyrics that are meaningful to them (Lightstone, 2012, p. 50–51). Engaging in music therapy is therefore an empowering process for the individual, and I can imagine the use of rap and hip-hop music in music therapy would then provide individuals the opportunity to engage in self-expression and resistance against oppression through music in the safe space of the clinical setting before connecting with the wider community.

The effect of music depends on how it is used. People use music to construct their emotional and social experiences and identity, and within music therapy we might relate empowerment to clinical processes that allow clients to participate, relate it to their musical performances, talk about clients that are empowered through the therapeutic process, or discuss the philosophy and the clinical perspectives it comprises (Rolvsjord, 2006). Therapy as empowerment involves therapist-client collaboration in the development of the client's ability to act and to participate in community, which has to do with individual strengths as well as the available and use of social, cultural, and economic resources (Rolvsjord, 2006). Assuming that the therapy approach taken is a collaborative one, there is a sense of agency for the client, as the therapist treats the client as the expert of one's own experiences and the client is able to work with the therapist to decide the goals and the directions that they want to take with their sessions.

## 9 Future Directions for Research

Despite hip-hop's liberating qualities and construction as a space relatively free from limiting expectations, its concentration on black hypermasculinity and objectification of women means that it can have narrow visions of acceptable presentations of masculinity and femininity and thus encounters limits to being accepted and individuals are relegated to the margins still dominated by narrow gender norms (McTaggart and O'Brien, 2017, p. 651–653). Therefore, when using hip-hop as a therapeutic device and a medium for empowerment, it is important to be mindful of these limits. Travis (2013) suggests further defining empowerment by the dimensions of esteem, resilience, growth, community and change, which are salient for those that engage music in casual everyday through their own self-expression within structured music therapy, and within commercial music that may be used in therapeutic interventions; and researchers can further examine distinctions among the functional value of music therapy versus music in therapy (p. 162). Moreover, qualitative research on hip-hop in counselling could explore how and under what circumstances counsellors in various settings integrate hip-hop into their practice while developing a repository of artists, songs, album titles, and lyrics counsellors find most useful (Washington, 2018, p. 102). As the existing literature on rap music in therapy focuses on receptive techniques (Elligan, 2000; Tyson, 2002; Wyatt, 2002; Tenny, 2002; as cited in Lightstone, 2012, p. 46), future research could also emphasize the outcomes from the use of rap in active music therapy techniques.

## 10   Conclusion

I reviewed the origins of rap and hip-hop music in New York among African-American youth, instances of oppression in a history of exclusion against Asian populations, and how they have and can use rap and hip-hop music in resistance of oppression and as a way of responding to the societal injustices that they may face. I have also considered rap and hip-hop music's function as a means to reaching empowering outcomes in music therapy and psychotherapy settings. I would like to further look into rap and hip-hop music's applications in clinical along with community practices, and whether this would be an appropriate means for myself as a clinician to use to practice music therapy in the future. While gender "norms" of hip-hop as well as rap and hip-hop's controversial nature require more discussion than I have offered in this chapter, rap and hip-hop nonetheless has its role as a form of resistance against stereotypes.

### References

Beighey, Catherine & Unnithan, N. (2006). Political rap: The music of oppositional resistance. *Sociological Focus, 39*, 133–143. doi:10.1080/00380237.2006.10571281.

Bradley, L. (2000). *Bass culture: when Reggae was king*. London: Viking.

Brown, L. S. (2004). Feminist paradigms of trauma treatment. *Psychotherapy: Theory, Research, Practice, Training, 41*(4), 464–471. https://doi.org/10.1037/0033-3204.41.4.464.

Bodden, M. (2005). Rap in Indonesian Youth Music of the 1990s: "Globalization," "Outlaw Genres," and Social Protest. *Asian Music, 36*(2), 1-26. http://www.jstor.org/stable/4098514

Bonilla-Silva, E. (2004). From bi-racial to tri-racial: Towards a new system of racial stratification in the USA. *Ethnic and Racial Studies 27*(6), 931–950. doi: 10.1080/0141987042000268530

Canadian Association of Music Therapists. (2016, June). *About music therapy.* https://www.musictherapy.ca/about-camt-music-therapy/about-music-therapy/.

Carr, E. S. (2003). Rethinking empowerment theory using a feminist lens: The importance of process. *Affilia, 18*(1), 8–20. https://doi.org/10.1177/0886109902239092.

Chang, J. (2007). It's a hip-hop world. *Foreign Policy, 163,* 58–65. www.jstor.org/stable/25462232.

Chin, F., & Chan, J. (1971). Racist love. In R. Kostelanetz (Ed.), *Seeing through shuck* (pp. 65-79). New York: Ballantine.

College of Registered Psychotherapists of Ontario. (2020). *What is psychotherapy?* https://www.crpo.ca/what-is-psychotherapy/.

Comas-Diaz, L., Hall, G. C. N., & Neville, H. A. (2019). Racial trauma: Theory, research, and healing; Introduction to the special issue. *The American Psychologist.* https://doi.org/10.1037/amp0000442.

Crane, D. (2016). Culture and globalization: Theoretical models and emerging trends. In D. Crane, N. Kawashima, & K. Kawasaki (Eds.), *Global culture: Media, arts, policy, and globalization.* New York: Routledge.

Dei, G. J. S. (2008). Schooling as Community: Race, Schooling, and the Education of African Youth. *Journal of Black Studies, 38*(3), 346–66. doi:10.1177/0021934707306570

Dennis, E. (2018). Exploring the model minority: Deconstructing Whiteness through the Asian American example. In Sefa Dei, G. J. and Hilowle, S. (Eds.), *Cartographies of Race and Social Difference.* (pp. 33–48). Springer Publishing.

Elligan, D. (2000). Rap therapy: A culturally sensitive approach to psychotherapy with young African American men. Journal of African American Men, 5(3), 27–37. doi:10.1007/s12111-000-1002-y

Gosine, K., & Tabi, E. (2016) Disrupting neoliberalism and bridging the multiple worlds of marginalized youth via Hip-Hop pedagogy: Contemplating possibilities. *Review of Education, Pedagogy, and Cultural Studies, 38*(5), 445–467. doi:10.1080/10714413.2016.1221712.

Herman, J.L. (1992). *Trauma and recovery.* New York: Basic Books.

James, C. E. (2012). *Life at the Intersection: Community, Class and Schooling.* Halifax, NS: Fernwood.

Kim, C. J. (1999). The racial triangulation of Asian Americans. *Politics and Society, 27*(1), 105–138. https://doi.org/10.1177/0032329299027001005

Kitwana, B. (2003). *The hip hop generation: young blacks and the crisis in African American culture.* New York: Basic Civitas Books

Kuwahara, Y. (1992). Power to the People Y'All: Rap Music, Resistance, and Black College Students. *Humanity & Society, 16*(1), 54–73. https://doi.org/10.1177/016059769201600105

Lee, S. J. (2015). *Unraveling the "model minority" stereotype: Listening to Asian American youth.* New York: Teachers College Press

Lee, J., & Zhou, M. (2004). *Asian American youth: Culture, identity and ethnicity.* New York: Routledge.

Lerner, G. (1993). *The Creation of Feminist Consciousness.* New York: Oxford University Press.

Li, G. and Wang, L. (2008). *Model Minority Myth Revisited: An Interdisciplinary Approach to Demystifying Asian American Educational Experiences.* Information Age Publishing Inc.

Lightstone, A. J. (2012). The importance of hip-hop for music therapists. In S. Hadley and G. Yancy (Eds.), *Therapeutic Uses of Rap and Hip-hop* (pp. 39–56). Routledge: Taylor and Francis Group.

McTaggart, N. and O'Brien, Eileen (2017). Seeking liberation, facing marginalization: Asian Americans and Pacific Islanders' conditional acceptance in hip-hop culture. *Sociological Inquiry,* 87(4), 634–658. doi: 10.1111/soin.12173.

Mistry, J., Li, J., Yoshikawa, H., Tseng, V., Tirrell, J., Kiang, L., Mistry, R. and Wang, Y. (2016). An integrated conceptual framework for the development of Asian American children and youth. *Child Development,* 87(4), 1014–1032. https://doi.org/10.1111/cdev.12577

Nguyen, J., & Ferguson, G. M. (2019). A global cypher: the role of hip hop in cultural identity construction and navigation for southeast Asian American youth. *New Directions for Child and Adolescent Development,* 2019(164), 99–115. doi:10.1002/cad.20279.

Nielson, E. (2012). 'Here come the cops': Policing the resistance in rap music. *International Journal of Cultural Studies,* 15(4), 349–363. https://doi.org/10.1177/1367877911419159.

Okihiro, G.Y. (1994). *Margins and Mainstreams: Asians in American History and Culture Seattle.* University of Washington Press.

Osajima, K.. (1988). Asian Americans as the model minority: An analysis of the popular press image in the 1960s and 1980s. In Y.G. Okihiro, S. Hune, S., A.A. Hansen, & M.J. Pullman (Eds), *Reflections on Shattered Windows: Promises and Prospects for Asian American Studies.* (pp. 165-174). Washington State University Press.

Poon, O., Squire, D., Kodama, C., Byrd, A., Chan, J., Manzano, L., Furr, S., & Bishundat, D. (2016). A critical review of the model minority myth in selected literature on Asian Americans and Pacific Islanders in higher education. *Review of Educational Research,* 86(2), 469–502. https://doi.org/10.3102/0034654315612205

Reyes, A. (2005), Appropriation of African American slang by Asian American youth. *Journal of Sociolinguistics,* 9, 509-532. https://doi.org/10.1111/j.1360-6441.2005.00304.x

Rolvsjord, R. (2006). Therapy as empowerment: Clinical and political implications of empowerment philosophy in mental health practises of music therapy. *Voices: A World Forum for Music Therapy,* 6(3). https://doi.org/10.15845/voices.v6i3.283

Said, E.W. (1979). *Orientalism* (1st ed.). New York: Vintage Books.

Suzuki, B.H. (1977). Education and socialization of Asian Americans: A revisionist analysis of the "model minority" thesis. *Amerasia Journal, 4*(2), 23-51. https://doi.org/10.17953/amer.4.2.x203l74863857108

Tai, C. (2018, May 28). *Asian hip hop: an homage to a genre or cultural appropriation driven by racism or ignorance?* South China Morning Post. https://www.scmp.com/lifestyle/fashion-beauty/article/2148143/asian-hip-hop-homage-genre-or-cultural-appropriation-driven?utm_source=copy_link&utm_medium=share_widget&utm_campaign=2148143

Tenny, S. (2002). Music therapy for juvenile offenders in residential treatment. *Music Therapy Perspectives, 20*(2). https://doi.org/10.1093/mtp/20.2.89

Travis, R. (2013). Rap music and the empowerment of today's youth: Evidence in everyday music listening, music therapy, and commercial rap music. *Child and Adolescent Social Work Journal, 30*(2), 139–167. doi: 10.1007/s10560-012-0285-x

Tyson, E. (2002). Hip hop therapy: An exploratory study of a rap music intervention with at-risk and delinquent youth. *Journal of Poetry Therapy, 15*(3), 131–144. https://doi.org/10.1023/A:1019795911358

Warren, A. and Evitt, R. (2010). Indigenous Hip-hop: Overcoming marginality, encountering constraints. *Australian Geographer, 41*(1), 41–158. doi: 10.1080/00049180903535659.

Washington, A. R. (2018), Integrating Hip-Hop Culture and Rap Music into Social Justice Counseling with Black Males. *Journal of Counseling & Development, 96*, 97–105. doi:10.1002/jcad.12181.

Wyatt, J. (2002). Clinical resources for music therapy with juvenile offenders. *Music Therapy Perspectives, 20*(2). https://doi.org/10.1093/mtp/20.2.80

World Federation of Music Therapy. (2011). *About WFMT.* https://www.wfmt.info/wfmt-new-home/about-wfmt/.

Wu, F. H. (2002). *Yellow: Race in America beyond Black and White.* New York: Basic Books.

Xiong, Z. B., Eliason, P.A., Detzner, D.F., & Cleveland, M.J. (2005). Southeast Asian Immigrants' perceptions of good adolescents and good parents. *The Journal of Psychology: Interdisciplinary and Applied, 139*(2), 159–175. https://doi.org/10.3200/JRLP.139.2.159-17

Zimmerman, M. A. (2000) Empowerment theory. In: Rappaport J., Seidman E. (eds) *Handbook of Community Psychology.* Springer, Boston, MA.

CHAPTER 12

# "L'Autore Ha Musicato Fin Qui, Poi è Morto": Diversity, Inclusion and Equity in Modern Staging of Classical Orientalist Opera

*Alison Lam*

A few weeks before his death, with his final opera *Turandot* yet unfinished, Giacomo Puccini told the famed conductor Arturo Toscanini that, if he could not finish writing the piece, he would like someone to appear on stage and say, "L'autore ha musicato fin qui, poi è morto." ("The author composed until here, and then he died.") While Toscanini honoured his wishes the night of the global debut of *Turnadot*, the opera was eventually completed and, to this day, features as a complete story from beginning to end.

And yet, Puccini's words that day were strangely prophetic, as it seems that, despite changes in social, economic, political, and cultural dynamics through the decades, classical opera has had very little advancement or evolution. Even though modern-era, and self-proclaimed "enlightened", opera companies have repeatedly made attempts to redress or recreate classical operas in order to eliminate all references that would today be considered as offensive, it seems they have only served to make the situation worse, as if underlining, highlighting, and even shining a spotlight on that which made it objectionable in the first place. As Rob Buscher, Festival Director of *Philadelphia Asian American Film Festival*, explains it:

> Turandot and other plays from the Orientalist canon differ from historically racist cinema because film exists in perpetuity. We study film as a primary source derived within the era in which it was produced because it will never change from its original state. A film produced in 1924 is the same film when watched in 2016. In the case of problematic films that use blackface, yellowface, and other negative ethnic stereotypes, we can still appreciate them from this historic context. However, a contemporary film production company could never justify a remake that included openly racist elements from the original.
> 
> BUSCHER, Turandot: Time to call it quits on Orientalist Opera?, 2016

For over a century, the Arts has had a fascination with all things Oriental. The Opera, in particular, has been an area in which predominantly white Europeans have chosen to exhibit their interest (Locke, 1993, p. 3133). And yet, are these supposed homages to Oriental culture more tribute or insult? Moreover, while these classical works were written and staged many decades ago, arguably before any periods of enlightenment, tolerance, and respect have developed for the numerous cultures of the world we share, how much have we learned in more modern times? This study performs an in-depth analysis of Mozart's *Die Entführung aus dem Serail* and Puccini's *Turandot*. Using the theories of Orientalism of Edward Said and intersectionality of Kimberlé Williams Crenshaw, this chapter seeks to determine how the racial implication and marginalization of the original European creations have been confronted in modern times by Canadian "multiculturalism" and, in each case, whether the treatment has proved to be an improvement or whether the updated versions simply serve to emphasize the original racial formation and intersectional encounters. How has diversity, equity and inclusion evolved and grown in Canada?

Edward Said's *Orientalism* is the study of the manner in which western society patronizes and diminishes their representations of the East. According to Mariela Nunez-Janes, he "argued that colonialism is sustained by the representation of cultural differences as binary opposites. Said showed that Orientalism was linked to the power of the West to authoritatively create and contrast the non-West." (Nunez-Janes, 2007, p. 41) The fascination with Orientalism was necessary because colonialism by definition requires the existence of diversity; one race must exert dominance over another. However, this version of diversity does not partner with equity in order to create an atmosphere of inclusion. Thus, although diversity is prominent in Orientalism, the fascination is fueled by the absence of equity and inclusion.

Said defines Orientalism as a "corporate institution for dealing with the Orient – dealing with it by making statements about it, authorizing views of it, describing it, by teaching it, settling it, ruling over it: in short, Orientalism as a Western Style for dominating, restructuring, and having authority over the Orient" (Said, 1978, pp. 3–4). And indeed, there are numerous time-honoured operas, by Verdi, Meyerbeers, Delibes, and countless works by Puccini, that serve to illustrate this point (Locke, 1993, p. 3125). Either through character archtypes or familiar plot devices, these operas encourage the dichotomized imagery of "Oriental despotism, Oriental splendor, cruelty, sensuality" (Said, 1978, p. 119).

The purpose of the operas in this study is to render the eastern societies more servile and to allow the nation state to exert more power. As Ralph

P. Locke explains, "the surface meaning of the allegory may have continued (and may continue even today) to operate separately from the deeper meaning and to reinforce – as Said and others rightly remind us – limited, distorted, or indeed entirely fictive and self-serving Western stereotypes of foreign culture" (Locke, 1993, p. 3134). While these two works were first staged over a century ago and such colonial implication is almost to be expected, the fact that they are also considered to be ingenious works of art and continue to be popular today, particularly among those who consider themselves to be sophisticated connoisseurs of impeccable taste, is troubling. High-end arts in general, and opera in particular, has a reputation for being elitist and exclusive, particularly for those who are not part of the white nation state. The fact that the opera-viewing public continues to be aficionados of works that are clearly party to racial formation in nature implies the need for this elite society to dominate over the inferior, impure one in eastern depiction.

## 1   Diversity

The UNESCO Universal Declaration on Cultural Diversity defines *cultural diversity* as "the set of distinctive spiritual, material, intellectual and emotional features of society or a social group, and that it encompasses, in addition to art and literature, lifestyles, ways of living together, value systems, traditions and beliefs." (UNESCO, 2002, p. 12) Diversity is about *difference* in a given setting, how the uniqueness of each individual defines the identity of a group or collective. According to Barbara Mazur:

> Diversity is a subjective phenomenon, created by group members themselves who on the basis of their different social identities categorize others as similar or dissimilar [...] Primary dimensions of diversity, those exerting primary influences on our identities, are gender, ethnicity, race, sexual orientation, age and mental or physical abilities and characteristics. The primary dimensions shape our basic self-image as well as our fundamental world views.
> 
> MAZUR, 2010, pp. 5–6

Of the two operas to be studied, the first to be completed and staged was Wolfgang Amadeus Mozart's *Die Entführung aus dem Serail* in 1782. This is a classic tale of East versus West, where the Western European characters are impeded from their future happiness by the evil Eastern Turks. Written to be a romantic comedy *singspiel,* the libretto opens by underlining the cultural diversity that becomes central to the opera's plot, telling the audience that our European heroines have been sold by pirates into slavery to the harem of the Turkish Pascha Selim.

Reflecting perfectly Edward Said's view on Orientalism, the Ottoman Empire is shown to be uncivilized and threatening. At the time, the real Ottoman Empire had just ceased to be a threat to Austria, where the opera was first mounted. It can be inferred that Mozart wrote his opera with the Viennese viewing public in mind, playing on their resentment of the Turkish culture and heritage. He sought to benefit from his audience's aversion to diversity with an opera that fuels their discomfort towards foreignness. Referring back to the writing of Mazur, Mozart was clearly using the *primary dimensions* of diversity to his advantage while wooing his audience.

The Pascha's harem, where much of the action occurs, is meant to evoke thoughts of sexual deviance and underline gender inequality in the way Eastern society denigrates women. As Yetka Kara, Artistic Director of the *Istanbul Opera Festival* has said, "You also can't escape the fact that Mozart strongly associates Turkishness with primitive, military masculinity which forms the opposite of the subtle and the vocal". (Hoile, 2018) According to Mazur:

> Secondary dimensions of diversity are less visible, exert a more variable influence on personal identity and add a more subtle richness to the primary dimensions of diversity. They include: educational background, geographic location, religion, first language, family status, work style, work experience, military experience, organizational role and level, income and communication style. The secondary dimensions impact our self esteem and self definition.
>
> MAZUR, 2010, p. 6

The Pascha's overseer, Osmin, is bad-tempered, vulgar, and represents the biggest obstacle to the freedom of the young female protagonists. While Osmin is described by his stage confrères to be detestable and abhorrent, for the audience, he represents the comic relief. He is the fool in our Turkish court; he brings the absurd to the story and allows the largely Western European viewing public to laugh at his strange, foreign antics. Although he is the principle antagonist, he is never taken seriously and easily succumbs to his foes. Even his own slaves, represented by Blonde, one of the female protagonists, do not submit to his authority.

The other main antagonist, also of Ottoman descent, is depicted as magnanimous. Instead of forcing Konstanze, the other Western European slave, to marry him or into a role of sexual slavery, the Pascha Selim demonstrates his integrity by setting out to win her heart. When he fails, upon foiling her plan to escape with her equally white love interest, he proves to be generous and forgiving by granting their freedom, thereby securing the happy ending for the opera.

However, while proven to be more likeable than Osmin, the Pascha Selim is still primitive and savage when compared to the civilized Western characters. He purchased slaves from pirates and gifts Osmin with Blonde, as if he had the right to gift a human being to another, according to these archaic, inferior, non-European laws. And, in the end, even though he has proven to be kinder, wiser, more honest, and more just than his romantic rival, the audience cheers when Konstanze leaves with her non-Muslim lover, which makes the latter the superior choice.

In 2018, the *Canadian Opera Company*, with a reputation for modernizing classical operas and putting a spin on the traditional (Weinman, 2009), mounted a brand new interpretation of *Die Entführung aus dem Serail*. This new version, a co-production with *Opéra de Lyons*, was re-written by Lebanese-Canadian writer and director Wajdi Mouawad "to prevent the opera from being 'an exercise in caricature or casual racism'" (Hoile, 2018). To achieve his goal, he added an extra 30 minutes of dialogue with the aim of undoing in the opera what he feels to be "an argument for the wholesale rejection of Islam and the East, thereby falling into larger patterns of Islamophobia in the West which would have us blame all our problems on the threat of an undifferentiated 'Arabic' Other" (Hoile, 2018).

Mouawad's version of *Die Entführung aus dem Serail* begins after the four Western European protagonists have returned home from escaping the Pascha's harem, the entire sequence of events of the original opera told in flashbacks. It is Konstanze and Blonde who represent Mouawad's voice of racial equality and cultural diversity. There is something about having these two characters defend the honour of the Eastern society that creates an inherent weakness in this voice; after all, they allowed themselves to be rescued and returned to Western society in order to ultimately become submissive to their male paramours. Yetka Kara's strongest argument for staging the opera as it was meant to be staged is that "Mozart gives a wonderful example of problems we still see today, fear of other cultures, lack of tolerance and the need to show understanding" (Hoile, 2018). However, Mouawad chooses to voice judgement to that fear and intolerance through his female leads.

Originally a light and lively *singspiel*, *Die Entführung aus dem Serail* already had more spoken lines than the traditional opera. With the addition of Mouawad's spoken dialogue, Mozart's work is transformed into something much more akin to a hybrid between a play and an opera, thereby already putting in doubt the true intent of the composer and alienating an audience in search of pure opera. Moreover, the tone of the subject Mouawad sought to treat is extremely heavy and introspective. It is certainly a subject that needs to be treated, but the vehicle he chose was a light-hearted comedy with upbeat music to match. The new dialogue slows down the pace of the entire performance, creating a start-and-stop between the heavy dialogue and the light music, something to which the audience is never able to adjust (Sumi, 2018). The effect created by the entire piece leaves both those seeking an entertaining comedy and those hungry for a lesson in cultural diversity completely unsatisfied by the outcome. The end result was a poorly-received opera with an opening night audience that even jeered at the production, something unheard of in the overwhelmingly polite Torontonian viewing public. Mouawad's intent, therefore, fails epically and falls largely on deaf ears.

## 2  Inclusion

Frequently described in economic terms, social inclusion was explained by Dan Allman in this way:

> In sum, the terms social inclusion and social exclusion have been used throughout the social science and humanities literature in a number of different ways—to describe acts of social stratification across human and animal societies, as a principle to reflect the ordering that occurs within societies to determine social position, and as a narrative to explain and at times justify why one or more groups merit access to the core or the periphery, to the benefit or expense of others.
> ALLMAN, 2013, p. 7

In *Die Entführung aus dem Serail*, social inclusion and exclusion is defined by race; the Europeans are clearly depicted as having the higher moral position in the social stratification, despite the fact that the Muslim characters seemingly have more power, wealth and prestige. In fact, while the European female protagonists are slaves to their Muslim captors, this seems to be nothing more than an illusion of social stratification. In the end, the European women regain the superiority of their social position at the expense of their Muslim captors by escaping with their European male counterparts.

Even Mouawad's modernized version dealing with the more offensive racial aspects of the opera seeks to emphasize the social stratification among European and Muslim societies. In the opening scene, an original written by Mouawad, those who are celebrating the return of the protagonists play a game of *tête-a-turc*, reminiscent of a carnival game, where the players take turns dropping a sledgehammer on a replica of the head of a Turkish man in a turban (Kaptainis, 2018). Though the point was ultimately to show how ignorant and prejudiced Western Europeans could be regarding a culture of which they know nothing, the scene also demonstrates the offensive and repugnant nature of Western society. As Allman explains:

> Gillies (2005) reflected that societies have a tendency to normalize the sins of the included while penalizing the sins of the excluded. This suggests that even if discourses about social inclusion are effectively rendered as policy and translated into practice, the act of revaluating the biases society's hold for marginal underclasses of excluded social actors may well remain. This is to say that were society able to find room within its social architectures for its marginal women and men (Park, 1928), the fact of their powerlessness coupled with their comportment could still relegate them to the periphery, occupying colonized spaces stratified on one side by accusations of nonnormative or deviant behavior and on another by power relations.
> 
> ALLMAN, 2013, p. 12

This concept of deviant behaviour juxtaposed with power relations is demonstrated in exemplary manner in Puccini's *Turandot*. Giacomo Puccini has always been known to be fascinated with the Orient, but he has never felt the necessity of thorough research before depicting the environment in his operas. In truth, he knew nothing factual about the culture with which he was obsessed, but he believed so much in his own music and talent that he was confident that his representation would make sense (Marsh, 2015). By not having bothered with the appropriate research on the topic and relying solely on his own musical talents and interpretations, Puccini provides a perfect representation of Said's version of Orientalism, where the Orientalist (in this case, the Western European) claims to know more about the Orient than do the Orientals themselves (Said, 1978, pp. 2–3). As Locke postulates, "the surface meaning of the allegory may have continued (and may continue even today) to operate separately from the deeper meaning and to reinforce – as Said and others rightly remind us – limited, distorted, or indeed entirely fictive and self-serving Western stereotypes of foreign cultures" (Locke, 1993, p. 3134).

Meanwhile, the titular character of Puccini's *Turandot* suffers from the same concept of intersectionality. The term *intersectionality* was first coined by Kimberlé Williams Crenshaw in 1989. When speaking of Black women and the court system, she wrote:

> Discrimination against the white female is thus the standard sex discrimination claim; claims that diverge from this standard appear to present some sort of hybrid claim. More significantly, because Black females' claims are seen as hybrid, they sometimes cannot represent those who may have "pure" claims of sex discrimination. The effect of this approach is that even though a challenged policy or practice may clearly discriminate against all females, the fact that it has particularly harsh consequences for Black females places Black female plaintiffs at odds with white females.
> CRENSHAW, 2018

The Princess Turandot is not only Asian, but also female, making the concept of inclusion nearly unattainable. This places her in an inferior position on two different planes; she must submit to both male dominance and the white nation state. Although, traditionally speaking, *Turandot* is resolved in a positive manner for all protagonists, it could be argued that the marginal destiny that awaits her is a tragedy for Asian women in general.

Likewise, when Liu, perhaps the only truly innocent character of the opera, is tortured by Turandot's ministers, her submission to male dominance immediately renders her the main heroine of the opera. Liu is considered one of Puccini's "little girls" (Innaurato, 2019), the trope of an Oriental girl, frail and small, who suffers greatly for her devotion and love. Her purpose is also to seduce and manipulate, not another character in the opera, but the audience. A favourite of the composer, Puccini's little girl entices and beguiles the viewing public with her wide-eyed innocence and tragic circumstances, ultimately breaking our hearts with her inevitable demise, usually in the form of a monumental personal sacrifice. At the same time innocent victim and irresistible temptress, she is Puccini's ultimate weapon of Orientalism used to threaten the stability and security of white privileged society. Speaking of the role of Black women as opposed to Orientalism, author and feminist bell hooks' comments nevertheless apply: "Then there were those spectators whose gaze was that of desire and complicity. Assuming a posture of subordination, they submitted to cinema's capacity to seduce and betray. They were cinematically "gaslighted."" (hooks, 2008, p. 260).

In this particular case, Liu is accepting the lack of inclusion in her role rather than challenging it as does Turandot, fitting perfectly into the mould defined for her by Western male society, not deviating from her expected position of subjugation and sacrifice to the superior populace. (Langford, 2016) As Locke explains:

> Liu is of course in a state of crisis and near despair here, confessing her long-unspoken love yet fearing all the while (rightly) that the Prince will ignore her plea and continue to pursue the seemingly fatal fantasy of winning Turandot's hand. In this sense, the harmonization succeeds at humanizing or de-Orientalizing Liu, much in the way that - as Carl Dahlhaus points out about national operas of Glinka, Moniuszko, and others - composers evinced sincere respect for certain of their peasant heroes and heroines by letting them sing, not in some watered down folk-song style, but in the "elevated" and emotionally varied, even noble and heroic, musical language of grand opera.
>
> LOCKE, 1993, p. 3127

Liu is therefore, on the one hand, given an exalted position in order for her to be able to play her role of seduction of the audience, through the process of de-orientalization in order to diminish or give illusion to negating her marginalization. On the other, she remains socially excluded, as the audience is well-aware that her advice will not be heeded, and her desires will not be fulfilled. She continues to be subjugated and powerless, particularly so in her position of intersectional encounters.

## 3    Equity

Equity is "an approach that ensures everyone access to the same opportunities. Equity recognizes that advantages and barriers exist, and that, as a result, we all don't all start from the same place. Equity is a process that begins by acknowledging that unequal starting place and continues to correct and address the imbalance." (Bolger, 2017) *Turandot*, completed posthumously in 1926, has an interesting take on equity. Like with the depiction of Turkey and the Ottoman Empire in *Die Entführung aus dem Serail*, Puccini's version of Peking is clearly created through a prejudiced and xenophobic lens, but where Mozart's Turkish harem is merely savage and uncivilized to the point of valuing slavery and the subjugation of women, Puccini's Peking is cruel and violent. The citizens of the city are at once vicious dictators and quivering subjects. When the opera opens with the execution of the Prince of Persia for the supposed crime of being unable to win their Princess's hand in marriage, they are originally bloodthirsty and crying for his head. And yet, when the Princess's cruelty is turned towards her own people, they cower in fear, preferring to torture and kill the aged and feeble in order to save themselves.

Equity here must be considered in relation to China, both in the real world and in Puccini's fictional Peking. In that historical era of colonization, China would be under formal territorial concessions for the next 85 years as a result of the Opium War of 1839. As Buscher explains, "With blessings from their government, British merchants flooded the Chinese market with opium to profit from addiction and intentionally destabilize society. When the Chinese government tried to intervene in the interest of their people the British actually went to war over it." (Buscher, Turandot: Time to call it quits on Orientalist Opera?, 2016) This led to an era where foreign governments had complete dominance over the Chinese populace and free reign over what they viewed as their vassal state. If a foreign national committed a crime against a Chinese local, the Chinese government had absolutely no jurisdiction over the former. If the British government found in favour of the foreign national, which was almost a given, there would be no repercussions for his actions. This impotence of the Chinese government and its inability to protect its own citizens weakened the country in the eyes of the world and made it a source of intense ridicule.

In Puccini's opera, equity is reversed, with China being the dominant race, but in a way that marks the Chinese as undeserving to the opera-going Western society. Though the female lead, the Princess Turandot does not have a single ounce of honour or decency as she misuses her power to instill fear in her people while displaying her lack of integrity in her refusal to keep her word. Turandot has promised to marry the suitor who can answer her three riddles, but those who fail must pay the ultimate price with their heads. Gleefully, she has mercilessly ordered the beheading of an endless number of suitors who have failed to answer her riddles. And yet, when the tables are turned and she loses her little game, she first begs her father, the Emperor, to release her from the requirement to wed the suitor who successfully answered her riddles. When the Emperor refuses, she attempts to shame her suitor into releasing her from her vow by asking if he was the kind of man who would force himself on a woman. When the suitor gives her one chance to break the vow if she can discover his name by daybreak, her vile and despicable personality grows in intensity as she unleashes a reign of terror on her own Chinese subjects that inspires them to turn on each other in fear, showing no regret in torturing and murdering innocents, all to indulge in Turandot's own selfish desires. She is a loathsome protagonist with not an ounce of likeability, and one would be forgiven if left to wonder if her numerous erstwhile suitors had chosen to sacrifice themselves to avoid the fate of being wed to her.

So, in the end, how does this stereotype of the "Asian Dragon lady" finally submit to the masculine protagonist? How is the fictionally superior but undeserving Chinese race brought to heel? The male protagonist, Prince Calaf, is identified by his foreign-ness to Peking society, thereby underlining his own otherness and inequity. He is known for honour and integrity (as is wont of those "other" than the Chinese race), but the moment he casts this aside and forces himself sexually upon Turandot, she is overcome, falls madly in love, and submits herself utterly and completely to male domination. This is a scene that not only encourages rape behaviour, it also affirms that Asian women would become vile, violent, vengeful, dishonourable and despicable if they are not properly controlled and subjugated by the appropriate male presence. Just like in history, the mighty Chinese power is brought down by the physical force of a foreign national.

As previously mentioned, both Turandot and Liu are victims of intersectionality. Liu is young and naïve, and Prince Calaf takes advantage of this, knowing that Liu would put him above her own life, sacrificing herself to protect his identity. Another form of discrimination against Liu is due to her class; in a battle for power between two royal families, her role as a servant immediately puts her at a disadvantage that eventually must result in her elimination. bell hooks explains in her book *Feminist Theory: From Margin to Centre*:

> Women in lower class and poor groups, particularly those who are nonwhite, would not have defined women's liberation as women gaining social equality with men since they are continually reminded in their everyday lives that all women do not share a common social status.
> HOOKS, 2014, p. 19

Likewise, Turandot, being both Chinese and female, cannot retain her power and privilege at the end of the opera; both must be relinquished in order for Turandot to conform to her expected place in society. Princess or not, as a Chinese woman, she cannot be allowed to wield all the power without being defeated. As Crenshaw explains:

> The point is that Black women can experience discrimination in any number of ways and that the contradiction arises from our assumptions that their claims of exclusion must be unidirectional. Consider an analogy to traffic in an intersection, coming and going in all four directions. Discrimination, like traffic through an intersection, may flow in one direction, and it may flow in another. If an accident happens in an intersection, it can be caused by cars traveling from any number of directions

and, sometimes, from all of them. Similarly, if a Black woman is harmed because she is in the intersection, her injury could result from sex discrimination or race discrimination.

CRENSHAW, 2018

Moreover, in this tribute to chinoiserie by Puccini (Innaurato, 2019), not one element is meant to be more representative than Turandot's three male Ministers. As their songs in Act II were inspired by a Chinese music box Puccini had discovered, it could be argued that Ping, Pang, and Pong were meant to be the most authentically Chinese of all the characters. However, they are snivelling, effeminate, and two-faced; even their names are offensive. On the one hand, they appear to be there to aid and guide the stranger, first attempting to deter him from his seemingly futile suit of the Princess, then trying to convince him to leave to spare his life. On the other hand, they do not hesitate to capture and torture Liu at the behest of Turandot in order to remorselessly save themselves from her wrath. There is not a single redeeming quality among any of the citizens of Peking, with the only sympathetic characters being the ones who are "foreign" to Peking and who are positioned in a place of inferiority, where their lives are nothing more than a game.

In 2019, the *Canadian Opera Company* mounted the opera *Turandot*, in yet another innovative and original production. They would not have been the only company to have done it in recent years, as *Opera Phila* had mounted a production in 2016 (Buscher, Addressing Yellowface in Opera, Theater and Film, 2016). The Philadelphia production was marketed with all the white actors wearing "yellowface" along with the offensive and particularly insulting tagline, "A Beautiful Exotic Adventure". At the *Beyond Orientalism* forum in Philadelphia late that same year, "the Caucasian theater directors and administrators spent about 20 minutes defending the lack of diversity in their productions and complaining about how difficult it was from their perspectives." (Buscher, Addressing Yellowface in Opera, Theater and Film, 2016)

In this Canadian version of *Turandot*, the artistic staging has the characters moving around the stage like chess pieces, never touching and never facing each other. All the characters wear the white and pink make-up of traditional Chinese opera, thereby hiding their true racial identity. In essence, this is a form of wearing yellowface, particularly when the characters are such absurd caricatures of what Asian stereotypes are thought to be.

The concept of "yellowface" is not new to Canada. In her book *Colonial Proximities: Crossracial Encounters and Juridical Truths in British Columbia*, Renisa Mawani tells a story of a "Lady Correspondent" who writes in a newspaper in British Columbia of the reopening of the Kincolith Church in 1900.

This re-opening included two days of festivities, with both white and aboriginal communities as guests. During the formal dinner on the second night, the Lady Correspondent described the entertainment as such:

> During the meal we were entertained by songs from the waiters, also by a funny Indian who dressed as a Chinamen [sic], acted his part splendidly, and added greatly to the amusement of all by joining in the songs, and giving his own squeaky solos from time to time.
> MAWANI, 2009, p. 2

This example of having an Indigenous man, already considered a colonial minority of the white nation state, dress up and encourage the belittling of another minority group by the dominant race, is horrific in its implications. The region was in the process of notable imperial expansion and the need to assert dominance was strong. The temptation to turn the Chinese community, which had been invaluable in contributing to this expansion, into a source of ridicule and to minimize their importance, is great. According to Said, with the use of Orientalism as the cultural norm, Western society erased and rewrote the identity of Asia in a way that took away their power and made them to be an impotent and inferior race. (Said, 1978, pp. 38–41)

While this explains the historical genesis in Canada of "yellowface", and also the overall sentiment towards Chinese culture when Puccini wrote the opera, it does not explain why Canadian culture, which takes pride in its acceptance and encouragement of the multicultural mosaic, continues to find the staging of operas where the characters wear "yellowface" to be artistically beautiful. This can also be explained by Said, along with the obsession with Orientalism. Western society has a dependence on creating a fictional world where the Orient is exotic but feminized, weak, and overall inferior. There are "immutable cultural essences" that will always exist, creating a perpetual inequality that underlines the strength of European (or white Canadian) society. (Said, 1978, pp. 65–7) It is this inequality, put on elegant display, which continues to feed the Western fascination with Orientalism.

## 4    Conclusion

bell hooks said it best when she explained, "Representation is the "hot" issue right now because it's a major realm of power for any system of domination. We keep coming back to the question of representation because identity is always about representation." (hooks, 2008, p. 221) What we present to our audiences today matters. The message that is given to the viewing public and society regarding diversity, inclusion and equity matters. We cannot simply perform a piece that was written at a time of extreme bias and bigotry without finding a way to address the injustices of the piece. As a source of representation of the world today, the arts have a responsibility to put forward a depiction that does not feed into the marginalization and oppression of a bygone era.

So, how do we do this? Rob Buscher believes that there are operas that should be retired forever. (Buscher, Turandot: Time to call it quits on Orientalist Opera?, 2016) Wajdi Mouawad believes operas can be reworked so they no longer serve the original purpose, risking unpopularity among opera aficionados and commercial failure.

Suffice to say, the worst possible solution is to ignore the inherent abhorrent racial formation. Nothing could be worse than continuing to perform these operas in "yellowface", while making what one can only assume are window-dressing changes. Whether by changing the original libretto of the opera or presenting it at its worst but openly inviting critique and criticism, the important thing is to not ignore the racist and misogynistic natures of classical opera.

Written during less tolerant and equitable eras, these operas are undoubtedly beautiful and masterful pieces of work. If not, they would never have withstood the test of time. However, universally accepted as an art form reserved primarily for the privileged classes in society, opera has among its audience the wealthiest and most powerful people on a global scale. With a viewing public that is by definition not equitable to the rest of society, it would be socially and ethically irresponsible for opera companies to continue to perpetuate the bigotry and prejudice so often espoused. Continually considered to be a luxury industry, the arts as a whole can count among its patrons those who have enough authority to dominate the world. The faults of the composers who created them may have been overlooked due to their artistic genius and talent for pandering to their dominant Western colonial benefactors, but with such spectators at its fingertips, today's modern world of Opera must carry the burden of at least attempting to influence society through the encouragement of open dialogue and the refusal to dismiss these challenging and problematic themes and ideas.

### References

Allman, D. (2013). The Sociology of Social Inclusion. *SAGE Open*, 1–16.

Bolger, M. (2017, October 24). *What's the Difference Between Diversity, Inclusion and Equity?* Retrieved June 27, 2020, from General Assembly: https://generalassemb.ly/blog/diversity-inclusion-equity-differences-in-meaning/.

Buscher, R. (2016, October 21). *Addressing Yellowface in Opera, Theater and Film.* Retrieved from Pacific Citizen: https://www.pacificcitizen.org/addressing-yellowface-in-opera-theater-and-film-2/.

Buscher, R. (2016, September 19). *Turandot: Time to call it quits on Orientalist Opera?* Retrieved from Opera Philadelphia: Opera Blog: https://www.operaphila.org/backstage/opera-blog/2016/turandot-time-to-call-it-quits-on-orientalist-opera/.

Crenshaw, K. W. (2018, May 13). *Demarginalizing the Intersection of Race and Sex: A Black Feminist Critique of Antidiscrimination Doctrine, Feminist Theory and Antiracist Politics.* Retrieved from PhilPapers: https://philpapers.org/archive/CREDTI.pdf.

Gillies, V. (2005). Meeting parents needs? Discourses of "support" and "inclusion" in family policy. *Critical Social Policy*, 70-90.

Hoile, C. (2018, February 8). *Reviews: The Abduction from the Seraglio.* Retrieved from Stage Door: http://www.stage-door.com/Theatre/2018/Entries/2018/2/8_The_Abduction_from_the_Seraglio.html.

hooks, b. (2008). *Reel to Real: Race, Sex and Class at the Movies.* New York: Routledge.

hooks, b. (2014). *Feminist Theory: From Margin to Centre.* New York: Routledge.

Innaurato, A. (2019). Turandot - Talking About Opera. On *Met Opera Guild Podcast* [Podcast]. Metropolitan Opera Guild.

Kaptainis, A. (2018, February 11). *Didactic, Sanitized Staging Abducts Mozart's Seraglio.* Retrieved from Classical Voice North America: https://classicalvoiceamerica.org/2018/02/11/didactic-stage-director-abducts-mozarts-seraglio/.

Langford, J. (2016). Turandot Pre-Performance Lecture. On *Met Opera Guild Podcast* [Podcast]. Metropolitan Opera Guild.

Locke, R. (1993). Reflections on Orientalism in Opera (and Musical Theater). *Revista de Musicología*, 3122–3134.

Marsh, J. (2015). Puccini Heroines - Tosca and Madama Butterfly. On *Met Opera Guild Podcast* [Podcast]. Metropolitan Opera Guild.

Mawani, R. (2009). *Colonial Proximities: Crossracial Encounters and Juridical Truths in British Columbia.* UBC Press.

Mazur, B. (2010). Cultural Diversity in Organisational Theory and Practice. *Journal of Intercultural Management*, 5–15.

Nunez-Janes, M. (2007). Diversity as an Orientalist Discourse. *Ethnic Studies Review*, *30*(1&2), 41–57.

Park, R. E. (1928). Human migration and the marginal man. *American Journal of Sociology*, 881-893.

Said, E. (1978). *Orientalism.* New York: Pantheon Books.

Sumi, G. (2018, February 9). *The Abduction From The Seraglio gets a culturally sensitive makeover.* Retrieved from Now Toronto: https://nowtoronto.com/stage/opera/the-abduction-from-the-seraglio-wajdi-mouawad-canadian-opera-company/.

UNESCO. (2002). *UNESCO Universal Declaration on Cultural Diversity, adopted by the 31st session of the General Conference of UNESCO, Paris, 2 November 2001.* Retrieved June 2020, from UNESCO Digital Library: https://unesdoc.unesco.org/ark:/48223/pf0000127160.

Weinman, J. (2009, May 7). *Why the COC's betting on the house.* Retrieved from Maclean's: https://www.macleans.ca/culture/why-the-cocs-betting-on-the-house/.

CHAPTER 13

# South Asian Representations in the Media
*Repetition or Progress?*

*Syed Fahad Ali*

1    Introduction

South Asians have largely been under-represented when it comes to the media. Furthermore, the few representations that do exist are often stereotypical and rarely stray from one-dimensional representations. However, just as there is progress being made on representations of Asians in general, there is also some progress being made on how South Asians are depicted. However, as someone who is of South Asian heritage, I feel that this progress is too slow and often done inauthentically. I also feel that one medium that can help portray South Asians as multi-dimensional is video games. Through representations in television, film, and video games, I want to focus on what 'progress' may look like and whether there a sense of repetition in these representations under the guise of inauthentic diversity. Lastly, I feel that in order to better reflect the changing demographic pattern in North America, a diverse workforce will lead to better representations in media, especially when it comes to South Asians.

2    South Asia – A Region within a Region

First and foremost, for the purpose of this chapter the region of South Asia or Southern Asia needs to be defined. For this, I have used the definition provided by the UN, which considers South Asia to be composed of the following countries: Afghanistan, Bangladesh, Bhutan, India, Iran (Islamic Republic of), Maldives, Nepal, Pakistan, and Sri Lanka (UNSD, 1999). It is important to emphasize South Asia in this chapter because there is little research done when it comes to depictions of South Asians (Muffuletto, 2018; Thakore, 2013), since most research tends to focus on East Asians, although it uses the umbrella term 'Asian.' This is misleading since South Asians are often excluded from 'Asia' or glossed over.

## 3   Representation in Film and Television

When it comes to film and television to say there has been progress would be somewhat misleading and an oversimplification, yet that is what the popular narrative appears to be. Just like the narrative of racial progress throughout history I feel like there are missteps in how cultural representations of South Asians have been presented. In a post-9/11 world South Asians have largely been cast as villains, particularly when it comes to males. Many representations of South Asians tend to portray Muslims as fundamentalists who are almost always male. Furthermore, representations that do not fall into the stereotype of the fundamentalist tend to fall into another stereotype. For these representations I would like to focus on some television shows that have become cultural staples such as *The Simpsons* or have become international hits such as *The Big Bang Theory* and *Silicon Valley*. I would also like to at films, such as the recent hit *Crazy Rich Asians* and *The Big Sick*.

The first character that I would like to focus on is Apu Nahasapeemapetilon from the animated show *The Simpsons*. Apu encompasses all of the stereotypical ideas that are held about Indian men. He works at a convenience store, he has a strong accent, and he lacks 'Western' social skills. Furthermore, the biggest shortcoming of Apu's character is that he is voiced by a non-Indian person. By having a non-Indian person voice an Indian character, Apu is set up as a character that is not only a caricature but also as someone that is being mocked through his appearance and his voice. However, there has been some progress made by the show. Recently, due to widespread backlash, and an outcry by South Asians who felt that they were mocked because of Apu's representation (Muffuletto, 2018, p. 23), Apu was retired from the show. Unfortunately, his existence in the numerous episodes form the past will not go unnoticed. Furthermore, rather than try to erase a racialized character from the show, *The Simpsons* could create a new character that is more authentic with input from racialized writers as well as being voiced by a racialized person.

The second character I would like to look at is Rajesh Koothrappali from the sitcom *The Big Bang Theory*. Despite no longer being on air *The Big Bang Theory* had huge ratings at the time of its airing and continues to be shown in reruns around the world. Unlike Apu, who is voiced by a non-Indian person in a stereotypical accent, Rajesh is represented by a British-Indian actor, yet his character has selective mutism in the show (Muffuletto, 2018, p. 16), which means that he is often unable to speak in front of women and can only speak around his friends who are all men. Furthermore, much like Apu, he has a strong accent and lacks social skills. The portrayal of Rajesh reinforces one of the stereotypes regrading Indian men. This stereotype is about placing the Indian male in the tech. world and only within the world of tech. can he exist. Furthermore, Rajesh's character is also played around with in terms of his voice. Much like Apu, who has a strong stereotypical accent, Rajesh is often left voiceless.

The third character I would like to look at is Dinesh Chugtai from *Silicon Valley*. Unlike Apu and Rajesh, Dinesh has been well received by the South Asian community (Muffuletto, 2018, p. 56). Despite not being too different from Rajesh, Dinesh came across as more 'authentic' for audiences. Reasons for this include, Dinesh having a love interest, being socially capable, and not forcing an accent (Muffuletto, 2018, p. 57). Yet, despite being less of a stereotype and more 'authentic' compared to other representations, Dinesh is still depicted as a South Asian in the world of tech., which will always place certain limitations on him and have certain expectations of him.

Moving on from television, I would like to focus on two films that made quite the impact recently when it came to representations of Asian and South Asians. The first of these films is *Crazy Rich Asians* which was a financial success but also seen as a cultural success and a milestone when it came to representations of Asians. Despite these claims to be true, the problem with the film, and the novel which it is based on, is with the use of the word 'Asians.' For this film, Asians is not inclusive but exclusive because it includes East Asians, mainly those who have a Chinese background. The representation of South Asians in the film is largely absent, except for brief scenes where there are South Asian men are seen as menacing guards for wealthy East Asians. Although this film was seen as a big success for Asians it was ultimately only a success for East Asians, and even then, it was only depicting an extremely wealthy, yet extremely small, group of East Asians at the expense of South Asians.

The second film that I would like to look at is *The Big Sick* and the character of Kumail Nanjiani. Much like the representation of Dinesh in *Silicon Valley*, who coincidentally was also played by Kumail Nanjiani. *The Big Sick* represents a South Asian character that is more complex than what is typically represented. This has largely to do with the production of the film. In the film Kumail plays a fictional version of himself which adds a sense of authenticity to the character. Furthermore, the film was written entirely by Kumail and his wife, Emily V. Gordon and was based on their story which meant that they had the freedom to represent themselves rather than have someone represent them. Since the story was based on true events the character of Kumail came across as being more genuine. While Kumail is a Muslim, he is not shown as a fundamentalist. Despite being Pakistani-American, his wife is a White American, which shows a more complex relationship. Finally, in the film Kumail is depicted as someone who goes through personal struggles with his culture which comes across as being relatable and authentic.

## 4  Representations in Video Games

I would like to shift my focus away from representation on film and television and focus on video games. Video games have become extremely popular in the last two decades (Slagle, 2006) and are now widely accessible due to advances in technology. Since video games as a medium are relatively new compared to other more traditional forms of media there has been little academic research done on representations in video games, especially when it comes to South Asian representations. Instead, most video game research tends to focus on the effects of violence depicted within video games while using research done in television as a parallel (Williams, 2009, p. 816). Furthermore, inadequate research on video games can lead to generalizations, such as stating that Asians are over-represented when, in a broader sense, they are greatly under-represented (Williams, 2009, p. 824), and also by not properly defining Asian or realizing that the term 'Asian' contains a great deal of diversity. However, despite there being little academic research, gamers themselves have decided to share their insights on representation. Despite gamers not being a traditional academic source, they do help provide insight into how representations in video games are seen because just like any other medium, video games are also used to negotiate one's identity (Patterson, 2018, p. 8).

When it comes to video games, representations tend be short lived, quickly forgotten, and not very memorable. However, one character in the video game world that does have some longevity and that I would like to focus on is from the popular video game series called *Street Fighter*, which is a franchise originating from Japan. Before delving into an analysis, it should be noted that despite this video game originating from Japan, the representation itself is not any less stereotypical than had it originated form the West. Furthermore, as a video game, *Street Fighter*, does very little to hide its racial stereotyping since it shows a flag next to its roster of characters to choose from (Patterson, 2018, p. 7). The character I would look at is named Dhalsim and is meant to be from India. Dhalsim's name has a strange origin story. The name was formed using a menu at an Indian restaurant in Osaka. The word 'dhal,' which means lentil in Hindi, was combined with the word 'shim,' which means hyacinth beans (Panesar, 2020). As for the character's background, he is said to have originated from a poverty-stricken village, which is a stereotypical view of Indian society. Finally, in terms of his physical appearance, Dhalsim appears as an old 'mystical' man with long stretched limbs who is originally a pacifist yet ends up becoming a fighter (Panesar, 2020). Overall, the character of Dhalsim does very little to stray from how Indians are traditionally depicted on film and television. What is even more disturbing is that despite all of the shortcomings of Dhalsim's character, he is the most prominent depiction of a South Asian in video games. Other examples of South Asians usually include them as the unplayable villains, much like fundamentals on television and film, in contrast to the white characters who are usually the playable heroes (Patterson, 2018, p. 5).

## 5 Absence or Stereotype

Overall, despite the agency and sense of freedom video games can provide when it comes to representation of South Asians and Asians in general, video games tend to follow the same shortcomings regarding representations as other media and further create stereotypes. Much like film and television, these shortcomings are also due to the fact that the creators themselves are not diverse (Williams, 2009, p. 830) yet they try to represent diversity which comes across as being inauthentic and negative. For the time being, South Asian audiences and other racialized groups in general, are left with two choices, absence of representation or a stereotypical representation.

## 6 Conclusion

Through this brief analysis of film, television, and video games, I have realized that representations of South Asians are categorized into stereotypes. Whether it is the convenience store owner, the tech. worker, or the fundamentalist, there is little complexity when it comes to representations of South Asians, and this is only when it comes to men. When it comes to women there is even more of an absence or a generalizing in representation. I have also come to realized that media representations of South Asians work in two ways. First, South Asians are othered (Said, 1978) through their appearance but also through their voices. Second, they are generalized (Spivak, 1995, p.25) into one-dimensional characters incapable of being complex or break out from stereotypes. Results are less stereotypical when media is created by a racialized person rather a non-racialized person's imagination. *Big Sick* is seen as successful when it comes to representations of South Asians because it was autobiographical, written by Kumail Nanjiani and his wife Emily V. Gordon about themselves and their experiences. Furthermore, the central character was played by Kumail

Nanjiani himself, although somewhat fictionalized for the purpose of the film. Going forward, I hope that tradtional mediums such as film and television as well as more emerging ones, suc as video games can progress in their representations of South Asians by reflecting the diverse demographics of their market, allowing content to be created by a diverse group of people, and embracing forms of hybridity rather than static stereotypical representations.

## References

Chu, J. M. 2018. *Crazy Rich Asians*. Film. Burbank, CA: Warner Bros. Home Entertainment.

Muffuletto, Samantha L., *Effects of American Media Representation of South Asian Americans* (2018). DCE Theses and Dissertations. 661. http://nrs.harvard.edu/urn-3:HUL.InstRepos:37799749.

Panesar, A. (2020). *Top 5 South Asian Video Game Characters*. DESIblitz. https://www.desiblitz.com/content/south-asian-video-game-characters.

Patterson, C. B. (2018). Asian Americans and Digital Games. *Oxford Research Encyclopedia of Literature*. Oxford University Press.

Said, E. (1978). *Orientalism*. New York, NY: Vintage Books.

Showalter, M. 2017. *The Big Sick*. Film. Santa Monica: Lions Gate Entertainment.

Slagle, M. (2006) 'Poll: 4 in 10 Americans Play Videogames', *Washington Post*, 8 May, URL (consulted 20 June 2007): http://www.washingtonpost.com/wp-dyn/content/article/2006/05/07/ar2006050700172.html.

Spivak, G. C. (1995). Can the subaltern speak? In Ashcroft, B., Griffiths, G. & Tiffin, H. (1995). In *The Post-colonial Studies Reader* (pp. 28–37). New York, NY: Routledge.

Thakore, Bhoomi K., *Just Like Everyone Else? Locating South Asians in 21st Century American Popular Media* (2013). Dissertations. 549. https://ecommons.luc.edu/luc_diss/549

United Nations, Statistics Division, *Standard country or area codes for statistical use (M49)*, M, No. 49/Rev.4 (1999), available from https://unstats.un.org/unsd/publications/catalogue?selectID=109

Williams, D. (2009). The virtual census: Representations of gender, race and age in video games. *New Media & Society*, 11(5), 815–834.

CHAPTER 14

# The Fallacy of Native-Speakerism in English Language Education

*Jasmine Pham*

## 1  Introduction

The hiring of Native English-Speaking Teachers (NESTs) to teach English as a foreign language in East Asia is not a new or uncommon practice. In fact, due to our increasingly interconnected world, the importance of English and English education has resulted in the expansion of English programs in countries like Japan and South Korea for decades (Wang & Lin, 2013). Since the launch of the English Program in Korea (EPIK) in 1995, and the Japan Exchange and Teaching Programme (JET) in 1987, thousands of English teachers have joined the two programs (Jeon & Lee, 2006). With the increase of NESTs stepping into South Korean and Japanese classrooms, there has been growing attention to the qualifications of NESTs as well as their impact on the professional identity and autonomy of Non-Native English-Speaking Teachers (NNESTs) (Ruecker & Ives, 2015). Current literature that addresses the professional identities of NNESTs reveals a lack of support in professional growth and legitimacy due to the prevalence of native-speakerism, a theory where native speakers are treated as "ideal" English teachers because of their English abilities as opposed to their teacher qualifications (Ruecker & Ives, 2015). As a result, NNESTs have difficulties upholding their professional autonomy and role as English teachers against the perception that NESTs are "superior" teachers of English (Ruecker & Ives, 2015).

As both the EPIK and JET programs have made very little changes since their inception, it's time for both programs to depart from the perception that one's "nativeness" such as race and nationality determines one's value as an English teacher. Through my research, I address the impact of globalization and native-speakerism on the hiring practices and policies of South Korea's EPIK program and Japan's JET program. I then discuss how native-speakerism not only undermines the professional identities of Korean and Japanese English teachers, but also the authenticity of NESTs of Asian descent and the English teaching profession in general. Finally, I offer policy suggestions and alternatives to native-speakerism that can improve the professional identities of both NESTs and NNESTs.


## 2   Globalization and English as a Global Language

English is currently the most spoken language in the world and the main language used for communication between world leaders and multinational organizations (Majhanovich, 2014). Through globalization, English has become a form of cultural capital that is "invaluable to aspiring populations and nations" (Luke, Luke, & Graham, p. 10, 2007). As a result, millions of non-English speakers are now expected to learn English in order to participate in our globalized world (Majhanovich, p. 169, 2014). The overwhelming hegemony of English is seen in the prevalence of English programs in East Asia as well as the practice of hiring NESTs to teach in said programs (Nunan, 2003). In implementing these changes to their education system, countries around the world are accepting the knowledge of English as a highly valued social capital and agreeing to abide by the rules and culture of the English-speaking world (Majhanovich, 2014). As a result, we see the influence of English not only in the teaching of English as a core subject, but also in the hiring process and perception of English teachers around the world.


## 3   Hiring Policies of Native English-Speaking Teachers

South Korea's EPIK program and Japan's JET program are both examples of how East Asian countries are responding to globalization and the rise of English as a dominant global language. The EPIK program was created with the intention to improve the English-speaking abilities of Korean students and teachers (EPIK, 2013), while the JET program was created with the purpose of "increasing mutual understanding between the people of Japan and the people of other nations" (JET, 2015). Although both programs hire NESTs to co-teach alongside NNESTs, the EPIK program focuses strictly on English, while the JET program emphasizes the importance of internationalization through the education of numerous foreign languages. Yet, despite the different rationales for the EPIK and JET programs, when looking at their hiring policies and program requirements, it is clear they both share the common goal of improving the English proficiency of their students (Wang & Lin, 2013. While seemingly innocent in nature, this shared goal actually reveals the prevalence of native-speakerism, the belief that native speakers are the best teachers of English (Holliday, 2006).

From the outset of EPIK's hiring process, the importance of nationality is highlighted as their prospective NESTs are required to be citizens from Australia, Canada, Ireland, New Zealand, the United Kingdom, the United States, or South Africa (EPIK, 2013). In stipulating the country of origin as a requirement, the EPIK program reinforces the belief that a teacher's nationality is essential in the teaching of English (Ahn, 2019). Likewise, when looking at the participation of countries for the NESTs hired by the JET program, 2 958 of the 6000 participants are from the United States, with the United Kingdom, Australia and Canada following closely behind (JET, 2015). With slightly fewer than half the teachers coming from the United States, and many more coming from English-speaking countries, it is clear that English is the dominant foreign language taught under the JET program.

The influence of native-speakerism is also found in the promotional materials which advertise the EPIK and JET programs. The two program websites as well as online blogs and advertisements often highlight the importance of one's nationality over teaching abilities and qualifications (Ahn, 2019). In fact, NESTs who apply to EPIK and JET are not required to have a teaching degree as their "nativeness" is what qualifies them to teach English (Ahn, 2019). Consequently, English teachers from countries outside of the approved list, regardless of qualifications, are rejected (Ruecker, 2015). So, the teachers hired are often young, untrained and inexperienced graduates hailing from predominantly white and English-speaking countries (Ruecker, 2015). It is important to note that "nativeness" goes beyond nationality and includes race, with white applicants favoured over other applicants (Rivers & Ross, 2013). In hiring teachers strictly for their nativeness, EPIK and JET sacrifices teacher professionalism and paints NNESTs as "inferior" teachers of English by "yielding to the myth [that] inexperienced NESTs can still be competent teachers" (Wang & Lin, 2013, p.13). As a result, NESTs of Asian descent are often denied teaching opportunities while local NNESTs continually face prejudice from their schools, students, and local governments (Ruecker, 2015).

## 4 Professional Legitimacy

Native-speakerism is problematic as it oversimplifies the complex realities of teaching English and undermines the qualifications of NNESTs and nonwhite NESTs, defining them "in terms of what they lack, rather than what they possess" (Wang & Lin, p. 12, 2015). What these teachers possess are qualifications earned through years of dedication and hard work; NNESTs in South Korea and Japan must pass "English proficiency tests, complete English teacher-training courses, and go through teaching practicums and a series of reviews so that they can become qualified English teachers in public schools" (Wang & Lin, p. 15, 2015). Meanwhile, NESTs are often fresh college graduates who have little to no teaching experience: studies show that nearly 90% of NESTs who participate in English programs abroad feel "unprepared or qualified for teaching" (Wang & Lin, p. 15, 2015).

Despite the clear difference in teacher training and qualification, the contracts NESTs receive often contain more benefits than local NNESTs. Additionally, the salaries of NESTs are usually on par with or even higher than local NNESTs. For example, NESTs under EPIK teach a maximum of 22 hours a week and are paid between 2300 CAD to 3100 CAD a month (EPIK, 2013), while local NNESTs often teach 25 hours a week and make 2500 CAD to 3500 CAD a month (EPIK, 2013). Although their pay scales are comparable, NESTs also receive additional vacation and sick days, monthly rent, and bonus pay for renewing their contracts (EPIK, 2013). NNESTs see none of these additional benefits in spite of working longer hours. Likewise, local English teachers in Japan make 34 802.13 CAD annually while their NEST counterparts make 43 195.77 - 50 909.30 CAD a year (JET, 2015). This disparity in salary demonstrates that local governments value the "nativeness" of their NESTs more than the qualifications of their locally trained teachers.

The double standards reflected in the recruitment practices and contract conditions between NESTs and NNESTs are also seen in the difference in the workload of NESTs and NNESTs on the ground. In both programs, NNESTs who work alongside their school's NEST oversee the paperwork needed for the NEST to settle into the school and their new homes. The NNEST is also in charge of the bulk of the lesson planning, marking, grading and classroom management (EPIK, 2013; JET, 2015). In fact, NESTs in both programs are not allowed to conduct lessons alone and must always be supervised by a local teacher, further adding to the responsibilities of NNESTs (EPIK, 2013; JET 2015). This difference in workload is then compounded when local NNESTs must also provide their NEST with teacher training and support as the NESTs recruited are typically "not properly trained to lead the class, has no experience as an educator, has little in-depth knowledge of the English knowledge, and is not responsible for the class" (Tajino & Tajino, 2000, p. 5).

## 5 The Fallacy of Native-Speakerism

The inability of numerous NESTs to lesson plan and teach English once in the classroom, demonstrates that recruitment policies aimed to recruit

NESTs to introduce "native" English to students have failed (Ahn, 2019). What native-speakerism has done instead, is increase the burden of local teachers and undermine the professional autonomy and legitimacy of NNESTs. Although NNESTs themselves have voiced their displeasure with having to work alongside inexperienced NESTs, native-speakerism is so rooted in both cultures, that both parents and students alike still view "nativeness" as an essential part of teaching English. This is because of the value both cultures place on "authentic pronunciation" (Ahn, 2019). Although parents and students are aware that the NESTs hired are generally underqualified and may not be the best teachers, their native speaking abilities and accents are an asset that local teachers are perceived to lack (Ahn, 2019). This is especially problematic as the emphasis placed on pronunciation as opposed to other aspects of language learning further paints NNESTs as inferior teachers (Ahn, 2019). It doesn't matter if they received an education in teaching English, or that they are experienced in teaching others how to read, write, and speak in English, parents and students will always prefer to have a teacher with the "proper" accent. As a result, regardless of their own training and qualifications, NNESTs lack confidence and see the introduction of NESTs in their classrooms as a "threat to their confidence in their own English competence" (Wang & Lin, 2013, p.15).

Due to the inequality created by the hiring policies of the EPIK and JET program, the conditions for co-teaching are not conducive to learning or teaching. With underappreciated NNESTs who have worked time and time again with inexperienced NESTs, NNESTs now have a prejudiced view of NESTs (Jeon, 2009). Instead of working together and combining teaching pedagogy to best meet the needs of their students, NNESTs have grown to resent all NESTs before new NESTs have even stepped into the classroom. Whether or not the incoming NEST is just as unqualified and inexperienced as the others that have come before them, the reputation of NESTs being inexperienced and underqualified newly grads looking for a short-term adventure in an exotic country, precedes them (Ruecker, 2015). For a qualified English teacher who moves abroad to teach English, this means they are fighting the perception that their "nativeness" is why they were hired and must convince their co-teachers that they are qualified educators as well (Jeon, 2009). So, even in the rare case that a qualified NEST has been hired, instead of learning from one another and working together, the qualified NESTs struggle to prove their capabilities to their co-teacher, while NNESTs struggle with balancing their autonomy with the general perception that NESTs are superior teachers.

## 6   Racial Hierarchies in English

Native-speakerism has resulted in tense relationships between NNESTs and NESTs and clearly plays a significant role in perpetuating racist assumptions (Rivers & Ross, 2013). While NESTs of all races are often privileged in comparison to NNESTs, these racist assumptions have created racial hierarchies that exist among NESTs as well; the experience of English teachers of Asian descent often differ vastly from their white counterparts (Wu et al., 2020). As I have noted above, the hiring of foreign teachers functions with the perception that an ideal English teacher is a native speaker hailing from a Western country. However, it is also important to note that the "ideal" NEST is also someone who is "Western looking" or "Caucasian" (Wu et al., 2020, p. 3). Studies conducted in Japan regarding student and parental preference for NESTs indicate that there is a "strong preference for White male teachers aged 30 to 35, originating from the United States" (Rivers & Ross, 2013, p. 334). Rivers and Ross' findings demonstrate a clear racial hierarchy with white raced teachers sitting at the top. This has resulted in the perception that white raced teachers are superior to teachers of other races, particularly those who are Asian (Rivers & Ross, 2013). This assumption that white teachers are better at teaching in English has then resulted in the perception that one's race plays a role in one's English language abilities and that an Asian teacher cannot teach "authentic" English. In fact, Korean American NESTs who decide to teach English in South Korea voiced they're constantly battling "with the suspicion of being inauthentic native English speakers" (Wu et al., 2020, p. 2). Despite speaking English as their first language and receiving their education in English speaking countries, NESTs of Asian descent often find themselves having to prove their English abilities. Consequently, NESTs of Asian descent tend to feel inferior to their "white counterparts" as Caucasian teachers are often put on a "higher pedestal" (Wu et al., 2020, p. 6).

Unfortunately, the influence of race on NEST experiences do not end here. Despite facing discrimination for their own teaching and English language abilities, NNESTs are also guilty of treating their White coworkers differently from their Asian coworkers. There appears to be a false assumption that being Asian or looking Asian means that these NESTs are "armed with sufficient cultural or even linguistic knowledge to live and work" in these new countries (Wu et al., 2020, p. 6). Because of this perception, Asian NESTs are rarely "evaluated on the same footing [as] their White peers" (Wu et al., 2020, p. 6). White NESTs are often provided with more assistance in the classroom and minor mistakes are brushed off as they are still settling into a new country. Meanwhile, Asian NESTs are often provided with less help in the classroom and expected to develop a rapport with their students early on despite rarely speaking the country's national language. As a result, in addition to not being "ideal" (white), NESTs of Asian heritages are also given less leeway when met with culture shock and difficulties in the classroom (Wu et al., 2020). So, Asian NESTs carry additional emotional labour and cultural expectations within the classroom despite being regarded as inferior to White NESTs (Wu et al., 2020).

## 7 Advocacy and Addressing Inequality

Though current research reveals the fallacy of native-speakerism, both the EPIK and JET program have done little to respond to the problems associated with their hiring policies. Unfortunately, this means that local governments continue to increase expenditure to fund these programs and hire more underqualified NESTs, while local English teachers in South Korea and Japan continue to face prejudice that leads to little pay, limited professional acknowledgement, and an increasing workload (Ruecker, 2015). Furthermore, voices that do speak up about these injustices often go unheard in the classroom despite research indicating the importance of departing from native-speakerism. For instance, although advocacy for changing English programs like EPIK and JET exists, current activism is confined to NNESTs themselves with minor community support and a major lack in NEST participation (Ruecker 2015).

While community support would be beneficial, the involvement of NESTs is even more crucial. This is because the lack of emphasis on professional credentials causes harm for both NNESTs and NESTs. NNESTs are painted as inferior teachers for lacking "nativeness" and "authentic accents", White NESTs are valued only for their "nativeness" whether they have teaching credentials or not, and Asian NESTs are seen as inferior to their White counterparts while also taking on more emotional labour. Therefore, it is vital that NNESTs and NESTs "work together in challenging the dominant discourses" in English language education (Ruecker, 2015). By working together, NNESTs and NESTs will have a greater impact by presenting a united front against the diminishing professional legitimacy and credentials of English language teaching. Standing together demonstrates the importance of their profession and asserts that they wish to be respected. In addition to NNESTs voicing their concerns, if NESTs stand up for the professional integrity of English language teachers and refuse to support a system that perpetuates prejudice against teachers for their "nativeness" and "race", it will send a stronger message to the policy makers in charge of these programs (Rucker, 2015).

If NNESTs and NESTs work together, it is possible that English programs like EPIK and JET may listen and make changes to their program so that their hiring practices and treatment of teachers are more equitable. To reduce racial assumptions, it is important that online advertisements and hiring boards should remove pictures and slogans aimed at hiring white teachers. To mitigate the inequality that NNESTs have been facing, it is imperative that local governments adjust their salary and contractual benefits so that NNESTs are treated as equals to NESTs and regarded with respect. Instead of putting additional funds to hire "more" NESTs, funding can be put in place to train underqualified NESTs and balance the pay disparity between NNESTs and their NEST counterparts. By making such changes, the resentment NNESTs feel towards NESTs may decrease, and the ability for NNESTs and NESTs to work together effectively may then increase.

## 8 Future Policy and Program Changes

As the current trend of English language education moves away from native-speakerism, the EPIK and JET programs should also make adjustments to their hiring policies. Where to begin and how these changes should take place though, must be considered carefully. As the importance of English continues to expand in our increasingly globalized world, it would be impractical to abandon these programs entirely or to completely stop the hiring of NESTs. It is important to remember that the root problem isn't with the act of hiring NESTs, but with the hiring of NESTs strictly for their "nativeness". Therefore, EPIK and JET need to redirect the focus of their hiring policies from native-speakerism to language teaching credentials and qualifications.

As of right now, anyone from a predominantly English-speaking country with a college degree is eligible to teach English in South Korea and Japan (EPIK, 2013; JET, 2015). To increase the professional legitimacy of this profession, EPIK and JET should change their criteria to one that requires their candidates to have a teaching degree. In doing so, NESTs walking into South Korean and Japanese classrooms will have the knowledge and experience required to teach English alongside local teachers. As for departing from native-speakerism, it is crucial that the EPIK program removes one's country of origin as a requirement to apply. Meanwhile, the JET program should hire a more diverse body of teachers from countries outside of the United States and Canada to teach English. In doing so, the English education industry in both countries will shift away from the idea that one's nativeness, nationality and race are what's important and emphasize the importance of a prospective teacher's qualifications and experiences instead (Rivers & Ross, 2013).

Finally, additional support systems are also needed to help underqualified NESTs who have already been hired. While new changes take place, firing NESTs who no longer meet the new requirements would only result in more resentment towards the EPIK and JET programs. What I suggest is to include teacher training workshops for NESTs to improve their teaching abilities and skills. Furthermore, workshops that focus on co-teaching and how NNESTs and NESTs can best work together, would also be beneficial. Such changes will not only improve the teaching abilities of NNESTs and NESTs, but also re-legitimize a profession that is so often stigmatized.

## 9   Conclusion

Moving forward, it is imperative that the EPIK and JET programs continue to reflect on the influence of native-speakerism on their hiring practices and make the appropriate changes to create an equitable environment conducive to learning and teaching. As for English language teachers, NNESTs should reflect not only on the prejudice that they face as educators, but also the prejudice that they may have towards NESTs. Likewise, NESTs should reflect on the importance of their role in instigating change in a profession where they hold a privileged position. Therefore, recognizing the fallacy of native-speakerism is the first step in moving towards an English education industry where one's native language, nationality and race do not determine one's professional legitimacy as an English language teacher.

### References

Ahn, S. (2019). Decoding "Good Language Teacher" (GLT) Identity of Native-English Speakers in South Korea. *Journal of Language, Identity & Education, 18*(5), 297–310. doi:10.1080/15348458.2019.1635022.

EPIK. (2013). In *English Program in Korea*. Retrieved from http://www.epik.go.kr.

Holliday, A. (2006). Native-speakerism. *ELT Journal, 60*(4), 385–387. doi:10.1093/elt/ccl030.

Jeon, M. (2009). *Globalization and Native English Speakers in English Programme in Korea (EPIK)*. Routledge. doi:10.1080/07908310903388933.

Jeon, M., & Lee, J. (2006). *Hiring Native-speaking English Teachers in East Asian Countries*. Cambridge University Press. doi:10.1017/S0266078406004093.

JET. (2015). In the Japan Exchange and Teaching Program. Retrieved from http://jetprogramme.org/

Luke, A., Luke, C., & Graham, P. (2007). *Globalization, Corporatism, and Critical Language Education.* Taylor & Francis Group. doi:10.1080/19313150709336861.

Majhanovich, S. (2014). *Neo-liberalism, Globalization, Language Policy and Practice Issues in the Asia-Pacific Region.* Routledge. doi:10.1080/02188791.2013.875650.

Nunan, D. (2003). The impact of English as a global language on educational policies and practices in the Asia-Pacific region. *TESOL Quarterly, 37*(4), 589–613.

Rivers, D. J., & Ross, A. S. (2013). *Idealized English Teachers: The Implicit Influence of Race in Japan.* Routledge. doi:10.1080/15348458.2013.835575.

Ruecker, T., & Ives, L. (2015). White native English speakers needed: The rhetorical construction of privilege in online teacher recruitment spaces. *TESOL Quarterly, 49*(4), 733–756. Retrieved from http://www.jstor.org.myaccess.library.utoronto.ca/stable/43893785

Tajino, A., & Tajino, Y. (2000). Native and non-native: What can they offer? *ELT Journal, 54* (1), 3–11.

Wang, L., & Lin, T. (2013) The representation of professionalism in native English-speaking teachers recruitment policies: A comparative study of Hong Kong, Japan, Korea and Taiwan English teaching: *Practice and Critique,* 5–22. Retrieved from https://eric.ed.gov/?id=EJ1017167.

Wu, M.H, Leung, G., Yang, J.H, Hsieh, I.H. & Lin, K. (2020): A different story to share: Asian American English teachers in Taiwan and idealized "Nativeness" in EFL, *Journal of Language, Identity & Education,* DOI: 10.1080/15348458.2020.1777870.

PART 4

*Community Resistance and Activism*

CHAPTER 15

# Feminization of Pandemics

*Experiences of Filipino Women in the Health Care System*

Rose Ann Torres

## 1     Introduction

There was an outbreak of cholera in the Philippines from 1899–1903 (Illeto 1995; Sullivan 1988). It was the beginning of one of the most terrible epidemics of modern times, lasting until February 1904 and, taking by official estimate 109,461 lives, 4,386 in Manila (Sullivan 1988, p. 284). People from all walks of life were affected and concerned by the way this epidemic decimated the population and left many wondering whether it was an act of God or just another human error. The Secretary of the Interior, Dean Worcester, and the Commissioner of Public Health, Dr. Victor Heiser, both American citizens, were charged with finding ways to stop the spread of cholera among the Filipino people. Illeto (1995) describes the therapy that individuals afflicted with cholera received: The cholera war proceeded along familiar military lines. Army surgeons, for one, were armed with trial magic bullets with which to shoot down the bacillus. One widely used drug was benzozone, the ingestion of which was found to burn the mouth and stomach linings. It eventually was diluted and mixed in with solutions used to irrigate the bowels and small intestines. Routine treatment involved the use of benzoyl-acetyl-peroxide, guiacol carbonate, calomel, potassium permanganate, two percent tannic acid, and dilutes sulphuric acid. These treatments were really experimental in nature, based on the assumption that some drug ought to be able to attack and destroy the cholera vibrio within the patient.

The American doctors' use of such and other, unfamiliar, methods of treatment only brought about an aversion in Filipino cholera patients so marked in many instances as to necessitate the use of force in the administering of medicine. In the end none of the medicine, at least in Heifer's experience in the Philippines, proved of any value. (p. 61) Nevertheless, despite assurances from the colonial government that Western trained doctors had the solution to this epidemic, the Filipinos continued to seek the help of Indigenous healers (Ileto 1995; Rafael 1995; Sullivan 1988).

Among the Indigenous groups whose knowledge and healing practices were sought were Aeta women healers (Krober 1919). Aeta are one of the Indigenous Peoples in the Philippines who resisted colonialism and —ensured the preservation of their customs and character as a people (Shimizu 1989, p. 11). According to Coloma (2004) colonialism is the conquest and direct control of other people's land and resources (p.2), however, Dei (2006) argues that the colonial in anti-colonial refers to anything imposed and dominating rather than that which is simply foreign and alien (p. 3). In this study, the word colonizer will be used to identify anybody who dominates and controls (or attempts to control) Aeta people. The Aeta healers use herbal medicine and offer prayers to the God or Apo Dios in healing the sick. To the colonial government, this was unacceptable because it was considered devoid of scientific rigor. For example, when one of the Aeta falls ill a culturally normal response is to offer food to the ancestor to seek forgiveness.

Scientific authenticity was a way to eliminate the self-sought directive prescriptions that Indigenous healers had proffered to Filipinos. This entered into direct conflict with Eurocentric beliefs centered on Euro cultural and historical supremacy as a means of taking control of the population and, in doing so, damaged the identity of the Indigenous People (Illeto 1995).

In this context, if the colonial government had allowed the Aeta women healers to heal, it would have demolished the claim by Dean Worcester that the war against cholera was a manifestation of American heroism and military skill (Illeto 1995). Since one of the goals of the colonial government was to portray that Filipinos needed help, —at times, [the] proscribed healer was the center of attention and [was] promptly suppressed; in other cases, the normal ritual life of the people was disrupted (Illeto 1995, p. 72). This American jingoism followed a well-established set of colonial governance tactics: when Spain established the Philippine as its colony, —the minorization of the Indigenous People started (Asian Development Bank (ADB) 2002, p. 9).

The ADB (2002) describes how the Indigenous Peoples were treated: They were labeled as barbarians, pagans, and all sorts of derogatory names. Soon, even the assimilated indios internalized these prejudices against Indigenous Peoples. (p. 10) However, Jocano (2000) explains that none of these labels characterizes their real lives (p. 17): They are not savage, primitive, or backward people. They only have different cultural ways of thinking, believing, feeling, and acting. They have complex social institutions and elaborate cultural traditions. The idea of their primitiveness has become deeply rooted in the consciousness of many lowland Filipinos because past writers, including scholars, have unnecessarily and negatively exaggerated many of the ethnic beliefs and practices ... In fact, many of the past and the present conflicts between and among the different ethnic groups (hinterland and rural) in the country are largely due to ignorance of one another's cultural or sub cultural orientation. (p. 17)

The consequence of colonization is too often the superimposition of foreign ideology and what Marx labeled as superstructure, and foreign institutions which change our understandings of the world, refocus our gaze and negate competing world views, institutions and sets of practices for self-governance and ruling (Fanon 1963; Memmi 1965). Colonization prescriptive bromide is that if I do not practice the Eurocentric way of living and knowing, we are not normal, intelligent, or civilized. From this perspective, the Filipinos who were assimilated through colonialism started to perceive the backwardness of these Indigenous healers as truth that was "taken for granted" (ADB 2002). This culminated into considerable elements of the Filipino population identifying with the Eurocentric cultures, ending with recognition by the dominant discourse (Constantino 1978).

Despite the internalization of these exogenous oppressive forces, resistances persisted. Rang-ay, one of the Aeta women healers, said in Ikolano, one of the dialects that they speak, in which I am also fluent, *ti kinapudno isu iti agballigi*, which translates to the truth shall prevail. This is stenographic shorthand testimony to the fact that their resilience, belief in them-their culture and healing powers - and steadfast fortitude cannot be demonized, characterized, or defined by ignorance and oppression. Their standards for intercultural evaluation and interaction are simple, and in their own way 'Universal': They want justice to prevail, and they lament cultural violence and lack of reciprocal cultural recognition. The attrition toll to their culture's data bases by these forces of domination is measurable in their memories: the women, as keepers of this shared knowledge, attest that much of the richness of the knowledge has been forgotten and couple with the failure to replenish and to remake these practices in cultural teaching, have culminated in their invisibility in the Philippine history (Pecson-Fernandez 1989).

## 2  Indigenous Healing Practices

This section of the chapter examines the Indigenous healers' ways of addressing health issues in the Philippines. This is necessary to include especially during this time of pandemic to highlight that these healers can also provide an assistance to our health care system in Canada and around the world.

There were 12 Aeta women healers who participated in the Talking Circle of my study (Torres, 2012), however, in this chapter, I only include two healers to give an example of their healing practices. Rang-ay is a healer who inherited her healing practices from her mother. At the time of the study, she had been a healer for twenty-eight years. When her mother was alive, Rang-ay used to help her in the healing processes. Her mother taught her how to heal the sick. She started healing when she gave birth to her first child. In her healing practices, she uses herbal medicine and rituals. Rang-ay states:

> Healing other people is a joy for me. I do not ask for money in exchange for my services. I heal because of my "ayat" or love for my people. I do not want my people to suffer. I try my best to help them. There are moments that I get very tired, but I know that if I do not carry out my responsibility to my community and to my people, I will not feel good. Healing is a gift from my Creator and therefore I have to use it for the benefit of my community.

Rang-ay is working on the notion of ayat or love. For Rang-ay, "ayat" means strong feelings or conviction that drives her to do great things for others. "Ayat" governs everything. It dismantles the notion of gura, or hatred that brings people to violate others. For Rang-ay, without ayat, she could never do anything for other people because —ayat possesses the qualities of responsibility, respect and compassion. Subsequently, Rang-ay always ensures that what she does conforms to the principles of ayat. That is why she was able to fulfill her responsibility to her community. For her, ayat means healing and, to her, healing is a way of preserving her identity and her community through tireless service. Rang-ay advocates for this knowledge.

Talna is another healer who inherited her healing practices from her brother. At the time of the study, she had been a healer for nine years. She uses herbal plants and prayer in her healing. According to Talna:

> I heal because of my love for my people. However, if they decide to go and seek another treatment, I am happy with that. To me, when people come and ask for help, I cannot say no. I have to help and to do my best to render my service. Healing is a way for me to continue the legacy of my people.

Talna shows one aspect of the traditions of the Aeta people: the fact that —you exist because of your people. She told me that she does not accept any payment because it is part of their practices that when you help, you do not expect anything in return. In addition, like Rang-ay, Talna also possesses the "ayat" that gives her the strength to fulfill her duty, a duty that will continue the legacy of her ancestors. In the community of the Aeta People, in the Philippines, they have been divided by decolonization. Some of them live in different towns in the Philippines, like Gattaran, Penablanca and Allacapan. Talna states that they have been divided by colonialists through the expropriation of their ancestral lands for mining purposes. The government of the Philippines passed the law of mining, empowering mining companies from other countries to legally mine. Some of the Aeta people are forced to relocate due to such legal tactics. One of her goals is to bring all the Aeta together by using her healing knowledge. How could this happen if they do not have enough land in Cagayan? Talna explains that the reason why she heals non-Aeta people is to share the idea of ayat. She believes that when a person feels the love of others, she or he can pass the same principles that govern them in their daily life. When this happens, non-Aeta people will not work on the notion of individuality, but, instead, bring back the idea that we are all connected and related.

The Isneg of Apayao sub-province occupies the cordillera mountain range. The scenery is very beautiful, and the land is covered with shrubs and trees. Isneg means upstream. The Isneg possess a very dignified and gracious attitude. When one goes to their village one can feel how gentle they are. Grant et al. (1973, p. 14) state that the Spaniards made an attempt to colonize the Isneg in 1890 when they succeeded in establishing three forts, however, after a period of Isneg raiding from Spanish punitive action, the Isneg defeated the Spaniards in a decisive battle in 1895. The Spanish did not try to penetrate their community again. This illustrates how they resisted colonization. They stood firm because they realized that if they allowed the invader to enter their village, they would subsequently lose their indigeneity. According to Grant et al. (1973), ...

> the people in highland Apayao conducted religious ceremonies. This responsibility was almost exclusively in the hands of women rather than of men. These shamans were called dururakit ... their service in a society which counted religion as of great importance helped to raise the status of women—(p.64).

In addition, if an Isneg woman has been consecrated as a shaman in her early childhood, she earns the respect not only of the household but of the neighbors as well. She inspired them with a kind of reverential awe, especially if she is advanced in years (Grant et al. 1973), . As such it can be seen that healing was both an inspiration to the society and a way of showcasing one's talent. This kept the society together by bringing forward (the talents of others), of sustaining the community and its pride. Thus, healing was a way of showing one's patriotism to her society. Through these ritualistic practices of unification, the Indigenous community was able to live as a unified entity even after outland intrusion. We can see that healing was seen as a political defensive bulwark meant to sustain the society.

Finally, Igorots' agency comes from the continuous interaction with everything else in the environment, acknowledging the existence of kabunyan (Igorot term for God) and that of their ancestors. They return to the songs, stories, rituals, values and beliefs, remembering the oral traditions that as rich reservoirs of the knowledge and wisdom of the Igorots or mountain people. In the early colonial days, the Spaniards needed to portray the Igorot as headhunting savages in order to justify their violence towards them. Later, the U.S. colonizers shipped their ancestors to be displayed in a sort of circus sideshow at the St. Louis Exposition in 1904, to show Americans what heathens they were and to justify President McKinley's Benevolent Assimilation policy (Dacog 2003, p. 4). Christianity in that arena of colonial hegemony was introduced to alter and abate the spiritual life of the Igorot. The settler taught Indigenous pupils that their Native beliefs were ineffectual, and unworthy of being acknowledged. The colonial platitude stressed that the only way to be saved was to adopt the Christian religion (Tauli-Corpuz 2006; Dacog 2003).

The Igorot People were made to believe that their Indigenous knowledge was apparently idiotic and that if they did not embrace the Western way of development, they would be considered backward and ignorant and would, thus, be prone to extinction (Tauli-Corpuz 2006; Dacog 2003). Igorots produce ten or more traditional rice varieties, and their rice terraces, found high up in the mountains, feature complex irrigation systems, testifying to Igorot expertise in hydraulics and engineering (Dacog, 2003). They continue to practice their cultural rituals during the agricultural and life cycles. Igorots do not claim to be the owners of the land, but rather see themselves as caretakers. They believe that they need to tend to the ancestral land because it is sacred ground where their ancestors were buried, and it will therefore be the homeland for the future generations. They consider their ancestral land part of their identity. That is where they see the connection between both their material and spiritual well-beings. According to Dacog (2003), at a very early age their parents and Elders taught them basic values deemed gawis (good): respect for nature and ancestors, honesty, collectivity, community solidarity, reciprocity, and love for Mother Earth (p. 4).

This implicit value of the Aeta is shared by many, perhaps even most, Indigenous Peoples. It is generally not framed this way, but acquisition as a central organizational tenant, Western colonization implicitly denies nature and shifts the standard of what is worthy from the collective to the self. Nature becomes a resource to be controlled, exploited and dominated rather than a force of creation. Tacitly, this belief in the power of one's own technological and cultural agency as the locus of control denies both the primacy of nature and our cultural dependence on one other. Healing is a technical problem, yet we must acknowledge that most of what heals us is given to us by the environment, our immune systems, the air, water and other biological and environmental processes.

Healing sees its own technology as Universal and all else as unscientific. It is surprising that an epistemology so divorced from the forces of creation and sustenance could, in such short geological and historical time, cause ecological disasters where water, air and land have been unsustainably degraded globally. (Earle 2009). Contrast this approach to health to the Aeta health paradigm. Igorot acknowledge *in-ina* or old lady who usually performs healing. Infante (1969) explains the healing practices in Ifugao which are performed by an Igorot woman as follows: When a person is very sick, an *in-ina* (old woman), who is a close relative possessing the sup-ok (power to heal the sick) is called. The *in-ina* summoned is left alone with the sick. In soft tones, she implores the help of a favorite or very close ancestor to find the anito (spirit) who brought the sickness to her family. After this concentrated talk with the supernatural, she discovers the guilty anito.

She talks to this anito and, feeling its presence, she now questions the reason for bringing bad things to the family; and reminds it of the many favors and good things they have given it on earth and that they never neglected to invite it to all their family *canaos* and *mangmangs*. Then she tells the spirit to go away, simultaneously breathing hard at the patient several times. The old lady then departs with good news … or is sad and lingers in the house of the sick to perform the *mangmang* as a sacrifice to the persistent spirit of sickness … The old *in-ina* or woman addresses the anito or the spirit of the dead ancestor of the family and tells him the reason for the offering. The dead chicken is placed over a fire; and when all the feathers are burned and removed, it is cut, and the viscera are removed to see the position of the gall bladder. If it shows good omens, the spirit is said to be pleased and all will be well for the family. When it is time to eat, the share of the spirits is set aside, and all dead ancestors are again invited to the feast. (p. 178–179)

Through this method of healing, the sick person's affliction is attenuated and he or she is told to be careful with his or her life. In-ina usually gives the sick person advice on how to pay respect both to the environment and to the ancestors. In-ina makes sure the infirmed learns not just to respect those things which he or she can see through his or her naked eyes but also non-tangible forces. The healing process is identified as a teaching arena through which societal teachings are passed on to the sick. It serves as a way through which the sick are taught what is right and told to discard that which is considered evil. To that extent, healing is identified as a key to asserting Indigenous wellbeing in society. As can be observed, Aeta, Isneg and Igorot have the same way of healing the sick. They believe that the spiritual and physical beings need to be cured before a person who is sick gets healed. They also believe that a person gets sick because of not respecting other creations and that before the healers can perform healing, they need to consult the spirit. This is the only time they can diagnose the cause of the illness. They also believe that spirits of the land, water, trees [are] also held to be influential and thus must also be appeased (Minoritized and Dehumanized 1983, p. 17). This is why they have a great respect for both living and non-living things. Their knowledge of the curing power of plants cannot be disregarded. They have illustrated the utility of this knowledge through the healing of the sick.

## 3   Indigenous Healing vs. Public Health Practice

The history of Philippine medicine historically required the use of herbs and followed to the belief that sickness was brought by the spirits. Historians thus, concluded that the earliest practice of medicine was in line with the Indigenous healer practices (de la Cruz 1984). Nevertheless, when Spaniards established their colony in the 19th century in the Philippines, they brought with them physicians from Spain. Indeed, the creation of public health and Western medicine were integral parts of the ideology of empire (King 2002 p. 765). This ideology of colonial healing is one of the justifications given by colonizers, on the pretext that they were bringing the best quality of life for Indigenous People. The idea that the Spaniards were out to save the newly found heathens from their uncivilized way of living was planted in the minds of the Indigenous People. It does not matter if the colonizers ravage, demonize, or dehumanize the lives of Indigenous People.

The colonial healing has been used to cover up the real work of colonization. In fact, history bears witness to several diseases in different countries where colonies were established. In other words, colonial medicine was a means of achieving the goal of colonization. The role that the Indigenous healers have played was completely disregarded. Alfred Crosby, in *The Columbian Exchange: Biological and Cultural Consequences of 1492* (Crosby, 1972), forcefully argues that the main destructive effects of the conquistadors and other settlers was the introduction of alien animals, plants and diseases and that much of the project of genocide was operationally realized by these forces.

In the case of North America, this led to over five million deaths and a radical alteration of population demographics and subsequently paved the way for the land expropriation, such as the Manifest Destiny in the United States. Similar analyses have been done and should be expanded to include the Philippines. In some ways the Aeta were protected from earlier ravages by their comparatively remote location.

Expansionism works on logic not unlike cancer: it is sustained by uncontrollable and unsustainable growth. In this respect it is hardly surprising that all people, including the Aeta, are exposed to its acidic forces. The Aeta women's work is therefore linked in the deepest ways to the connections between Nature, health and society and is a counterpoint to what may be seen as the crisis medicine approach imposed from the West. The Aeta women healers explain the differences between their healing practices and the Western way of healing. Singli: In my healing I use herbal medicine and prayers. I believe that without the help of my Creator, the herbal medicine that I apply for my patient's body will be useless.

Holmes (2002) states that, ways of knowing are not based on the limits of one's own physical sense and may include prayer, prescience, dreams, and messages from the dead (p. 37). This has been affirmed by the Aeta women healers who state that their healing practice does not only focus on using herbal plants but also focuses on other ways of healing. Cena states: Before I start healing, I ask my God to give me the wisdom so that I know which herbal medicine I should use. Through this, I get the courage to diagnose and at the same time to give my patients the necessary herbal medicine. Cena corroborates that she can diagnose diseases without going through any Western training and knows what herbal medicines she can prescribe for her patients. What Cena is trying to do here is tell us that her knowledge is authentic, as Hurtado (2003) explains, the important thing was for the world to hear their hollering and to claim an intellectual space not by only complaining and deconstructing but by being fruitful and multiplying (pp. 218–219).

Cena knows that by sharing her knowledge she will be heard. She does not complain if others do not recognize her but rather continues to assert her place as an Aeta woman healer. Other Aeta women healers explain their ways of healing. Rang-ay states: I prepare my own medicine depending on the needs of my patients. I do not just heal the physical body but also the spiritual aspect. Sometimes you look at the patient and it seems that she is okay, in this I can tell it is the physical that needs healing the spiritual or the emotional being.

Aly also notes: Before a patient comes to me, I dream about him or her. So, before I meet my patient, I already know the problem. However, I usually consult my patients first. I believe that I and my patients have a way to heal her or him. Actually, I always give power to my patients to heal themselves. Wila further explains the difference between her healing and the Western way of curing diseases: Aeta healing is not all about healing the physical body of a person but also bringing back that person into the good relationship with the other creations. Our practices always encourage our people to be respectful to others. In our community among us healers we do not compete, in fact, we help each other. There are times that I need the help of my fellow healers to heal the sick, so I usually ask them to help me.

These observations bear witness that the Aeta women healers neither ignore nor compete with the public health healing system. They work on the basis of their worldview. Despite the knowledge that the Aeta women healers have, the public health system does not recognize them. Indeed, Philippine public health administrators are aware that having Western trained doctors and nurses in health centres does not adequately solve the health problems of the Filipino people. Torres, 2012 has profiled some problems faced by this health care system, including insufficient funds; lack of medical and paramedical manpower; inefficient use of scarce health services available; and lack of community support for health programs.

The World Health Organization (WHO) and various United Nations entities have been giving out medical and humanitarian aid to the Philippines to treat different kinds of diseases. As much as this help is of immense importance, illnesses such as respiratory infections, tuberculosis, malaria, and skin infections, still persist. This has also been worsened by the fact that, despite the advancement of the medical system, they fail to reach the majority of those who are at risk, due to rising costs, and complex and expensive technologies that limit accessibility and availability of health care (Marks 2006, p. 473). Tan (1987) has a different explanation of these health problems in the Philippines. According to Marks (2006), the need to recognize plurality in our society is especially important for health care as it has become clear that the deficiencies of the health care system are partly rooted in our inability to understand even the most basic concepts of health and illness among our people (p. 1). Gonzalez (1998), who situates himself from a Eurocentric perspective, refutes these claims, because Tan suggests recognition of the notion of health from the Filipino people, including the Aeta women healers.

Other aspects of life like spirituality and connectivity with the environment play a marginal role in the contemporary health care arena. Non-recognition of these factors in the contemporary medicine world has been the cause for its minimal performance in seeking the precise way of curing illnesses among the population. In spite of this shoddy treatment of the Aeta women healers by the public health system, the healers still want to be represented on the basis of their healing practices.

They believe that if they are represented based on the knowledge that they hold, the readers who do not know them will finally get to know and respect them. They want to change the negative characterizations about them. It is time to change the current norm into a reality: a reality that speaks honestly about the Aeta women healers. In fact, they believe that public health has played a tremendous role in helping the people who are sick. The only concern that they have is that public health is claiming to be the dominant player in curing diseases. This claim is extremely problematic to them because they recall that empirically, there are more diseases than before. Despite all the claims about the technical mastery of nature and science, the colonized people suffer from highly toxic aliments like high blood pressure, diabetes, and obesity, among others. Before the introduction of Western medical models and its monopoly over health care, which came with credentials and certification, these illnesses usually did not exist in their community because the traditional Aeta person walks, climbs the mountain, eats fresh food, and wild animals and drinks herbal medicines to cleanse his or her system.

Increasingly, even in the West it is now being understood that it is the body's immune system, not medical interventions per se, which sustain wellness. All pharmaceuticals are, after all, chemicals and all such chemicals are generally found in their most complex and useful forms in Nature. The Aeta clearly embrace this, and it is built into their practices. For example, aloe vera mixed with lemon juice and honey is issued for cleansing. For the Aeta women healers, representation is about writing and talking about their authentic identity, but their identity is very much grounded in what the West glosses as scientific fact.

## 4 Recommendations Relating to Public Health

### 4.1 Local Public Health

The narratives of the Aeta women healers in Cagayan serve as a paradigm to other Aeta Peoples in different parts of the Philippines. The women healers speak to the non-Aeta people about the healing knowledge that they possess and tell the story of their struggle against colonization. Hopefully in this way the normative discourse about the Aeta will change and the space for inclusion in a more robust health model for all will evolve.

## 4.2   National Public Health

For the period between 2005–2010, Francisco Duque III (2005), the Secretary of Health in the Philippines, identified several challenges that the Department of Health (DOH) was facing, including macroeconomic and political issues, fragmented local health systems and private health care markets, limited capacity for quality assurance of health care products and services, many essentials drugs still excessively priced out of reach for the poor, low investments in health, and the mal-distribution of health professionals compounded by their massive out-migration (p. iv). The DOH does not consider the Aeta women healers their partners in the eradication of health problems among the Filipino people (National Objectives for Health Philippines 2005–2010). At the national level, the DOH focuses on addressing the health crisis by placing: public health nurse, rural sanitary inspectors and midwives (Cuevas 2007, p. 32) in the hospital or health care facilities. The Aeta women healers are not part of the team involved in resolving the national health crisis. Moreover, the DOH focuses on solving the health crisis in the Aeta community by deploying Western trained practitioners, who do not understand the culture of the Aeta people. Instead, this practice violates their well-being as a community. This is because such a move is imposed on the Aeta people without consulting them. This study recommends that the DOH learn a lesson from the voices of the women healers heard during the course of this research. The Postcolonial Aeta women healing practices do not only take the form of healing people, but also recognize the whole community as part of the healing process. Talna, who is also one of the Aeta women healers in Cagayan, stated:

> in our community during my healing rituals everybody is involved. Some are part of singing and dancing, others are part of drumming and the rest are part of praying or being present to give support to the ill person. Through this, an ill person feels the support and love of his or her people. Maya, an Aeta woman healer, pointed out that —one of my ways of healing is using herbal medicine, for example, boiled aloe vera mixed with honey cures amoeba.

The DOH can learn from the practices of the postcolonial Aeta women healers by including not only the health practitioner who has undergone Western training but also other entities in a society, including the postcolonial Aeta women healers when addressing the health crisis. This will not only lessen the financial burden on the health care system but will also encourage the postcolonial Aeta women healers to contribute their skills in treating diseases. This is what this study is calling for in the face of major medical catastrophes. Ellerby (2001) notes that, most elders and cultural teachers view the sharing of knowledge and collaborative treatment of an individual as important (p. 47). Moreover, using herbal medicines that are already available in the forest or farms in the Philippines can address financial problems and can accommodate some members of the society who cannot afford to buy medicine. Furthermore, such collaboration brings back the recognition of the indigeneity of every person and disrupts the mentality that was induced by colonialism in the Philippines. This thesis presents the Aeta women healers' knowledge of healing. It showcases the sociology of health from the Indigenous perspective, which has been sidelined by central government. Collaboration brings about the awareness of the people in the Philippines showing that the Aeta women healers possess the healing power that is available to everybody. It highlights the agency and spirituality of the Aeta women healers that gives them the strength and knowledge to heal. It gives another way of understanding the root cause of illness, that of the Aeta women who have resisted colonization. This study recommends that the public health in the Philippines recognize the knowledge of the Aeta women healers in order to have a more effective way of addressing the health problems of the people.

## 4.3 *Global Public Health*
Certainly, Indigenous healing is important to most people in the world, as has been noted in the World Health Organization (WHO) 2004 report. Dr. Margaret Chan, the Director-General of WHO does not include them in the decision-making platform when addressing the global health crisis (WHO 2004). Instead, Chan calls on governments and a host of agencies, foundations, non-governmental organization, and representatives of the sector and civil society when talking of efforts to resolve the global health crisis which is plagued by illnesses such as malaria, women's and children's health, tuberculosis, venereal disease, nutrition and environmental sanitation, including HIV/AIDS (WHO 2004). Chan recognizes the participation of different stakeholders in resolving these health crises. As much as this may be appreciated as the way forward, Chan fails to explicitly state the role that the Indigenous Peoples, such as the Aeta women healers, need to play in resolving the health crisis. This not only sets the stage for the perpetual marginalization of the Indigenous Peoples' role in knowledge production, but also denies them a part in resolving the world's health crisis. Furthermore, Chan states that the WHO standards help protect the safety of everyone's food and the quality of medicines and vaccines (WHO 2004). This strategy only focuses on curing the physical health of a person. The

Aeta women healers focus not only on healing the physical health, but also the whole well-being of a person. This holistic healing focuses on the physical, emotional, spiritual and cultural aspects of living. Rang-ay, an Aeta woman healer in Cagayan, believes that a person gets sick partly because of disrespecting the spirit world. That is why the body is affected. For Rang-ay, healing the sick person includes calling on the spirit that brings the sickness and asking for forgiveness. According to her, if there is no conversation between the healer and the spirit, healing will not be completed. It is, therefore, important for Rangay to teach her patients to be respectful to the spiritual world in order to avoid illnesses. What lessons can the WHO learn from this healing practice of Rang-ay? It provides an understanding that health crises exist in part because of a lack of consideration of the spirit world. The treatment of one's disease does not focus solely on the physical well-being of a person but also on the inclusion of other parts of a human being. Ellerby (2001), a healer in North America, states, all aspects are important in a person's health: spiritual health, mental health, emotional health, physical health (p. 3). This study recommends the inclusion of the Indigenous Peoples of the world, including Aeta women healers in the global public health policy-making process when combating diseases. The WHO should also be more proactive in sharing the experiences of initiatives in different countries that have started to unite Western medicine and traditional healing.

## 5   Conclusion

This chapter discusses the healing knowledge of Indigenous peoples in the Philippines. It also includes a discussion of how they have been discriminated on the basis of their healing practices. We are in the midst of a Covid-19 pandemic; as I listen to the news, I have never heard any report that Indigenous healers are being consulted in addressing the pandemic. The question is, why is that? Why is it that the public health is not consulting the Indigenous healers? In Canada, there are many Indigenous healers, however, I have not heard any consultation between the public health and healers too. I wonder what could happen if we include Indigenous healers in finding a solution to this global pandemic? It has been a year, but, until now there is no vaccine that can address this pandemic. If we ask the Indigenous healers of the world, what would they say? My hope is that we can consider the knowledge and contributions of the Indigenous peoples of the world in finding a solution for the Covid-19 pandemic.

## References

Asian Development Bank. (2002, June). ADB Publications. Retrieved from: http://www.adb.org/Documents/Reports/Indigenous_Peoples/PHIdefault.as p

Coloma, R. (2004). Empire and education: Filipino schooling under United States Rule, 1900–1910. (Doctoral dissertation). Ohio State University, Columbus. Retrieved from http://etd.ohiolink.edu/send-pdf.cgi/Coloma%20Roland.pdf?osu1086209087

Constantino, R. (1978). *Neocolonial identity and counter-consciousness: Essays on cultural decolonization.* London, England: Merlin Press.

Crosby, A. (1972). *The Columbian exchange: Biological and cultural consequences of 1492.* Westport, CT: Praeger.

Cuevas, F. P. (Ed.). (2007). *Public health nursing in the Philippines.* Manila, Philippines: National League of Philippine Government Nurses.

Dacog, M. (2003). Remembering my roots, interrogating the present, envisioning my future. Educational Insights, 8(2). Retrieved from http://www.ccfi.educ.ubc.ca/publication/insights/v08n02/contextualexplorati ons/sumara/dacog.html.

Dei, G. (2006). Mapping the terrain-towards a new politics of resistance. In G. Dei & A. Kempf (Eds.), *Anti-colonialism and education: The politics of resistance* (pp. 1–24). Rotterdam, Netherlands: Sense.

De La Cruz, J. (1984). Defending our inalienable rights: We cannot fail our children. Retrieved from http://www.cwis.org/fwdp/Americas/joe

Duque, F. (2005). Foreword. In M. Villaverde, M. Beltran, & L. David (Eds.), *National objectives for health 2005–2010* (iii-v), Manila, Philippines: Department of Health.

Earle, S. (2009). Wish to protect our ocean. Retrieved from http://www.ted.com/talks/sylvia_earle_s_ted_prize_wish_to_protect_our_ocea ns.html

Ellerby, J. (2001). *Working with Aboriginal elders: An introductory handbook for institution based and health care professionals based on the teachings of Winnipeg-area Aboriginal elders and cultural teachers*: Winnipeg, Manitoba, Canada: Native Studies Press.

Fanon, F. (1963). *The wretched of the earth.* London, England: Penguin Books.

Grant, F & Reynolds, H. (Eds.) (1973). *The Isneg of the northern Philippines: A study of trends of change and development.* Dumaguete City, Philippines: Silliman University, Anthropology Museum.

Holmes, L. (2002) Heart knowledge, blood memory, and the voice of the land: Implications of research among Hawaiian Elders. In Dei, G., Hall, B., & Rosenberg, D. (Eds.), *Indigenous knowledges in the global contexts: Multiple readings of our world*, (pp. 37–53). Toronto, Ontario, Canada: University of Toronto Press.

Hurtado, A. (2003). Theory in the flesh: Toward an endarkened epistemology. *Qualitative Studies in Education*, 16 (2), 215–225.

Illeto, R. (1995). Cholera and the origins of the American sanitary order in the Philippines. In Rafael, V. (ed.), *Discrepant histories translocal essays on Filipino cultures* (pp. 51–82). Philadelphia, PA: Temple University Press.

Infante, T. (1969). *The woman in early Philippines and among the cultural minorities.* Manila, Philippines: University of Santo Tomas.

Jocano, F.L. (2000). *Filipino Indigenous ethnic communities: Patterns, variations, and typologies.* Manila, Philippines: Punlad Research House, Inc.

King, N. (2002). Security, disease, commerce: Ideologies of postcolonial global health. *Social Studies of Science*, 32 (5–6), 763–789.

Kroeber, A. (1919). *People of the Philippines.* New York, NY: American Museum Press.

Marks, L. (2006). Global health crisis: Can Indigenous healing practices offer a valuable resource? *International Journal of Disability, Development and Education*, 53 (4), 471–478.

Memmi, A. (1965). The colonizer and the colonized. Boston, MA: Beacon Press.

Minoritized and Dehumanized. (1983). Reports and reflections on the condition of tribal and Moro peoples in the Philippines. Retrieved from http://daga.dhs.org/daga/press/urm/dehumanized/contents.htm

Pecson-Fernandez, A. (1989). Why women are invisible in history. In: *Women's role in Philippine history: Selected essays*, (2nd Edition), (pp. 1–21). Quezon City, Philippines: University Center for Women's Studies, University of the Philippines.

Rafael, V. (Ed.). (1995). *Discrepant histories: Translocal essays on Filipino cultures.* Philadelphia, PA: Temple University Press.

Shimizu, H. (1989). *Pinatubo Aytas: Continuity and change.* Quezon City, Philippines: Ateneo de Manila University Press.

Sullivan, R. (1988). Cholera and colonialism in the Philippines, 1899–1903. In Macleod, R., Lewis, M. (Eds.), *Disease, medicine, and empire: Perspective on western medicine and the experience of European expansion* (pp. 284–300). New York, NY: Routledge.

Tan, M. (1987). Usug, kulam, pasma: Traditional concepts of health and illness in the Philippines. Quezon City, Philippines: Alay Kapwa Kilusang Pangkalusugan (AKAP).

Tauli-Corpuz, V. (2006). Our rights remain separate and distinct. In Tauli-Corpuz, V. & Mander J. (Eds.), *Paradigm wars* (pp. 13–21). San Francisco, CA: Sierra Club Books.

Torres, R. (2012). The Aeta Women Healers in the Philippines: Lessons and Implications. Toronto: University of the Philippines. (Unpublished Dissertation).

World Health Organization (2004). A World Free of TB Antibiotic Resistance. Retrieved http://www.euro.who.int/en/what-we-do/health-topics/diseaseprevention/antimicrobial-resistance/antibiotic-resistance.

CHAPTER 16

# Multiculturalism

*A Case for Continued Resistance for Space for Race*

Tika Ram Thapa

## 1   Introduction

Let me begin by defining some terms used in this essay. Firstly, 'Multiculturalism' refers to the Canadian Multiculturalism Policy, 1971, which was later reinforced by the Canadian Charter of Rights and Freedoms, 1982. Secondly, 'race' has been used to refer to "a socially constructed system of classifying humans based on particular phenotypical characteristics (skin color, hair texture, and bone texture)" (Sensoy et al., 2017, p. 45), which often coincide with geographical origins of people both native and immigrants to Canada. Such a categorisation has real, social, political, and economic implications. For example, in Canada, data on origins of Canadians is recorded as ethnic origins such as Asian origins, Caribbean origins, North American Aboriginal origins and European origins (Statistics Canada, 2017). Diversity of this geographical origin suggests rich sources of immigrant origins.

The term 'space for race' is rooted in a number of assumptions from critical race theory (CRT). Firstly, all individuals are members of social groups and not all social groups are valued equally. This unequal access to resources between social groups leads to real injustice, and racism pervades in the dominant culture. Racism is a system in which one race maintains supremacy over another race through a set of attitudes, behaviors, social structures, and institutional power (Love, 2000). This means the power structures are set up to continue to perpetuate the marginalisation of non-dominant groups.

Thus 'space for race' is an aspirational ideal which envisions people of all social groups have a sense of belonging, a right to *be*, and equal access to full benefits of citizenship and freedom. Given that the membership of certain social groups has often placed limits to equal access to citizenship and freedom, the need for continued resistance is proposed in this essay. Thus 'continued resistance', in this essay needs to be understood as any *ongoing* action and engagement with an expressed commitment to ending social injustice. Consistent with this activist intent, recognizing how the relations of unequal social power are enacted both at the micro (individual) and macro (structural) level is the first step necessary in our resistance to realize the ideal of a more socially just society. As Delgado (2009) reminds:

> As marginalized people we should strive to increase our power, cohesiveness, and representation in all significant areas of society. We should do this though, because we are entitled to these things and because fundamental fairness requires this allocation of power. (p. 110)

Frequent media portrayal of both Canada's successful adoption of Multiculturalism as its official policy, and the nation's rising stature in world stage as an arbiter of plurality appears to be more of an imagined ideal than the reality. Approximately 300,000 immigrants (most of whom are racialized) arrive in Canada every year – a fact often used to corroborate the attractiveness of Canadian policy on Multiculturalism. Writing from the perspective of immigrant experiences, this essay introduces migration-based entry points into discussion of multiculturalism, immigrant positioning and the politics of possible. My analysis will be primarily informed by anti-racism framework within Critical Race Theory (CRT). Anti-racism theory analyzes/critiques racism and how it operates, and the theory provides a basis for taking action to eliminate racism (Henry & Tator, 2009).

Modern Canadian history is a narrative of immigrants beginning with the first European settlement in 1604. With the exception of indigenous people who alone predate this narrative; everyone else has been in this land as a consequence of immigration of one form or the other. Given this historical backdrop, the promotion of multiculturalism as a policy in 1971, which was reinforced by the Canadian Charter of Rights and Freedoms of 1982, lays strong legal foundations for a society based on equality and freedom. Having said that, if multi-culturalism is conceptualized and perceived in an unnuanced way as the mere existence of multiplicity of cultures in a social landscape, then Canada, as well as many other countries, can serve as an excellent example of a thriving multicultural nation. Such a simplistic conceptualization, however, is fraught with problems, not the least because the dominant norms, forms and structures go unchallenged in such a theorisation.

But, in its scope and intent, the policy on Multiculturalism is much deeper and broader than its vision of Canada as a biblical garden of flowers of different kinds blossoming to the delight of onlookers. In fact, the policy not only promotes the idea of tolerance but also intends to foster understanding between different groups of people. It aims to prevent both assimilation and ghettoization of minority groups. It envisions that people of different groups participate fully in civil life and promote shared values of Canadian society while accepting the difference that characterize other different groups in our society, for the greater good of the nation.

As such, the policy emphasises maintenance of heritage, culture and identities on the one hand, and encourages full and equitable participation in the life of larger society on the other. The act assumes these two stances are not mutually exclusive, although they are opposing to a degree, and they need to be pursued in tandem since a) active maintenance of heritage without participation in wider societal life is likely to lead to segregation and ghettoization and b) active participation in the wider social life without maintenance of one's heritage is a project of assimilation (Canada Multiculturalism Act, 1988). The act reminds, pursuit of either of these positions at absolute exclusion of the other, is to be dreaded and avoided as history has taught us some costly lessons.

Understanding race and racism must center on understanding the experience of racialized people. This means looking beyond superficial, although meaningful to racialized Canadians, differences such as cultural dresses, foods, and dances. "Anti-racism is the practice of identifying, challenging, and changing the values, structures, and behaviors that perpetuate systemic racism" (Government of British Columbia, 2020).

Positioning myself as an immigrant, I will contextualize and evaluate a set of experiences that I have had using an anti-racist framework. Doing so will allow me to achieve three specific aims of this essay. Firstly, I examine theoretical/conceptual basis of multiculturalism in an attempt to problematize it. Specifically, I will delve into the underlying logic, assumptions, purposes, and intended beneficiaries of this operationalization of multiculturalism. Secondly, I discuss the construct of racialized 'Other' and then demonstrate the continued salience of 'Othering' when discussing immigrants' negotiated belonging in Canadian context. This, I argue, is foundational to Canadian consciousness and that it is used to justify the logic of domination. Finally, I celebrate the agency and spirit of immigrants in order to make a case for continued resistance.

## 2    Multiculturalism: For Whom?

In September 2019, during the first week of school, I noticed my child deeply engaged in her artwork. I asked her what she was doing. Totally absorbed in her task, she told me that she was drawing a Hindu God since they were celebrating Hindu heritage month in school. Every month she would complete a different project (not always artwork) related to a different religion. Often, fueled by my questioning, she would enthusiastically share some facts about her learning on the topic. At times, such questioning provided an opportunity to engage in a conversation for the whole family and some quick research. On one occasion, I believe it must be around Orange T-Shirt day, the conversation revolved around residential schools. Curious as she was, because the characters in the narratives were school-going children, she asked a series of questions. I answered them in as much detail as I think was appropriate for her age. We discussed how knowledge is power and how it is important to know about these things in sufficient details before jumping to conclusions. I was careful not to impose my own reasoning or judgements. However, this prompted me to question my being in Canada, my participation in civic/social life in Canada and the policy of multiculturalism. In this section, I will evaluate immigrants' being and their experiences viz a viz the policy of Multiculturalism in Canada and discuss effects of its deployment in politics and our everyday life. Consider:

> Multiculturalism has acquired a quality akin to spectacle. The metaphor that has displaced the melting pot is the salad. A salad consists of many ingredients, is colorful and beautiful, and it is to be consumed by someone. Who consumes multiculturalism is a question begging to be asked.
> DAVIS, 1996, p. 45

In the light of recent events of early 2020, it is too naïve to believe that the policy of Multiculturalism has ensured a level playing people field for all Canadians. For instance, Black Lives Matter (BLM) rally swelled in Canadian streets protesting police and state violence and anti-racism. Although the killing of George Floyd in the USA occasioned this rally in the first place, there is no dearth of anti-black racism in Canada. Canadian Human Rights Commission (CHRC) issued a statement on June 02 acknowledging that anti-black racism is pervasive in Canada, and that "many people of African descent in Canada feel threatened or unsafe every day because of the colour of their skin" (CHRC, 2020). Unsurprisingly, the dominant narrative often has been that racism is either the thing of the bygone era or happening *elsewhere*. Scholars such as Henry and Tator (2009) and Lund (2006) note that historical and contemporary evidence of racism are too often not given serious consideration by majority Canadians.

Similarly, new data from a survey conducted by Angus Reid institute in partnership with University of Alberta revealed the extent and depth of racism directed at people of Chinese (and other East Asian) descent. The report finds that negative media portrayal and exposure to racist graffiti or messaging on social media has been particularly high since the Covid-19 pandemic began. The respondents noted that just 13 per cent believe others in this country view them as fully Canadian "all the time" (Angus Reid.org, 2020) and this emphatically challenges the Asian- Canadian's the right of belonging and the 'right to be here'.

Recent killing of members of First Nations community and a series of police violence led Prime Minister Trudeau (2020) to state:

> Systemic racism is an issue right across the country, in all our institutions, including in all our police forces, including in the RCMP. That's what systemic racism is ... It is recognizing that the systems we have built over the past generations have not always treated people of racialized backgrounds, of Indigenous backgrounds, fairly through the very construction of the systems that exist.
>
> CBC.ca, June 11, 2020

I feel it was a welcome development to hear such an acknowledgment from the Prime Minister because, as Henry and Tator (2009) maintain, Canadians commonly ignore the fact that racism and discriminatory laws and policies are the foundation of significant political, economic, social, and cultural institutions today.

There is a growing widespread perception in the world, particularly in Europe and Australia, that multiculturalism has failed(Cuperus et al. 2003). The Council of Europe recently declared that multiculturalism is simply the flip side of assimilation, equally based on an assumption of an irreconcilable opposition between majority and minority, leading to 'communal segregation and mutual incomprehension' (Council of Europe, 2008, p. 10). It is important to be mindful of how this is being played out in Canada.

Unsurprisingly, Canada has not been immune to these rising global anxieties about multiculturalism. In Canada, popular support for multiculturalism remains relatively strong (although gradually declining over the years, and none of the major national political parties has proposed to step back from multiculturalism). Yet, many Canadians feel that Canada is gradually losing its sense of national identity, and that the smug complacency is blinding Canadians to evolving racial stresses and tensions. An excerpt from Standing Committee on Citizenship and Immigration report that many Canadians believe "Diversity is our strength" but "worry that their country is becoming fragmented, and it is becoming a loose collection of parts each pursuing its own agenda rather than a cohesive entity striving for the collective good of Canada" (CIC, 1994, p. 10, in Li, 2001, p. 84 ).

Often expressions of a backlash against immigrants is rooted on racism. It would appear that in the social imaginary, it is the construed image of hordes of black/brown/yellow immigrants who look and speak different, are seen as challenging the implied cohesiveness of Canada. While analysing Canada's immigration discourse, Li (2001) argues that a racial subtext can be discerned and that the questions in opinions polls reify the notion of race and legitimize the right of Canadians to pass judgements on newcomers' worth based on their superficial features.

Canada does not appear to have a special talent to deal with its diversity and minorities. Were it the case, as Hansen (2017) observes, Indigenous Canadians, who are the oldest 'minority' "would be well incorporated into Canadian society and the Canadian economy" (p. 712). The unemployment rate and median income is significantly lower amongst Indigenous Canadians compared to national average. Economic outcomes amongst immigrants is also declining over the years as "the past 25 years has seen a more or less continuous deterioration in the economic outcomes for immigrants entering Canada" (Picot, 2008, p. 5) and this trend of immigrants earning lower than Canadian-born population has not changed much (Chui & Kelly, 2005). The latter is a worrisome trend to those who view multiculturalism as promoting equality. An immediate debate on the utility of multiculturalism centres on its fundamental assumptions and values.

Multiculturalism in Canada encourages immigrants to integrate into society and take an active part in its social, cultural, economic, and political affairs while at the same time retain their heritage and culture if they choose to. It is obvious that Canada has chosen a social imaginary whereby existing hierarchical relations and racial hegemony go unchallenged. This also detracts our attention from an analysis of the complexity of inequalities. Melamed (2006) argues that neoliberalism manages to employ multiculturalism in a self-justificatory way, all the while 'obscuring the racial antagonisms and inequalities on which the neoliberal project depends' (p. 1). Bannerji (2000) notes that diversity discourse portrays society as a horizontal space, in which there is no theoretical or analytical room for social relations of power and ruling, of socio-economic contradictions that construct and regulate Canadian political economy and its ideological culture (p. 555).

Essentially, normalizing of whiteness is what multiculturalism achieves. Thus, adoption of anti-racist perspective that problematizes whiteness is necessary to understand how multiculturalism reifies both the culture and status of immigrants as *outsiders*. Different from the normative whiteness, immigrants are socially, politically and economically marginalized. It is not difficult to discern the notion of 'national unity' and national sentiments embedded in the ideals of multiculturalism. When defined in relation to white normativity, immigrants represent a threat to 'national identity' – i.e., the dangerous 'Other' in this binary. Thus, the need to contain and control the 'others' is justified, and multiculturalism fulfils this role readily.

One major tenet of multiculturalism is that it proposes discourse of diversity within a framework of unity. Yet, at the same time, it repeatedly works to undo the same. It seeks to erode that very sense of unity among and between diverse groups. For example, the policy has theoretically a somewhat uneasy relationship with Quebecois and Indigenous people as it regulates the terms of belonging and national unity. Similarly, the technology of securitization, surveillance and policing of racialized people is deployed to 'regulate' foreignness and perceived threats of these 'dangerous internal foreigners' (Dhamoon & Abu-Laban, 2009). Given this, it is not difficult to see that multiculturalism positions racialized peoples and can serve as a technology of control.

Melamed (2006) is highly critical of the relationship between multiculturalism, anti-racism and neoliberalism,"Race continues to permeate capitalism's economic and social processes, organizing the hyper-extraction of surplus value from racialized bodies and naturalizing a system of capital accumulation" (p.1). This leads to inequality, divisiveness and ghettoization. In fact, the ideal of multiculturalism is at the service of hegemonic norms and forms. As a technology of control and containment and as an ideology to manage racial contradictions, neoliberal multiculturalism in Canada is poised to perpetuate difference, maintain structural inequalities and prescribe a recipe of tolerance in relation to a hegemonic normative whiteness.

## 3  Othering – Negotiated Being and Belonging

Countless times, I have been asked, "Where are you from?" and I respond sometimes saying "I'm from Toronto". Sometimes this answer is sufficient. However, sometimes I sense that my interlocutor is clearly not satisfied with the specificity of my answer and throws an inquisitive look, and/or often adds, "No … where are you actually/originally from?" I am usually an agreeable person but a few months ago I once instinctively mentioned that "I am from central Africa". He looked surprised. I nodded with a smile and said, "We all are!". All humans have in fact evolved in Africa before navigating the face of the planet.

It is wrong to assume that I do not like being asked where I am from – in fact I am proud of my identity and ethnicity. One can argue, surely the person could simply be curious, and the question is harmless and that I could be reading more into it than it actually is. Well, it is not difficult to differentiate between a genuine effort to get to know me and my background, and a subconscious response that defies his/her conception of how people like me speak, behave and possibly 'be' in this space. It is the latter kind of questioning that bothers me with its embeddedness of an implicit suggestion/hint in that question - that it is an anomaly that I am here, or rather I cannot fully belong here, and that I must be defined by my belonging to some other place somewhere else. I wonder, who does *not* get asked such a question? This leads me to reflect on 'negotiated belonging', 'right to be' and citizenship in this section of the essay. This also relates to the idea of 'Othering' from the previous section.

Given that we are all equal in the eyes of the law, do we have equal access to citizenship, and all that it confers? Having said that, could anything define your limit to autonomy and equality/freedom? Using both historical and contemporary example, I demonstrate that the technology of 'othering' backed by race-thinking appear to punctuate access to full enjoyment of citizenship, and right to 'be', and right to be 'here'. This relates to the notion of space discussed in the essay.

Rooted in a deep existential fear of the 'Other', anti-immigrant racism in Canadian discourse is used to affirm Canadian national identity, particularly White identity. This self/Other binary manifests itself in race-thinking which presupposes congenital and logical grounds for categorizing people into naturally constituted immutable groups. Such classification is based on the "assumption that groups, categories or classes of objects have one or several defining features exclusive to all members of that category" (Ashcroft, Griffiths & Tiffins, 2007, p. 73). Although self is complex and fluid and has multiple dimensions and that our race intersects with class, gender, sexuality etc., this race thinking of self/Other binary foregrounds race. Such a way of exaggerating difference, presumption of white-superiority and representations of Other, to borrow an insight from Edward Said (2003), is a means for domination and control.

Contrary to the policy of multiculturalism, the deeply entrenched nature of systemic racism in Canadian society acts as an effective barrier to integration and economic success for many racialized people. Differences in skin color and ethnicity are often factors that are used to exclude racialized immigrants from the workforce and marginalize them. This evokes the question of belonging and access to full benefits of citizenship. Such examination of power imbalances racialized and non-racialized is necessary to start conversation about anti-racism.

In the past (and even today), this reified and legitimated difference lent superiority to whites, and institutionalized racism. This race-thinking was then deployed not only to spur ongoing colonial projects but also to justify management of supposedly 'inferior' population who were 'non-whites'. Some examples are the introduction of a Chinese head tax and internment of Japanese-Canadians. When white superiority was yoked with imperialist enterprise, subjugation of others based on race-classification was rationalized. It is curious to observe how race thinking was coopted to suddenly reimagine indigenous people from idealized 'noble' savages to 'degenerate and disposable' savages worthy of exploitation and homicide. It is also equally curious how this race-thinking of 'othering' was embedded in social imaginary, enshrined in law, and operationalized in order to justify oppression against racialized minorities.

An important anti-racism action that one can take is to recognize, acknowledge, and demonstrate how racism has been crucially important in the construction of society as we know it today. Examining the relationship between discourses of security, racialization, and foreignness, Dhamoon and Abu-Laban (2009) argue that that "foreignness" is produced and regulated in historically specific ways with consequences for how "the nation" is viewed, and how this is especially evident in relation to racialized constructions of "internal dangerous foreigners" (p. 163). Canadians of Arab or Muslim background became the targets of hostility, harassment, and racism when the Canadian government went to war against Iraq in 1991. In the post-9/11 Canada, Muslims and Arabs began to endure various forms of discrimination (Razack, 2008). In today's Covid-19 crisis, Canadians of Chinese and East Asian backgrounds have been subjected to similar hostility and racism, and they have often been blamed for bringing about the pandemic. In Critical Race Theory, this is differential racialization whereby the dominant society racializes different minority groups in different ways at different times in response to its shifting needs and priorities of the dominant group (Abrams & Mojo, 2009; Omi & Winant, 1994).

Often loyalties (and most fundamentally, their very 'being in this space') of racialized Canadians are questioned and that they have at times been portrayed as dangerous/unwanted aliens. The introduction of a Chinese Head tax and Japanese Internment are cases in point. Evidently, the "right to be here" and "right to be" was questioned; and methods of surveillance and discipline were embodied in a range of different white subjects and institutions. Minority groups were relationally made through these processes but so too were notions of Canada and its citizens. For example, during internment of Japanese-Canadians, the Canadian settler nation used racial and colonial technologies to implement the law and ensure white settlers' right to place. Arrangement such as this is hardly surprising because, as Sherene Razack argues, '[R]ace thinking becomes embedded in law and bureaucracy so that the suspension of rights appears not as a violence but as the law itself' (in Oikawa, p. 97). Who belongs or gets to belong and how is belonging negotiated amid such strong anti-immigrant stance? These questions become particularly problematic for racialized immigrants and citizens.

Walker (1985) notes that although "legal reforms have restrained openly hostile behaviour; they have not affected the essential factors leading to discrimination ... The basic issue in Canada has been racial stereotyping" (p. 24). I think it is much more than stereotyping, it is systemic racism that pivots on unequal access and distribution of resources in relation to marginalized communities. Everyone has racial prejudice and bias but, as DiAngelo (2018) established, "When you back a group's collective bias with lingering authority and institutional control, it is transformed"(Chapter 10, Section 3, para 5). Introduction of the 1885 Head tax, and the 1923 Exclusion Act are some examples of structural/systemic racism – that is inequalities rooted in the system-wide operation of a society that excludes substantial numbers of members of particular groups from significant participation in major social institutions (Henry & Tator, 2006, p. 352). This again raises the question of negotiated belonging.

## 4  Immigrants and the Politics of Possible

As discussed in previous sections, immigrants are positioned in a way that marginalizes them and that neoliberal multiculturalism policy is poised to perpetuate difference, which maintains existing hierarchical relations. The logic of othering is foundational to the Canadian nation-building project and the logic of domination is the modus operandi.

Despite all this, I believe there is hope. In Section 15 of the Canadian Charter of Rights and Freedoms, Equality rights are proscribed as follows:

> Every individual is equal before and under the law and has the right to the equal protection and equal benefit of the law without discrimination, and in particular, without discrimination based on race, national or ethnic origin, colour, religion, sex, age, or mental or physical disability.
> CANADIAN CHARTER OF RIGHTS AND FREEDOMS, 1982

This marked not only the end of legalized racism but also the beginning of change centered on freedom and equality for all. And this section 15 needs to be our ally for change while moving forward to realize the politics of possible towards a just society. I share some examples of successful mobilization of racialized immigrants/citizens even when the times were hostile and challenging.

During the Exclusion era, Chinese immigrant power brokers mitigated even the most direct processes of exclusion. Collaborating with ruling party machines to foil anti-Chinese laws, the Chinese Canadians embraced Canada's legal system, and capitalized on its rule of law to defend their interests in both internal and external conflicts (Mar, 2010). They did not resign to passivity. Instead, they were agents of change, albeit small but their actions helped reunite families and inspired hope in the community.

Johnson (2011) documents how a Sikh family from India successfully navigated barriers to establish themselves "despite weathering decades of social and legal discrimination" (p. xiii). Despite living amidst one of the most hostile periods of Canadian history, the Sidhoo family managed to provide for themselves and contributed to wider community.

Filipino immigrants in Canada are using innovate ways to make their stories heard using drama. In doing so, they are making a strategic choice "to reject entombing. ... in their victimhood" (Pratt, 2012, p. 110). It is a testament to their fighting spirit and agency that despite hardship and marginalized status, they are speaking out. They are defying expectations and shaking status quo. It is no mean feat.

Similarly, by taking up a traditionally female role, Filipino-Canadian male caregivers are challenging Canadian hegemonic and masculine perception of gendered roles and care-giving policy (Nyaga & Torres, 2017). The caregivers are also asserting their rights and actively defining and negotiating their new identity increasingly in their own terms. It is a moment of agency and resistance!

Chinese restaurants in small towns in Canada invite us to see the possibilities of diasporic agency located in the everyday menus of these restaurants (Cho, 2010). Japanese-Canadians are similarly resisting forgetting. Oikawa (2012) notes, "The imagining of the nation and its proper citizens as white necessitates this forgetting of the Internment, an act that renders Japanese Canadians' histories invisible; racist speech marks their visibility and reinscribes the violence forgotten" (p. 300). Women in school resist the institutionalization of forgetting of the Internment in the white space of the school. This form of resistance is important to them because Japanese Canadian women remember the nation as one in which they and their families have struggled against racism. Resisting to forget and remembering "in distinct and diverse ways" (p. 302), reveals the cracks in the mythology of the nation as an always stable entity (ibid). Such counter-storytelling, as critical race theory argues, lends centrality to the experiences of marginalized people and those who have been silenced (Dixon & Rousseau, 2006). Such a storytelling preserves the history and experiences (of the marginalized group) which have been excluded from the master narrative.

The racialized immigrants are impacted in multiple but reinforcing ways through policy, governance and systemic racism in society. Simultaneously, as shown in example above, such a condition provides basis for inspiring unity and solidarity-building for counter-hegemonic resistances and struggle. Examples of immigrant resistance (ranging from affirming one's being to collective resistance to effecting wider social change) highlight our might and agency. They may sometimes not be adequate, but they offer hope in our struggle towards a more just and equitable society. Therefore, we must celebrate these acts of resistance, these moments of agency, be they individual or collective, even when the gains are not as great as we would like.

Mindful of the enduring presence of inequality and the structures that maintain it for quite some time, we should continue to resist because resistance is, as Caygill (2013) reminds us "one of the most important and enduring expressions of twentieth-century political imagination and action" (p. 6). Revolutionary change is not always fundamental or instantaneous;it is incremental (Noguera, 2014, p.72) and that resistance is essential to human life; even when we know we may lose, we make the effort because it is how we are human – this is humanness of resistance (Fordham, 2014, p.101).

## 5 Conclusion

Often marked by several forms of exclusion and multiple forms of vulnerability, immigrant experiences serve as a useful framework to understand the origins and institutionalization of othering. Racialized immigrant experience also provides a useful lens to understand multiculturalism in Canada in relation to lens of white normativity. Similarly, persistent resistance and active agency of racialized immigrant also provides an understanding of change and changemaking process.

A critical step toward change is acknowledging Canada's part and continuing role in the perpetuation and maintenance of power hierarchies and structures. We need to employ anti-racist strategies and actions, to challenge and counter racism, inequalities, prejudices, and discrimination based on racial classifications. Systemic racism needs to be opposed and systemic barriers to equal participation need to be dismantled. This is a political endeavour and can take various forms. Kobayashi and Peake (2000) advise, the political task of anti-racism as 'situat[ing] antiracist struggles in those sites where they will have most effect' (p. 398).

Rightly, developing effective resistance, however, is challenging. As Gramsci (1971) implied with his notion of hegemony, even when agency is apparent, oppressed/disadvantaged groups must operate on a complicated terrain where common sense and prominent institutions tend to align with the interests of dominant norms/groups. This is not an easy terrain to navigate. As Roseberry (1994) reminds, in hegemony 'the words, images, symbols, forms, organizations, institutions, and movements ... are shaped by the process of domination itself' (p. 361). In short, there is a possibility that struggles 'from below' such as the immigrant resistances will, in the end, lead to reinforcing existing power relations. Nevertheless, examples of inspiring resistances abound as discussed in the preceding section. Mindful of the limitation as well as the potential of these resistances, continued resistance is necessary in order to realize the goal of "eliminating racial oppression as a broad goal of ending all forms of oppression" (Solórzano, 1998, p. 122).

Resistance encapsulates our courage to challenge dominant power structures in our fight for social ills such as injustices, inequality and racism, which Cacho (2012) describes as a killing abstraction. Samudzi and Anderson (2018) remind that we fight not because we love to fight, we fight because we're worth fighting for. In any case such resistances assert humanity, dignity and agency of those who resist (Noguera, 2014, p.71) and also, as Kelley (2014) notes, produces a new reality, a new condition for further resistance/radical work.

### References

Abrams, L. S., & Moio, J. A. (2009). Critical Race Theory and the Cultural Competence Dilemma in Social Work Education. *Journal of Social Work Education, 45*(2), p. 245–261.

Angus Reid Institute (2020). *Blame, bullying and disrespect: Chinese Canadians reveal their experiences with racism during COVID-19*. Retrieved on 28 June 2020 http://angusreid.org/racism-chinese-canadians-covid19/

Ashcroft, B., Griffiths, G. & Tiffin, H. (2007) Key Concepts in PostColonial Studies, London and New York: Routledge..

Bannerji, H. (2000). The Paradox of Diversity: The Construction of a Multicultural Canada and 'Women of Color". In *The dark side of the nation: Essays on multiculturalism, nationalism and gender*, 15–61. Toronto: Canadian Scholar's Press.

Cacho, L. M. (2012). *Social death: Racialized rightlessness and the criminalization of the unprotected*. New York: New York University Press.

Canada Multiculturalism Act, (1988). https://laws-lois.justice.gc.ca/eng/acts/c-18.7/page-1.html. Ottawa: Parliament of Canada.

*Canadian Charter of Rights and Freedoms*, s 15, Part I of the *Constitution Act*, 1982, being Schedule B to the *Canada Act* 1982 (UK), 1982, c 11,

Canadian Human Rights Commission (CHRC). (2020). *Statement - Anti-Black racism in Canada: time to face the truth.* Retrieved on 20 June 2020 https://www.chrc-ccdp.gc.ca/eng/content/statement-anti-black-racism-canada-time-face-truth

Caygill, H. (2013). *On resistance: A philosophy of defiance.* London: Bloomsbury.

CBC.ca (2020). *Systemic racism exists in RCMP, Trudeau argues — after commissioner says she's 'struggling' with the term.* Retrieved on 22 June 2020, https://www.cbc.ca/news/politics/rcmp-systemic-racism-lucki-trudeau-1.5607622

Cho, L. (2010). *Eating Chinese: Culture on the menu in small town Canada.* Toronto: University of Toronto Press, 2010.

Chui, T., & Kelly, T. (2005). Longitudinal survey of immigrants to Canada. Progress and challenges of new immigrants in the workforce. *Statistics Canada Catalogue no. 89-615-X.* https://www150.statcan.gc.ca/n1/en/catalogue/89-615-X

Council of Europe Committee of Ministers, (2008). *White paper on intercultural dialogue.* (Brussels: CoE).

Cuperus, R., Duffek, K. and Kandel, J. (2003). *The challenge of diversity: European social democracy facing immigration, integration and multiculturalism.* Innsbruck: Studien Verlag.

Davis, Angela Y. (1996). Gender, Class and Multiculturalism: Rethinking "Race" Politics. In A. Gordon & C. Newfield (Eds.), *Mapping multiculturalism* (pp. 4–48). Minneapolis, MN: University of Minnesota Press.

Delgado, R. (2009). Affirmative Action as a Majoritarian Device: Or Do You Really Want to be a Role Model? In *Foundations of critical race theory in education* (pp. 109–116). New York: Routledge.

Dhamoon, R., & Abu-Laban, Y. (2009) "Dangerous (Internal) Foreigners and Nation-Building: The Case of Canada." *International Political Science Review 30*(2), p.163–183.

DiAngelo, R. J. (2018). *White fragility: Why it's so hard for white people to talk about racism.* [Kindle version].Retrieved from Amazon.com.

Dixson, A. D., & Rousseau, C. K. (2006). *Critical race theory and education: All God's children got a song.* New York: Routledge.

Fordham, S. (2014). What Does an Umbrella Do for the Rain? On the Efficacy and Limitations of Resistance. In Tuck, E., & Wayne, Y. K. (Eds). *Youth resistance research and theories of change,* pp. 82–96. New York: Routledge.

Government of British Columbia. (2020). *Anti-Racism.* [website]. Available: gov.bc.ca/gov/content/governments/multiculturalism-anti-racism/anti-racism

Gramsci, A. (1971). *Selections from the prison notebooks.* Q. Hoare and G. Nowell Smith (Eds.). New York: International.

Hansen, R. (2017). Why Both the Left and the Right Are Wrong: Immigration and Multiculturalism in Canada. *PS: Political Science & Politics, 50*(3), p. 712–716.

Henry, F. & Tator, C. (2006). The Colour of Democracy: Racism in Canadian Society. 3rd Ed. Toronto, ON: Nelson.

Henry, F. & Tator, C. (2009). *The color of democracy: Racism in Canadian society (4th ed)*. Toronto, ONT: Thomson Nelson Canada.

Johnston, H. J. M. (2011). *Jewels of the Qila: The remarkable story of an Indo-Canadian family*. Vancouver: University of British Columbia Press.

Kelley, R.D.G. (2014). Resistance as Revelatory. In Tuck, E., & Wayne, Y. K. (Eds). *Youth resistance research and theories of change*. pp. 82–96. New York: Routledge.

Kobayashi, A., & Peake, L. (2000) Racism Out of Place: Thoughts on Whiteness and an Antiracist Geography in the New Millennium. *Annals of the Association of American Geographers 90*, p. 392–403.

Li, Peter. (2001). "The Racial Subtext in Canada's Immigration Discourse". *Journal of International Migration and Integrations* 2(1):77–97.

Love, B. (2000). Developing a Liberatory Consciousness. In M. Adams, W. J. Blumenfield, R. Castañeda, H. W. Hackman. M. L. Peters, & X. Zúñiga (Eds.), *Readings for diversity and social justice* (2nd ed.), pp. (470–474). New York: Routledge.

Lund, D. E. (2006) Waking Up the Neighbours: Surveying Multicultural and Antiracist Education in Canada, the United Kingdom, and the United States. *Multicultural Perspectives, 8*(1), p. 35–43.

Mar, L. (2010). *Brokering belonging: Chinese in Canada's exclusion era, 1885–1945*. Toronto: University of Toronto Press.

Melamed, J. (2006). The Spirit of Neoliberalism: From Racial Liberalism to Neoliberal Multiculturalism. *Social Text 24* (4), p. 1–24.

Noguera, P. (2014). Organising Resistance into School Movements. In Tuck, E., & Wayne, Y. K. (Eds). *Youth resistance research and theories of change*. pp. 71–81. New York: Routledge.

Nyaga, D. & Torres, R. A. (2017). Gendered Citizenship: A case study of paid Filipino male live- in caregivers in Toronto. *International Journal of Asia Pacific Studies* 13 (1): 51–71, http://dx.doi.org/10.21315/ ijaps2017.13.1.3.

Oikawa, M. (2012). *Cartographies of violence: Japanese Canadian women, memory, and the subjects of the internment*. Toronto: University of Toronto Press.

Omi, M. & Winant, H. (1994). *Racial formation in the United States: From the 1960s to the 1990s*, 2nd ed. Routledge.

Picot, G. (2008). "Immigrant economic and social outcomes in Canada: Research and data development at Statistics Canada." *Analytical Studies Branch Research Paper Series. No.319*. December. Statistics Canada Catalogue no.11F0019M (accessed April 2020).

Pratt, G. (2012). *Families apart: Migrant mothers and the conflicts of labor and love*. Minneapolis: University of Minnesota Press, 2012.

Razack, S. (2008). The Muslims are Coming: The 'Sharia Debate' in Canada. In *Casting out: The eviction of Muslims from Western law and politics*, 154–172, Toronto: University of Toronto Press.

Roseberry, W. (1994). Hegemony and the language of contention. in Joseph, G.M & Nugent, D. (Eds.) *Everyday forms of state formation: revolution and the negotiation of rule in modern Mexico.* pp. 355–366. Durham, NC: Duke University Press

Said, E. W. (2003). *Orientalism.* London: Penguin Books.

Samudzi, Z., & Anderson, W. C. (2018). *As black as resistance: Finding the conditions for liberation.* California: AK Press

Sensoy, O., DiAngelo, R. J. & Banks, J. A., (2017). *Is everyone really equal?: An introduction to key concepts in social justice education.* New York, NY: Teachers College and Columbia University.

Solórzano, D. G. (1998). Critical Race Theory, Race and Gender Microaggressions, and the Experience of Chicana and Chicano Scholars. *International Journal of Qualitative Studies in Education, 11*(1), 121–136.

Statistics Canada (2017). *Census in brief. Ethnic and cultural origins of Canadians: Portrait of a rich heritage.* Retrieved on 20 June 2020. https://www12.statcan.gc.ca/census-recensement/2016/as-sa/98-200-x/2016016/98-200-x2016016-eng.cfm

Walker, J. W. S. G. (1985). *Racial discrimination in Canada: The Black experience.* Ottawa: Canadian Historical Association.

CHAPTER 17

# Brokering Belonging, Shattering Silences and Examining Erasures

*Grace Garlow*

## 1   Introduction

This chapter explores the relevance of new framings of Critical Anti-Racist Theory (CART) to mobilize theory into praxis for educators and leaders in Canadian K-12 schools. As a theory, it raises questions about power and domination central to race. It also serves as an intervention to unsettle the maintenance and reproduction of hierarchical paradigms by raising critical awareness of different expressions of racism through reflexive practice. CART offers implications for substantive social changes through curriculum development, pedagogy, teacher education and policy. In sharing a personal incident, I will write through my reflections to analyze and interpret this experience by grounding myself to the specificities of my subject location as a feminized Taiwanese-Canadian. In doing so, I aim to interrogate erasures and expound on how these relations link to power and domination. The chapter concludes with a discussion to initiate a renewed dialogue towards building a shared understanding of equity, inclusive education, and the significance of embodiment as a personal and political subject in knowledge production and a site of recovering the self and recovering the 'Other' by mapping pathways toward intercultural and "relational solidarities" (Gaztambide-Fernández, 2012). Central to this discussion is a desire to support educators and leaders in understanding decolonizing educational practices and our collective responsibility to engage in different iterations of respectful relationships and reciprocity to improve the lives of our youth.

Questions I seek to problematize are: What does it mean to enter discourses on anti-racism as an East-Asian woman? How do we perceive the orientation of a feminized East-Asian woman in a leadership role? How are the historical legacies of race, gender, class, and sexuality in East-Asian women's identity understood when it materializes in our interactions? The reframing of CART (Dei, 1999, 2013, 2017; Gillborn, 2006) examines how we can learn about the complexities and specificities of relationships to support social and political activism. This challenge is a collective endeavor to reconsider the reading of race, racism, and relationships in plural societies.

## 2   Beginning with the Personal and the Site of Struggles

> History despite its wrenching pain cannot be unlived, but if faced with courage, need not be lived again.
> MAYA ANGELOU

Drawing on Dei (2013), I am entering this piece from the personal through embodiment and my lived experiences as an Asian-Canadian woman. More accurately, as a Taiwanese-Canadian woman living on the traditional territories of the Wendat, the Haudenosaunee, the Anishinaabe peoples, and the treaty lands negotiated as the Williams Treaty and Treaty 13 on Turtle Island. While benefiting from the privileges as a second-generation Canadian, it also conceals oppressive and dispiriting experiences navigating racial discrimination and the vestiges of colonial education. Despite holding privileges attending post-secondary school and employment as an educator at a school board in the Greater Toronto Area (GTA), my schooling experiences from K-OAC did not affirm a sense of belonging nor illuminate an imagined future of possibilities that one imagines education would do for its learners. Instead, Euro-Canadian education conditioned racism and epistemic violence, alienated me from being connected to my past and knowing who I am in the present.

Growing up in the GTA, I was raised primarily by my maternal grandmother, who followed a spiritual path. Observing and learning from her was disrupted when I entered Kindergarten in public school, where reciting Christian prayers was enforced whether or not we were Christian. This process discounted diverse belief systems and multiple readings from plural communities by imposing a singular worldview. It disregarded how that may estrange children from their families and communities. The notion of alienation proliferated through my teachers, classmates, and our overwhelmingly White community. White voicings in the exclusionary Euro-Canadian curriculum solely affirmed Western, historical, and intellectual knowledge systems and simultaneously omitted any representation, histories and the futurities of a plural world. The persistent questioning of my citizenship reinforced the temporality of my existence. My peers targeted me through spiritual violence linked to racism and social ostracism. I was lost and profoundly disconnected from a strong sense of self that deepened with my grandmother's passing— wrestling with notions of being myself where I felt dislocated and trying to find my voice in spaces where my voice only mattered when I remained silent.

Straddling multiple worlds feeling invisible and maneuvering through tensions by resisting and yearning for my being to feel and be whole. This fractured existence became an integral part of reading the world through multiple ways of seeing, feeling, and knowing. Even when I did not have the words to express the expansive weight of brokering my belonging, I was fractured and knew I was the *Other*. As Swartz (1992) informs us, "others become marginalized and disconnected from their time and place, and their contributions are severed from the eras or movements that constructed them and which they, in turn, collectively constructed" (p. 343).

The past, present and future transcended through space and time when I became a mother. My children are the first generation from their patrilineal family to be raised outside of the Six Nations of the Grand River First Nations Reserve since 1784. They have gifted my life with a deepened perspective of community and renewed purpose to reshape history and futurities. I acknowledge this profound responsibility to root them with a strong sense of cultural pride in their Taiwanese, Onyota'a:ká: (Oneida) of the wolf clan with English and Irish ancestry. Thus, the commitment and desire to affirm cultural pride, recover ancestral knowledges and histories for all students connect to rooting my children with a strong sense of belonging through affirming their multiple identities. Braided into this journey is my spouse's story as a Federal Indian Day School survivor and the journey of coming to know who I am and reacquainting with my being. As Wane (2020) insightfully shares, "getting to know the self is very important because I as a parent, I cannot parent my child if I do not know my history." Essential to this commitment is the responsibility for all educators to "weave a connective pathway" (Smith, Tuck & Yang, 2019, p. 16) for our collective futures and communities.

## 3    Critical Incident

Education is a political arena "legitimizing" dominant epistemologies and ontologies while normalizing the practice of obscuring non-hegemonic worldviews. This discussion makes a case for considering the reframing of CART (Dei, 1999, 2013, 2017; Gillborn, 2006) in educational theory and praxis to support teacher practitioners and leaders in developing their critical and collective understanding of decolonial approaches in education. Against overwhelming pushback to greater inclusion, equality, and social justice, critical practitioners who commit to anti-racist and decolonizing education face violent backlash for their activism. As such, the social practice of erasures has become a normalized practice eluding critique. It questions institutions and structures enforcing a one-dimensional worldview, racist oppression and addresses broader critical conversations around White supremacy, capitalism and neoliberal practices that maintain these structures. This discussion focuses on examining erasures in social justice and equity and anchoring race in anti-racism discourses. At the heart of theorizing the Asian-Canadian identity is finding meaning, building relational solidarities across communities, and rethinking the purpose of education and futurities.

As a teacher practitioner in various leadership capacities, I have spent much of my career working toward strengthening critical consciousness and reconstituting a sense of hope for a better world. While I am only focusing on a particular incident, it captures various dispiriting experiences linked to historical relations of power and domination in education. In sharing this piece, it is essential to note that the imperative to theorize this incident is not to point to any victims nor vilify anyone. Instead, it is to critique the internalized practice and material impact of ideologies through an essential lesson to understand the reading of East-Asian women within particular structures and how these unresolved histories morph and reshape in our present day. This critical incident evokes the instrumentalization of racism and neoliberalism as an engine of capitalism to maintain the accumulated power and wealth for a few through education. Fundamentally, it presents challenges to dismantle colonial institutions reproducing White supremacy through neoliberal policies and practices (Lopez, 2020), as exemplified in the domination of the White middle-class teachers throughout my teaching career at various schools within the Greater Toronto Area (GTA). Despite changing demographics in the community reflecting greater lingual, social, and cultural diversity from a growing immigrant population, the school staff remains exceedingly White. Not surprisingly, collaborating with my colleagues who interpreted the world and the curriculum from a different perspective and lived experience has provided rich opportunities for growth and challenge.

Within this backdrop, the Ministry of Education has identified the urgency to eliminate systemic barriers in schools to address Ontario's education system fraught with equity and human rights issues. Professional development and staff meetings became contested sites of push-back and resistance for space to "talk back" (hooks, 2014) and question institutional dysfunctions including systemic racism, barriers to essential resources to support academic outcomes, harsher disciplinary actions on students of colour and streaming in the school-to-prison pipeline for Black, Indigenous and racialized students (Dei, 1995, 2000; James & Turner, 2017; Lopez, 2016; Tuters & Portelli, 2017). Many teachers on staff challenged data that presented systemic racism in Ontario education, repudiated the valuable opportunity to work collaboratively and build capacities and pedagogical practices to create more inclusive environments. Some recast equity and social justice education as "extra work" and "not part of the curriculum" and expressed "over-servicing" marginalized students and denied the legitimacy of lived experiences shared by students in their spoken word poetry and the school's "brave space" (Palfrey, 2017).

In response to a few staff members who approached our administrator seeking a resource to approach culturally relevant and responsive practice, my administrator asked if I could help put something together to support staff learning and student improvement. As a result, I worked with a colleague to create a framework supporting creativity, encourage cross-curricular connections, space for agency and collaborative work with grade partners, families, and the community. It challenged traditional thinking and deepened conversations around instructional practice through anti-racism theory and equity towards more inclusive practices in education. Recognizing its potential to advance meaningful changes, my administrators asked if my colleague and I could present it at our next staff meeting.

When it was our turn to present at the staff meeting, I felt the tension in the room as I stood up and walked to the front of the room. Within a few moments, a White male colleague brusquely disrupted the presentation and quickly dismissed the work for social justice and equity. He questioned the purpose of the resource before I had a chance to share and eroded any goodwill. As I explained the context of the resource to support student success and well-being, he raised his voice and spoke over me while asserting his power to silence my voice. I continued to justify the imperative of responsive practices to achieve a collective goal of inclusion and removing barriers while warring emotional and spiritual violence, undermining my lived experiences, professional knowledge, and dignity. I shared some experiences disclosed by youths and implored the sense of urgency, to which he quashed with an audible scoff and a brush-off with a hand gesture. The children and I were dismissed, just like that.

Research from multiple critical theories advancing culturally relevant and responsive pedagogies (Battiste, 2013; Dei et al., 2000; Dixson & Rousseau, 2014; Gay, 2000; hooks,1994; Ladson-Billings, 1995a, 1995b; Lopez, 2016) discredited, devalued and relegated to the space of deficiency. Hours of work reconceptualizing how to subvert character education to create purposeful opportunities to include the community as valuable resources to support students and the school, framing questions to prompt critical conversations to co-construct knowledge and forward critical consciousness from K-8 delegitimized under the White gaze. Each time I spoke, my responses were quashed and muted, constraining my humanity from being fully realized.

The permanence of "settler colonial patterns and logics" (Rojas, 2016) taking shape in the present moment at the nexus of race, gender, class, and sexualization linked to the history of "racial formation" (Omi & Winant, 1994) in the Canadian nation-building project (Dua, 2007; Miki, 2000; Omi & Winant, 1994; Razack, 2002; McKittrick, 2006). Not a single person stepped forward to intervene or put an end to the spectacle. Approximately sixty educators, including my administrators, were present observing in silence, maintaining their power and privilege and complicit in normalizing a spiritually violent assault rooted in power and domination. As the fracturing of my spirit began, I could not help but wonder if the problem was indeed truly about sharing a resource to assist the staff or if it had more to do with me. What was it about my particular presence or a shared resource that necessitated such discord and hostility?

The co-presenter expressed her annoyance that the presentation had been derailed and continued. While my White colleague spoke, not a single person, including the other White educator who hijacked the presentation, interrupted or uttered a single word. The interrogation and barrage of questions altogether ceased fire. I stood in silence, taking it all in. Believing there would be an opportunity to pick up and contribute to the presentation, it concluded while I stood there, observing like a prop. Muted and disempowered once again. At that moment, it illuminated the workings of Whiteness through neoliberal globalisation (Narayan, 2017), converging to deny and disempower through racial discrimination while diverging to attain individual power through self-congratulatory acts of superiority. I returned to my seat and watched a different White colleague present and was warmly received. Once more, not a single person interjected as she shared a resource with the staff. While I observed what was unfolding, I became enraged and clutched onto my dignity while the fracturing splintered the mind, body, and soul. Once the meeting concluded, a few other colleagues came to admonish the male colleague's egregious behaviour. The co-presenter also joined in and expressed how she was received much differently when she presented, sharpening the notion of being othered.

## 4   New Framings of CART toward Decolonial Praxis

Reframing Critical Anti-Racist Theory (CART) is an alliance of critical theoretical frameworks to restructure education through decolonizing efforts. It draws on the wisdom, strength, and support of communities to better understand relations within ourselves and the interconnection beyond the self. As a theory, it helps draw meaning from experiences and practices that are the legacies of our history and White imaginations by interrogating colonial ideologies and Western practices as *the* singular reading informing our plural world (Dei, 2013;

Thobani, 2007). CART is also a practical approach to activism by connecting the theory into transgressive practices to live more wholly and authentically. In this paper, I will explore three principles from CART to analyze anti-racism in the context and specificity of a feminized East-Asian educator.

The first principle is the centrality of race in discourses on anti-racism. The saliency of race has become a symbolic representation reinforcing racist actions, behaviors, access to resources and ideologies supported by policies in our social, institutional and state structures. As Donnor and Ladson-Billings (2018) posit, race and racism are enmeshed in social, economic, and political institutions functioning as the primary determinant inequitable outcomes for people of color. The need of "confronting racism, then, is confronting racial superiority and its legacy, not only in history but also in contemporary experience" (Battiste, 2013, p. 125). This experience of empowerment or disempowerment varies along a continuum of skin colour and human characteristics that remain unresolved injustices that discern the saliency of race and racism in people's lives (Dei, 2013, p. 5). The nebulous concept of race positions Whiteness as *the* normative in a racialized society by ranking and categorizing from this vertex (Dei, 2013; Ladson-Billings, 1998). Omi and Winant (1994) argue, this concept of regulating who is "raced" has been a determining factor "over natural and legal rights, over the distribution of resources, and indeed, over who shall live and who shall die" (p. 54).

The second principle of CART is understanding how markers of social difference are anchored to conceptualized notions of Whiteness as a baseline and materializing into real and felt experiences as a process of being othered. These White imaginaries create polarizing constructs based on the assumption that Whiteness is superior and *the* normative. By default, everything else is "inferior" and invisible. As Dei (2013) explains, the "oppressive process of 'Othered' and a signification of difference in the dominant's imagination" (p. 5). It is further complicated when multiple identities intersect with historical legacies and compounded by the multiplicities of oppressions (Collins, 2000; Crenshaw, 1991; hooks, 2015). As Jones and Guy-Sheftall (2015) posit, this framework captures a broader and more holistic experience to analyze women of color through an intercultural and intersecting analysis of individual and social factors that challenge interrelated systems of domination, race, gender, sexuality, and class. Collective action must address the root cause of White supremacy and racism: power and domination. Only when we recognize and redress core issues can we begin disseminating how racism has permeated our structures, institutions, curriculum and ideologies, practices that reproduce the same harmful outcomes.

The third principle in discourses on anti-racism is the permanence of race in reproducing and reinforcing social structures limiting access to resources and social mobility. The permanence of racism is a process of using power and privilege to disempower, estrange and disconnect marginalized subjects from knowing themselves, thereby obstructing the experience of their whole life and full humanity. Liu (2020) asserts, "within a sociological imagination, our personal situations become indivisible from social structures" (p. 6). It brings to the fore critical discussions anchoring the reading of anti-racism through an anti-colonial gaze (Dei, 2013). As Dei (2013) argues, it is imperative to link the role of anti-racism in colonial histories, imperialism, and current contexts related to capitalism, global capitalism, and xenophobia in our plural societies and how these manifest into intersecting identities shaped by capitalism and modernity. This positions CART as a relevant and practical theory to push forward ways to challenge systemic barriers and the material consequences of racism and colonialism. Essential in this process of decentering is creating the space for genuine inclusion of hegemonies, ontologies, epistemologies and cosmology to challenge Eurocentric normativity. Thus, CART creates space to "decolonize the mind" (Lopez, 2020, p. 35), build relationships and empower marginalized and racialized communities through opportunities to experience wholeness and inclusion.

Reframing CART is a collective struggle for justice that insists on embracing a radical pedagogy of decolonial praxis (Dei, 2017) for both the colonized and oppressed peoples (Freire & Macedo, 2018). It must critically interrogate ongoing settler colonialism (Alfred & Corntassel, 2005; Tuck & Yang, 2012) and see beyond our sites of differences towards sites of convergence and relational and collective solidarities (Gaztambide-Fernández, 2012; hooks, 2003). CART calls upon a collective movement of action for our shared communities by critically examining the particularities of our actions as it relates to all our relations and relationships (Tuck & Yang, 2012). We must also be honest and examine our complicities in the "ongoing colonial project" (Dei, 2013; Lawrence & Dua, 2005, p. 123) and think about what it means to be "accountable to Indigenous sovereignty and futurity" (Tuck & Yang, 2012, p. 35). This evocation of living in the spirit which Thích Nhất Hạnh illuminates as committing to open-heartedness and recovering one's self, integrity and our true existence by returning home (as cited in hooks, 2003, pp. 161–162).

## 5   The Resistances

Many teachers and leaders push back transformative changes that embrace inclusion. However, it raises some questions to critically self-reflect why there is push back and what ideologies are maintained. How do we understand the consequences of our actions and their unwitting harm without a critical understanding? Drawing on my personal experiences, this section will highlight common social practices of erasures in social justice and human rights education. I will examine these erasures through CART's new framings to clarify how race, gender, class, sexuality, religion and other identifications play out in education and the specificities of my identity as a Taiwanese-Canadian woman. This tool helps to analyze our intersecting identities and the compounding impact of intersecting oppressions to engage in a dialogue and build a greater understanding by taking actionable steps to disrupt the nebulous expressions of racisms (Dei, 2013; Dei & Lordan, 2013; Ladson-Billings, 1998; Omi & Winant, 1994).

### 5.1   *Colourblind Approaches:* "I Don't See Colour"

One of the ways educators deny an anti-racist curriculum is by projecting a colorblind perspective. As a society, we have learned that colorblind approaches address racial disparities. However, detrimental inequities due to racism have made social constructions a reality. Colorblindness discounts race when making decisions and reinforces a false notion that the problem rests at the individual rather than a social level by excusing racism's functioning. The negation of race as a social organization excludes race and racism from being recognized as a legitimate factor and its symbiotic relationship with the disempowerment, exploitation, and disenfranchisement of people of color (Creshaw, 1991; Donnor & Ladson-Billings, 2018; Omi & Winant, 1994). It disproportionately fails to provide equitable access to wealth and resources by engendering this notion of people's inability to achieve academic success. The damaging outcomes of a narrative, according to Ladson-Billings (1998), are "cast in a language of failure" (p. 19) and a refusal to see color by rendering it invisible. Colorblindness absolves accountability for the disproportionate number of Black and Indigenous students streamed into predetermined pathways, criminalized for student behavior, and "pushed out" (Dei, 1995) of schools with an alarming and undisputable school-to-prison pipeline (Dei, 1995; hooks, 1994; James & Turner, 2017; Lopez, 2019).

### 5.2   *Pushback:* "Extra Work"

Teachers pushing back equity and social justice education through discourses of "extra work" are choosing a stance of inaction and a deliberate choice to dismiss the concerns and existence of Others. It comes from a position of power and privilege and discounts the educators' responsibility to engage reflexively on the curricula, ideologies, histories, cultures, and social contributions being advanced and remembered while negating voices from the oppressed that continue to be absent. Taking a stance of inaction to deliver a curriculum of erasures reproduces harm and needs to be challenged. It is a deliberate action to maintain an oppressive structure and practice that do not permit equal opportunities for all to access resources, experiences, wealth and increased engagement that advances success (McMahon & Portelli, 2004).

### 5.3　*Maintaining Power to Disempower:* "Teaching to the Curriculum"

The curriculum perceived as objective and "race-neutral" (Ladson-Billings, 1998) has excluded the existence and contributions of other civilizations, reframed histories of conquest in settler nation-building projects that erase narratives of genocide (Dua, 2007; Alfred & Corntassel, 2005; Swartz, 1992; Tuck & Yang, 2012) and presented through the lens and interpretation of predominantly White educators. Master scripting in education is present in theories, methods, instructional materials and practice grounded in White supremacy and Eurocentric ideologies (Swartz, 1992, pp. 341). It institutionalizes an agenda of White, patriarchal, upper-class as the universal standard in education. The limited inclusion of Others is through the imaginary (mis)representation, distortion, and denigration to ensure the severing of Others from knowing themselves to realize a curriculum of assimilation (Bernal & Villalpando, 2002; Ladson-Billings, 1998; Swartz, 1992).

Standards and knowledge believed to be neutral and objective empowers or disempowers specific populations from accessing knowledge and opportunities in life through the process of racial division and epistemological racism (Bernal & Villalpando, 2002; Scheurich & Young, 1997; Smith, 2012). Consequently, the curriculum has created an "apartheid of knowledge where the dominant Eurocentric epistemology is believed to produce "legitimate" knowledge, in contrast to the "illegitimate" knowledge that is created by all other epistemological perspectives" (Bernal & Villalpando, 2002, p. 177). It silences multiple voices, culturally diverse perspectives, and existence in a "multicentric" (Dei et al., 2000) world through omissions that impart a "monological and monovocal expression" (Swartz, 1992). Fylkesnes (2019) argues that this socially accepted exclusionary practice as the "pedagogy of amnesia" concealing institutionalized Whiteness and the colonial legacy of racism by "forgetting" diverse communities, the totality of their histories, concerns and lived experiences to produce a "lost generation." These experiences disconnect critical relations to the past, present, and future by robbing opportunities of knowing who they were, who they are, and who they will be.

### 5.4 Silencing Voices from Other Ways of Knowing: "Free Speech"

Silencing "dissonance to the status quo" (Dei, 1999, p. 22) is a spiritual assault disconnecting critical perspectives and multiple ways of making meaning and interpreting our world from taking place. A social practice critical scholars (Dei, 1999, 2013, 2017; Swartz, 1992; Thobani, 2007) argue, mutes counter-narratives, experiences theories, and knowledges from marginalized bodies. Liu (2020) forwards this notion of being seduced by the imperialist fantasy of White masculine dominance, strength, and power in tandem with that which has bestowed upon White men the "right to command and control humanity" (p. 17). Ong (Ong, 1999, as cited in Pon, 2000) critiques essentialist notions of Confucian cultural values promoting collectivism, filial piety, devotion, and respect for all elders and superiors, misconstrued under the Western gaze as obedient, inferiority, subserviency, and passivity without an intimate understanding of the underlying philosophies (Liu, 2020, pp. 29–32; Ong, 1999).

The colonial construction of Asian women's identities is inseparable from neoliberal ideologies to maintain the state's capitalist interest and relationship in sustaining gender and racial power hierarchies through institutionalized, systemic oppression (Dua, 2007; Mohanty, 2003; Pon, 2000). Within the specificity of this context, the embodied racial identity of a feminized East-Asian woman holding a leadership role in a colonial institution offers counter-hegemonic readings and interpretations entrenched in the racial formation of Canada as a nation-state and a White settler project (Omi & Winant, 1994). My presence as a woman and person of colour occupying a leadership role and speaking to equity and social justice betrayed my colleague's ability to recognize me outside of the White imagination of an Asian woman. There are "political consequences" (Mohanty, 2003) for being a woman and as an embodied East-Asian woman in Canada where my racialized and gendered identities were constructed as immoral prostitutes in the building of the White settler nation, ensured the legitimization of regulating Asian women. The exclusionary Acts prevented the reunification of families and the settlement of Asian men in Canada and later regulated as the embodied solution through inclusion to address mixed-race relations between Chinese men marrying White women (Dua, 2007, pp. 450–458).

These tensions in the asymmetrical power axes of my intersecting identities of race, gender, class, and sexuality unsettled the White male since my existence is essential in maintaining the neoliberalism in education. Talking back to the inequities of these structures and seeking change poses a threat. To maintain his power and sustain the status quo, he redirected his aggression by exerting his social power to control, mute, and erase my existence through a racist act under the guise of "free speech." According to Rajchert (2015), this behavior is a psychological defence mechanism to displace the source of anger by projecting it onto a less threatening person or thing to circumvent consequences. The entire staff maintained their privilege as our colleague dismissed my knowledge and lived experiences and concerns I was addressing to maintain a single narrative, ultimately preventing Others from being empowered and making sense of the world. In aligning with dominant conceptions of "internalizing the stereotypical images that certain elements of society have constructed to maintain their power" (Ladson-Billings, 1998, p. 14). Their complicities preserved their privilege and simultaneously implicated them in racial and gender discrimination. Subjugating, interrogating, challenging, delegitimizing, dismissing, omitting, erasing, and devaluing are numerous ways of erasing and silencing voices. These acts are violent, dehumanizing, and engenders marginalization.

## 6   Discussions to Pursue towards Decolonial Praxis

> A journey of a thousand miles begins with one step.
> LAO-TZU

This chapter reviewed some reactionary practices that maintain and reproduce racial and gender hierarchies and injustice by teachers and school leaders. Theorized through new framings of CART), it centers the self with the tension of transformative praxis in education by unsettling current practices and ideologies. It creates discomfort by opening up space to engage in discussions with diverse standpoints. Recognizing there is no singular solution to perennial problems in education, I propose renewed critical understandings of resistance to initiate a dialogue that builds on the shared experience of struggles that sustain unequal relationships.

### 6.1   *Strengthening Critical Consciousness Beginning with Self*

Leading transformative changes to center and reaffirm our diverse identities in education remains a profoundly complex issue within colonial structures that maintain and reproduce the same outcomes. Without engaging in critical self-examination of our biases and strengthening critical knowledge about how we are entangled in the social structure, we cannot effectively lead against the grain and transform how we educate. Dei's (2013) assertion that "histories tell us the anti-racist/colonial is about praxis and being able to self-determine through critical consciousness" (p. 13) resonates as a critical practice. Dei explains that "engaging in social justice leadership and culturally responsive leadership as a critical educator is a political act, and one needs to know the self to engage in political action, find out what needs to be done and how to do it" (as cited in Lopez, 2016, p. 74). It is a learning process of unlearning and relearning that begins with self (Lopez, 2016). Reflexivity is not only critical, but a necessary process in which we are engaged in the process of reshaping the way we see and interact with the world to be humanized, advance equity and social justice (Freire, 2018; Lopez, 2016; Tuters & Portelli, 2017), and build community (hooks, 2003).

### 6.2  *Culturally Responsive Teachers and Leaders*

As globalization continues to rise, expand and diversify student populations (Statistics Canada, 2019) in Canadian schools, it will require educators and school leaders "to change the way race is understood and thereby mitigate the effects of racism" (Dei & McDermott, 2019, p. 3). Culturally responsive teachers and leaders must rethink how they educate for all learners' success and engagement in a plural society. These entanglements of relations and relationality stresses the importance of creating space to embed culturally relevant (Ladson-Billings, 1995a, 1995b; Lopez, 2016) and culturally responsive (Gay, 2000; Lopez, 2016) practices to create authentic connections and respectful partnerships between the school and the community (Khalifa, Gooden, & Davis, 2016; Lopez, 2016). This understanding is central to disrupting, institutionalized practices that silence dissenting voices from the margins struggling to find a sense of belonging within spheres of power and privilege.

### 6.3  *Relational Solidarity*

Gaztambide-Fernández (2012) challenges us to rethink educational change as a commitment to decolonization through relational solidarity and to engage in purposeful ways. He argues that it cannot be subsumed under antiracism theory. As "antiracism does not begin with, and reflect, the totality of Native people's lived experience - that is, with the genocide that established and maintained all of the settler states within the Americas" (Lawrence & Dua, 2005, p. 121). It must unsettle settler colonialism relations and our witting and unwitting complicities in perpetuating contemporary colonialism (Alfred & Corntassel, 2005; Bernal & Villalpando, 2002) and solely settler futurities (Tuck & Gaztambide-Fernandez, 2013, p. 73). As Thobani (2007) asserts,

> Citizenship emerged as integral to the very processes that transformed insiders (Aboriginal peoples) into aliens in their own territories, while simultaneously transforming outsiders (colonizers, settlers, migrants) into exalted insiders (Canadian citizens). The category citizen, born from

the genocidal violence of colonization, exists in a dialectical relation with its Other, the Indian, for whom the emergence of this citizenship was deadly, not emancipatory. (p. 74)

Intentional and collaborative community engagement must reimagine ways of responding to relational solidarity committed to Indigenous sovereignty, repatriation and relations (Smith et al., 2019; Gaztambide-Fenández, 2012; Tuck & Gaztambide-Fenández, 2013). A collective resistance for justice to reconstitute the existence of Indigenous communities and their self-determining rights, beginning with a critical self-examination that recognizes the tensions of our existence and what Gaztambide-Fenández (2012) points out are histories that "bring us together into treaty relations based on a commitment to decolonization" (p. 61).

## 7  Conclusion

By understanding historical evolution processes, we are better informed to respond to dehumanizing practices when we see them. Reframing of CART challenge us to analyze how racism functions in maintaining the same education structures. As a theory, it is worthy of consideration as it approaches the historical inequalities and injustice experienced by racially marginalized bodies and moves beyond discussions of differences that sustain inequities. The centrality of anti-racism in discourses about race mobilizes the discussion centered on race theory into reflexive praxis and transformation. It must challenge practices to speak back to the dynamics in power relations linked to existing beliefs, values grounded in past legacies manifesting into systemic practices, and policies that enforce the state's political, social and economic interests.

Many teachers and leaders who embody Whiteness in education have a limited understanding of critical theories and social justice (McMahon, 2007; McMahon & Portelli, 2004; Tuters & Portelli, 2017). Engaging from a learning stance and humility can help reframe how they understand conflicts in education. Interrogating enduring resistances is part of the process of unsettling entrenched beliefs and creating discomfort. By doing so, it creates space for dialogue, different perspectives and voices from the margins. This space creates opportunities to ask questions, welcomes diverse perspectives, and critical self-reflection to reexamine the construction of current beliefs and practices enshrining neoconservative ideologies as the normative. The very practice of disrupting is an essential part of the inquiry process that explores diversity and ideologies. It problematizes the notion of not *what* you know but coming to the place of realizing education as a practice of freedom (hooks, 1994). This process is widely misunderstood in education and needs to be re-conceptualized as a courageous act of hope instead of being problematic. Hope offers new awakenings and alternative views to open up the possibility for political action. As Achinstein (2002) clarifies, teachers often relate community as one that should have a shared vision and a 'culture of niceness'; however, the practice of 'niceness' seldom creates radical change. Anti-racist and decolonial work is profoundly complex and messy work.

The converging interfaces of theory-pedagogy-praxis is an ongoing struggle towards equity and emancipation for subjugated subjects to (re)claim space. The demarcation of the hyphenation between Asian-Canadian / Taiwanese-Canadian links our ancestors. It also marks the inability to fully assimilate as citizens (Dua, 2007) in tandem, embracing multiple citizenships. This identity marked by the punctuation materializes into an ongoing colonial project on Indigenous land and rendered invisible within the temporality of the bordered hyphenations and contested sites fraught with a duelling consciousness. The hyphenation marks an internalized struggle which Wah eloquently pens as a "marked (or unmarked) space that both binds and divides... the operable tool that both compounds difference and underlines sameness. Though it is in the middle, it is not in the centre" (as cited in Suarez, 2002, p. 29). Building on Wah, the obscured Others read emotionally felt experiences that continue to exist when past legacies take shape in the present. They offer insight into a fuller account of our existence and multiple readings to map terrains of promise and possibility that benefit our students and society. We exist straddling various lifeworlds. I live within a space that binds and divides, punctuated in the middle while knowing I am not centered.

### References

Achinstein, B. (2002). Conflict amid community: The micropolitics of teacher collaboration. *Teachers College Record, 104*(3), 421–455. DOI:10.1111/1467-9620.00168.

Alfred, T., & Corntassel, J. (2005). Being indigenous: Resurgences against contemporary colonialism. *Government and Opposition, 40*(4), 597–614. https://doi.org/10.1111/j.1477-7053.2005.00166.x.

Battiste, M. (2013). *Decolonizing education: nourishing the learning spirit*. Purich Publishing.

Bernal, D. D., & Villalpando, O. (2002). An apartheid of knowledge in academia: The struggle over the "Legitimate" knowledge of faculty of color. *Equity & Excellence in Education, 35*(2), 169–180. https://doi.org/10.1080/713845282.

Collins, P.H. (2000). *Black feminist thought: Knowledge, consciousness, and the politics of empowerment*. Routledge.

Crenshaw, K. (1991). Mapping the margins: Intersectionality, identity politics, and violence against women of color. *Stanford Law Review., 43*, 1241–1299. http://www.jstor.org/stable/1229039?seq=1&cid=pdf-reference#references_tab_contents

Dei, G. J. S. (1999). The denial of difference: Reframing anti-racist praxis. *Race Ethnicity and Education, 2*(1), 17–38. https://doi.org/10.1080/1361332990020103.

Dei, G. J. S. (2013). Chapter one: Reframing Critical Anti-Racist Theory (CART) for contemporary times. *Counterpoints, 445*, 1–14. http://www.jstor.org/stable/42982029

Dei, G. J. S., & Lordan, M. (2013). Chapter eleven: Conclusion: Where Does Critical Anti-Racism Theory Lead Us? Considering educational, policy, and community implications. *Counterpoints, 445*, 183–185. http://www.jstor.org/stable/42982039

Dei, G. J. S. (2017). Foreword. In: A. Abdulle & A. N. Obeyesekere (Eds.), *New framings on anti-racism and resistance: Volume 1 – Anti-racism and transgressive pedagogies* (pp. ix-xii). Sense Publishers. https://10.1007/978-94-6300-950-8

Dei, G. J. S., Holmes, L., Mazzuca, J., McIsaac, E., & Campbell, R. (1995). *Drop out or push out? The dynamics of Black students' disengagement from school*. Ontario Institute for Studies in Education. https://ia600100.us.archive.org/30/items/dropoutorpushout00deig/dropoutorpushout00deig.pdf.

Dei, G. J. S., James, I. M., Karumanchery, L. L., James-Wilson, S., & Zine, J. (2000). *Removing the margins: The challenges and possibilities of inclusive schooling*. Canadian Scholars' Press Inc.

Dei, G. J. S., & McDermott, M. (Ed). (2019). *Centering African proverbs, indigenous folktales and cultural stories in curriculum: Units and lesson plans for inclusive education*. Canadian Scholars.

Dixson, A. D., & Rousseau, C. K. (2014). And we are still not saved: Critical race theory in education ten years later. *Critical race theory in education* (pp. 45–68). Routledge. https://doi.org/10.1080/1361332052000340971

Donnor, J. K., & Ladson-Billings, G. (2018). Critical race theory and the postracial imaginary. In N. K. Denzin & Y. S. Lincoln, *Handbook of Qualitative Research* (5th ed., pp. 195–213). SAGE Publications.

Dua, E. (2007). Exclusion through inclusion: Female Asian migration in the making of Canada as a White settler nation. *Gender, Place & Culture, 14*(4), 445–466. https://doi.org/10.1080/09663690701439751

Freire, P., & Macedo, D. (2018). *Pedagogy of the oppressed* (4th ed.). Bloomsbury Academic.

Fylkesnes, S. (2019). Patterns of racialised discourses in Norwegian teacher education policy: Whiteness as a pedagogy of amnesia in the national curriculum, *Journal of Education Policy, 34*(3), 394–422, DOI: 10.1080/02680939.2018.1482503

Gay, G. (2000). *Culturally responsive teaching: Theory, research and practice*. Teachers College Press.

Gaztambide-Fenández, R. A. (2012). Decolonization and the pedagogy of solidarity. *Decolonization: Indigeneity, Education & Society, 1*(1), 41–67.
Gillborn, D. (2006). Critical Race Theory and education: Racism and anti-racism in educational theory and praxis. *Discourse: Studies in the Cultural Politics of Education, 27*(1), 11–32. https://doi.org/10.1080/01596300500510229.
hooks, b. (1994). *Teaching to transgress: Education as the practice of freedom*. Routledge.
hooks, b. (2003). *Teaching community: A pedagogy of hope*. Routledge.
hooks, b. (2014). *Talking back: Thinking feminist, thinking Black*. Routledge.
hooks, b. (2015). *Feminist theory from margin to center*. Routledge.
James, C. E., & Turner, T. (2017). *Towards race equity in education: The schooling of Black students in the Greater Toronto Area: April 2017*. York University. https://edu.yorku.ca/files/2017/04/Towards-Race-Equity-in-Education-April-2017.pdf.
Jones, L.V., and Guy-Sheftall, B. (2015). Conquering the Black girl blues. *Social Work Volume* 60, (4), 343–350. https://doi.org/10.1093/sw/swv032.
Khalifa, M., Gooden, M., & Davis, J. (2016). Culturally responsive school leadership: A synthesis of the literature. *Review of Educational Research, 86*(4), 1272–1311. https://doi.org/10.3102/0034654316630383.
Ladson-Billings, G. (1995a). But that's just good teaching! The case for culturally relevant pedagogy. *Theory Into Practice, 34*(3), 159–165. https://doi.org/10.1080/00405849509543675.
Ladson-Billings, G. (1995b). Toward a theory of culturally relevant pedagogy. *American Education Research Journal, 32*(3), 465–491. https://doi.org/10.3102/00028312032003465.
Ladson-Billings, G. (1998). Critical race theory and what's it doing in a nice field like education? *International Journal for Qualitative Studies in Education, 11*(1), 7–24.
Lawrence, B. & Dua, E. (2005). Decolonizing antiracism. *Social Justice, 32*(4 (102)), 120–143. https://www.jstor.org/stable/29768340.
Liu, H. (2020). *Redeeming leadership: An anti-racist feminist intervention*. Bristol University Press.
Lopez, A. E. (2016). *Culturally responsive and socially just leadership in diverse contexts. From theory to action*. Springer. https://doi.org/10.1057/978-1-137-53339-5.
Lopez, A.E. (2019). Anti-Black racism in education: A school leader's journey of resistance and hope. In K. Arar & K. Beycioglu (Eds.), *Handbook on promoting social justice in education*, 1935–1950. https://doi.org/10.1007/978-3-030-14625-2_37.
Lopez, A. E. (2020). *Decolonizing educational leadership: Exploring alternative approaches to leading schools*. Springer. https://doi.org/10.1007/978-3-030-62380-7.
McKittrick, K. (2006). *Demonic grounds: Black women and the cartographies of struggle*. University of Minnesota Press. http://www.jstor.org/stable/10.5749/j.ctttv7n.
McMahon, B. (2007). Educational administrators' conceptions of whiteness, anti-racism and social justice. *Journal of Educational Administration, 45*(6), 684–696. https://doi.org/10.1108/09578230710829874.

McMahon, B., & Portelli, J. (2004). Engagement for what? Beyond popular discourses of student engagement. *Leadership and Policy in Schools*, (3), 59–76. DOI:10.1076/lpos.3.1.59.27841

Miki, R. (2000). Altered states: Global currents, the spectral nation, and the production of "Asian Canadian". *Journal of Canadian Studies, 35*(3), 43–72. https://doi.org/10.3138/jcs.35.3.43.

Mohanty, C. T. (2003). *Feminism without borders*. Duke University Press.

Narayan, J. (2017). The wages of whiteness in the absence of wages: racial capitalism, reactionary intercommunalism and the rise of Trumpism, *Third World Quarterly, 38*(11), 2482–2500. https://doi.org/10.1080/01436597.2017.1368012.

Omi, M., & Winant, H. (1994). *Racial formation in the United States: from the 1960s to the 1990s* (2nd ed.). Routledge, 53–76.

Ong, A. (1999). *Flexible citizenship: The cultural logics of transnationality*. Duke University Press.

Palfrey, J. G. (2017). *Safe spaces, brave spaces: Diversity and free expression in education.* MIT Press. https://10.2307/j.ctt1vz4994.

Pon, G. (2000). Importing the Asian model minority discourse into Canada: Implications for social work and education. *Canadian Social Work Review / Revue Canadienne De Service Social*, 17(2), 277–291. http://www.jstor.org/stable/41669710.

Rajchert, J. (2015) Emotional, cognitive and self-enhancement processes in aggressive behavior after interpersonal rejection and exclusion. *Eur J Psychol. 11*(4), 707–721. doi:10.5964/ejop.v11i4.934

Rojas, C. (2016). Contesting the colonial logics of the international: Toward a relational politics for the pluriverse, *International Political Sociology*, 10(4), 369–382. https://doi.org/10.1093/ips/olw020.

Razack, S. (2002). *Race, space, and the law: Unmapping a white settler society*. Between the Lines.

Smith, L. T. (2012). *Decolonizing methodologies: Research and Indigenous peoples*. Zed Books.

Smith, L.T., Tuck, E. & Yang, K.W. (2019). *Indigenous and decolonizing studies in education: Mapping the long view*. Routledge.

Statistics Canada. (2019). *Canada's Population* (July 1, 2019) [Data set]. https://www150.statcan.gc.ca/n1/pub/11-627-m/11-627-m2019061-eng.htm.

Suárez, M. I. C. (2002). Hyphens, Hybridities and Mixed-Race Identities: Gendered Readings in Contemporary Canadian Women's Texts. *Caught between Cultures: Women, Writing & Subjectivities*, 15–33.

Swartz, E. (1992). Emancipatory narratives: Rewriting the master script in the school curriculum. *The Journal of Negro Education, 61*(3), 341–355. doi:10.2307/2295252.

Thobani, S. (2007). Nationals, citizens, and others. In *Exalted subjects: Studies in the making of race and nation in Canada* (pp. 67–102). University of Toronto Press. http://www.jstor.org/stable/10.3138/9781442685666.6.

Tuck, E. & Gaztambide-Fenández, R. (2013). Curriculum, replacement, and settler futurity. *Journal of Curriculum Theorizing, 29*(1), 72–89. https://journal.jctonline.org/index.php/jct/article/viewFile/411/pdf.

Tuck, E., & Yang, K. W. (2012). Decolonization is not a metaphor. *Decolonization: Indigeneity, Education & Society 1*(1), 1–40. https://uwaterloo.ca/faculty-association/sites/ca.faculty-association/files/uploads/files/decolonization_is_not_a_metaphor_a.pdf.

Tuters, S., & Portelli, J. (2017). Ontario school principals and diversity: Are they prepared to lead for equity?. *International Journal of Educational Management, 31*(5), 598–611. https://doi.org/10.1108/IJEM-10-2016-0228.

Wane, N. (2020, February 19). *OISE's Black Faculty in conversations with our communities about our collective futures* [Panel conversation Day 1]. Social Justice Education Department Conference, OISE, University of Toronto, Toronto, ON, Canada. https://www.youtube.com/watch?v=5e9E2PQfGCo.

CHAPTER 18

# Filipina Activism from a Transnational Theoretical Framework

*Rose Ann Torres*

## 1    Introduction

There are different meanings associated with activism. One of them is the engagement of issues that focus on a global level (Healy, 2000; Lundy, 2004; Mullaly, 2002; Riaño-Alcalá & Lacroix, 2008). This form of activism addresses how "globalization changes the structural divisions in society (for example, who is poor, who is marginalized, who has power) and how it shapes human needs, as well as how it affects the provision of welfare and services" (Ross 2017, p. 130). Such global activism also looks at the different issues that members of the community face from broader perspectives. Jackson and Thomas (2017) clearly illustrate an example of a structural issue that immigrants deal with in Canada:

> Racist discourses and ideologies continue to play a central role in the construction of Canada's migrant labour policies, with migrant workers constructed by policy-makers as "problems" for Canadian society. For example, in the late 19th and early 20th centuries, male Asian workers who immigrated to Canada were employed in a range of low-wage, labour intensive occupations, but were denied access to permanent residency and citizenship. (p. 131)

This issue stems from the labour policy created to discriminate against foreign workers in Canada. Structural-level activism works with international alliances and engagement. The advocacy work targets systemic matters. For example, White supremacy is not a problem that can be resolved solely an individual; there is a need for collective action to address this problem. Structural-level activism calls for international commitment in finding a solution for an issue that is affecting not only an individual but also others who are from different countries. However, Ross (2017) points out a limitation to structural-level activism and reiterates that "it is integral for us to consistently connect with the individual people with whom we work because these connections can serve as a significant motivator sustaining our macro-level social justice activism" (p. 313). I agree with Ross and underscore the importance of connecting structural level-activism to a direct service level of activism.

Direct service activism addresses issues at the individual level. Aronson notes that "workers are engaged at crucial intersections between people and the various faces of the state, between institutions and community, between medical and social, market and government, public, and private spheres" (as cited in Ross, 2017, p. 309). In other words, the service is directed at the individual. The focus of my chapter is my mother's direct service level of activism. She focused her service on the individual who needed an assistant. Though it is a direct service level of activism, this does not mean that it is not connected to the systemic issues that we face in the Philippines, a colonized country. The legacy of colonization is embedded in every aspect of our community. It is embedded in laws, regulations, administration, and in every practice that we have. Colonization is an ongoing process in the Philippines and this time, colonization has transformed into different faces. For example, in the Philippines' educational system, English has been a mandatory medium of instruction, except when the course is Filipino. These are just some examples of ongoing colonization in the Philippines. This chapter then does not only show cases of activism pertaining to my mother but also presents activism as a form of resistance against colonization.

Antrobus (2004) states that

> the stories of local struggles ... provide the kind of inspiration needed at a time when so many of our gains are jeopardized by the spread of neoliberal globalization and religious fundamentalisms; solidarity among women challenged by resurgent racism; and our very lives endangered by militaristic responses to the "war on terrorism" and the AIDS pandemic. (p. 9)

My mother's story is about fighting for the rights of others, a local struggle and a direct service level of activism that needs to be told. Her life as a woman was full of joy, challenges, and meaningful relationships. Writing about her life is challenging only because her life was composed of many intricacies that made her life meaningful. My mother was born in a village in the Philippines. She was a very wise woman (see Torres, 2011). She lived a life for others. Her official name is Norma Llaneza Torres but she was known as Noring. She was a very loving mother, wife, sister, daughter, and a friend to everybody. She was very patient, generous, kind, and a fighter for social justice (Torres, 2011). And most of all, she was a woman who stood for the rights of others. She went with the

Lord in 2017. She was a Christian who loved the Lord Jesus Christ. She believed that her absence in this world is the beginning of her eternal life with our Lord.

Her activism is about fighting for others. For her, others were her family, neighbors, friends, the weak, the orphans, the widows, and people she did not know. She believed that if others are not well, she also is not well. Others for her are as important as her life and her family. Levinas's (1987) notion of the other states that:

> The Other as Other is not only an alter ego: the Other is what I myself is not. The Other is this, not because of the Other's character, or physiognomy, or psychology, but because of the Other's very alterity. The Other is, for example, the weak, the poor, "the widow and the orphan," whereas I am the rich and the powerful. (p. 49)

My mother's motivating force in helping others was to serve God. To serve God for her was to serve others. She believed that to love God is to love others—especially those who are in need. Levinas (1969) explains this form of service as follows:

> The true life is absent. But we are in the world. Metaphysics arises and maintained in this alibi. It is turned toward the "elsewhere" and the "otherwise" and the "other." For in the most general form it has assumed in the history of thought it appears as a movement going forth from a world familiar to us, whatever be yet unknown lands that bound it or that it hides from view, from an "at home" ["chez soi"] which we inhabit, toward an alien outside-of-oneself [hors-de-soi], toward a yonder. The term of this movement, the elsewhere or the other, is called other in an eminent sense. ... The other metaphysically desired is not "other" like the bread I eat. ... The metaphysical desire tends toward something else entirely. (p. 33)

My mother used "love" as her guiding principles to serve others as she lived her life in this world. My mother lived in the Philippines her entire life. My father, Abraham Torres loved her so much until my father went with the Lord in 2002. They loved each other so much that when my father was gone, it was so difficult for my mother to live in the absence of my father. They were together for 55 years. My brothers, Danilo and Ferdinand, and my sister Emely, and I are very fortunate to have had them as parents. They dedicated their lives for us and others. My mother devoted her life to her family. My family used to own land in the middle of the Sierra Madre mountain range in the Philippines, where we had a house growing up as siblings. I was born during the Marcos regime (Torres, 2012). During this time, it was very difficult for my parents to continue to live in this place because of the military presence. It became a terrifying scene to be surrounded by a military group. The very daunting moment at the time was the prospect of a clash between the military and the Communist Party of the Philippines. My parents became so unsettled in our former home to the point of not being able to sleep in our house. We had to go to our friends' house to spend the night because it was close to other people's houses. Our house was located on top of a hill, far from other homes. Our location was so unique because we were close to the river, farms, and the forest. The farm was full of animals, fruit trees, and vegetables. My mother and father did not lose joy and hope at that time; instead, they continued to be the best parents we ever had, even in the midst of difficulties.

My mother continued her dedication to serve her community. Every time they harvested rice, she made a point of keeping enough so that when others needed some, they could always ask her. This is one of the things that my mother did that I will never forget, because in neo-colonial times it is hard to serve others who do not regard you as a human being due to your race, class, gender, ethnicity, sexuality, and other forms of differences. However, my mother was very focused on helping others no matter who they were. I agree with Shiva's (2004) assertion that "women are the leading experts in, and custodians of, biodiversity. They have been society's seed keepers, food processors and healers" (p. 25). My mother carried these characteristics of a woman that Shiva talks about. My mother was not only a friend to everybody but also one of society's seed keepers, food processors, and a healer (Torres, 2011). In this chapter, a transnational framework guides me as I theorize my mother's activism and how I use her activism as my inspiration to achieve my dreams in serving others.

## 2   Transnational Framework

I am applying this framework in this chapter because it theorizes my relationship with my mother and her influence in my life. My mother resided in the Philippines and considered herself a woman who never was influenced by colonization (Torres, 2011). Though she experienced the impact of colonization in her life, she chose to stay true to her Indigenous roots. The Philippines was colonized by Spaniards for 500 years (Torres, 2012) and then experienced ongoing colonization by Americans, and because of these outside forces my mother and other women suffered. My mother was not able to go to school and faced challenges as a woman living under the regimes of patriarchy. At an early age she had to work on the farm. This experience may seem hard for others, but for her this was the time she developed resiliency, agency, and power. She used this time not only to help her family but also to help others. This experience of my mother has helped me to live a life in Canada. Transnational feminism is a framework that acknowledges "the condition of cultural interconnectedness and mobility across space" (Ong 1999, p. 4). It also "interrogates the 'in-between' space of the local and the global as a site of analysis and centres women within this analysis" (Mayuzumi, 2008, p. 169). My experience and her experience are interconnected in so many ways. We both experience(d) the patriarchal systems of governance. While there have been many changes in terms of women's conditions, there still are many things that need to be addressed. In Canada, racialized women have been experiencing discrimination in the workplace (Jackson & Thomas, 2017). In the Philippines, women also experience discrimination. Although she spent all her time in the Philippines, and I now live in Canada—we lived in different spaces, time, politics, and culture—we share the same beliefs of helping and serving others. We both have the desire to transform the world that we live, and this make our experiences interconnected.

My connection with my mother helps me realize that my experience in the West is not an isolated incident but is also connected to both historical and ongoing colonization. My experience is not something that I can address alone; I need my mother and the whole community to help me in my struggles. As I focus on my struggles, I also cannot forget that others are also facing the same struggles, though perhaps to a different degree. One example of this struggle is the difficulty of finding a job when your education is from other countries (Jackson & Thomas, 2017). According to Jackson and Thomas (2017), racialized women have a high rate of unemployment in Canada. One of the reasons for this is because they do not possess the Canadian experience and education. Canadian experience is one of the major requirements of an employer in addition to having a Canadian certificate. A transnational framework

> problematizes the ideology of universality or hierarchy in nations, knowledges, and people, and critiques superficial understandings of "differences" and "diversity." It ruptures the reductionist nature of West-centric viewpoints, which fail to acknowledge the heterogenous and plural formations of economies, cultures, and populations such as women of colour, the poor, and immigrants.
> MAYUZUMI, 2008, p. 169

These experiences of racialized women in Canada and the Philippines show how different spaces are interconnected in terms of their struggles. It shows how a hierarchy of nations exists based on how Canada treats Filipino women (Torres & Nyaga, 2017) in terms of their race, class, and gender. It also shows how the Canadian labour system serves as a tool to marginalize these women. For example, Filipino women who came to Canada as caregivers must spend 2 years in their employer's home (Torres & Nyaga, 2017). The question is, how do we know that these women were able to work only eight hours per day while staying in their employer's home continuously? How can we protect these women's rights when the governments that are supposed to protect them are the ones that impose this legislation? What kind of diversity does Canada practice when racialized people experience discrimination and work in unhealthy workplaces?

A transnational framework recognizes the in-between and beyond involvement, knowledge, skills, practices, understanding, and familiarity of women who now live in other countries. Living in other countries does not necessarily mean that they forget their original countries. They live in both countries. They live physically in their present country, while living in spirit in their original country. The question is: How do you live in a country in spirit? It means the relationships that they had in their original country remain. For example, their relationship with their parents continues to exist in the way they assist them with their financial needs or through their continued communication. This relationship helps them to face their struggles in their current country. The experiences that they go through are recognized through the use of a transnational framework. My relationship with my mother has helped me make sense of the life that I live in Canada.

## 3   Well-Being of the Family

My mother knew that family is one of the most important units in society. This teaching from the Book of Proverbs exemplifies who my mother was. She was a woman of wisdom. She is a pure love. She never relied on her own knowledge and instead she allowed God to direct her path. She did not belong to any congregation; instead, she developed her personal relationship with the Lord. She possessed a spirituality that was rooted to God (Torres, 2010; 2011). Her faith made her achieve her dreams—a dream to take care of the family and others, to fight for women's rights, and to serve her community. She did not have a university degree, yet she was able to accomplish her dreams. She took full responsibility for taking care of the needs of our family. She demonstrated the principle of working together. She demonstrated how to work together with the family and the community members. And that working together with my father was necessary for the family to stand. She knew that women's place is in the struggle based on the ongoing colonial processes and how society internalizes coloniality. My father too believed in equity and equality of men and women, so the idea of working together for the family and society was not a struggle for my mother. Her love of her family is related to Butler's (2004) description in terms of mourning:

> One mourns when one accepts that by the loss one undergoes one will be changed, possibly for ever. Perhaps mourning has to do with agreeing to undergo a transformation (perhaps one should say submitting to a transformation) the full result of which one cannot know in advance. (p. 21)

For my mother, loving and caring for her family was about losing herself; however, while she lost herself, she transformed into a loving and caring human being. From a colonial perspective, this kind of service means oppression but to my mother it meant joy and caring for others. While she loved the others, she saw herself also in that love.

## 4     Community Responsibility

My mother had to work hard for her entire life in helping, assisting, and contributing to the community. However, she always reminded us that she always did alongside other members of the community. She knew that being a member of a community meant working together. I remember seeing her going to the neighbor when there was someone who was so sick. She went to the house to either bring food or give advice or ask them what she could do to help them. I also remember when other members of the community came to our home and asked her if she could give them some rice or other kinds of food. I saw her giving freely to them. I was young at that time, so I asked her why she kept giving people our food. And she said, "We need to help others especially when they need it. … Responsibility is not only to provide for the family, but also, to share what we have with others … and do not worry … because we have more than enough to sustain us and others." My mother's words puzzled me. I did not understand. Butler (2020) states that "Once we see that certain selves are considered worth defending while others are not, is there not a problem of inequality that follows from the justification of violence in the service of self-defence?" (p. x). My mother did not choose which one to defend or to serve;

instead, she chose to help everybody. She knew that everyone is important, and that if she serves one and not the other then it will only create inequality. What is the point of serving some and not everybody? For her, this was not the right thing to do. She wanted to share whatever she had with the whole community.

One of the principles underpinning my mother's service to the community is about responding to the needs of others. For her, the only way to live was to be with the community and to work with the community. For her, community responsibility was about giving back and, while you are giving back, it is necessary to work with the community. According to Wehbi (2011),

> when working with community members, we have the responsibility of not taking their role. Concretely, this means understanding and believing that we are working alongside (or with) communities, not for them. ... At times, the principle of "not taking their role" is easier said than done. ... First, community trust will not be so easily gained, thereby impeding our work. Second, if we leave when our particular job or task is done, the community loses an important resource; in other words, "doing for" the community does not reinforce and strengthen its own existing resources. Third, the sense of community ownership of a particular job or initiative is not fostered if we choose to work for a community and not alongside or in solidarity with its members. Finally, our own sense of ourselves as co activist contributing to an anti-oppressive vision of society is not reinforced. (p. 140)

Wehbi explains well what working with the community looks like and how my mother was doing her calling in her community. It is important to remember that when we want to engage in any work in the community, we have to understand and believe that we are not working for them but rather with them. The moment we think that when we go to the community, we are there to serve them and it has nothing to do with us, then this kind of mentality will invalidate the principle of community responsibility. It strips their sense of power and belonging. Who are we to imagine that we can only do the work on our own? Who are we to say that they need our help, when they are not even asking us to help them? Who are we to say that we are more powerful than them? What kind of power do we have that we think we can use in the community? These are some critical questions that we need to ask ourselves before we embark on the idea of working in the community. My mother always reminded me that while we belong to our community, it does not mean that we are the only important entity. She reiterated that one of the ways to live in a peaceful community is to recognize that everyone is important—and that everyone has the power to contribute to the growth and development of the community as a whole.

One example of an issue that she advocated was the violence against women. For example, every time she would hear about a woman being mistreated, she would go and talk directly to the abuser, not to insult but to educate about respect and love for one another. Violence against women is predominant in our society today and the Philippines is no exception to this phenomenon. According to Crow and Gotell (2009), "violence against women is another issue that profoundly affects women's health, and also affects and is affected by their socio-economic status" (p. 79). Violence against women affects every aspects of life. It affects the physical, mental, psychological, and spiritual well-being of a person. It diminishes the capacity of the individual to participate in the economic, political, social, and cultural facets of life. This will lead to more complicated conditions, and these conditions will disempower the individual and the community as a whole. As Butler (2004) reminds us,

> Violence is surely a touch of the worst order, a way a primary human vulnerability to other humans is exposed in its most terrifying way, a way in which we are given over, without control, to the will of another, a way in which life itself can be expunged by the willful action of another. To the extent that we commit violence, we are acting on another, putting the other at risk, causing the other damage, threatening to expunge the other. In a way, we all live with this particular vulnerability, a vulnerability to the other that is part of bodily life, a vulnerability to a sudden address from elsewhere that we cannot pre-empt. (pp. 28–29)

Butler explains well the results of violence to the victim and the person who commits the act. The other who is a victim of violence suffers immeasurably. One of the reasons why violence exists is because our society is deeply structured by gender, sexuality, race, and class.

My mother's principles in terms of community responsibility have been ingrained in me—that whoever I am today, community responsibility also becomes the centre of my research and teaching. Thus, in my research, I focus on community health and wellness, community development and engagement, economic security, social wellness, and women and gender issues.

## 5 Conclusion

This chapter showcases my mother's direct service level of activism and how it helps me in my own activism today. Activism is about engagement with issues that we face in the community and in the whole society. It is also about our involvement in our community in terms of the social, political, economic, and spiritual well-being of an individual. I also believe that our struggles at the individual level connect to other struggles. To me, structural- and direct service-levels of activism cannot be separated; these activisms are interconnected. My mother's direct service level of activism cannot be separated to the broader perspective of activism because we are a product of our society. As individuals, our experience is connected to the whole society. This chapter highlights my mother's activism and I believe that because of her examples, I was and am able to engage in different issues that we face. To my mother-Norma Torres and father-Abraham Torres, a*ya-ayaten kayo unay unay nanang ko ken tatang ko!*

### References

Antrobus, P. (2004). Preface. In L. Ricciutelli, A. Miles, & M. H. McFadden (Eds.), *Feminist politics, activism and vision: Local and global challenges*. New York: Zed Books.

Butler, J. (2020). The Force of Non-Violence: An Ethico-Political Bind. London. New York: Verso.

Butler, J. (2004). *Precarious life: The powers of mourning and violence*. Verso.

Crow, B. A., & Gotell, L. (2009). *Open boundaries: A Canadian women's studies reader*. Pearson Prentice Hall.

Healy, K. (2000). *Social work practices: Contemporary perspectives on change*. Sage.

Jackson, A., & Thomas, M. P. (2017). *Work and labour in Canada: Critical issues* (3rd ed.). Canadian Scholars.

Levinas, E. (1969). *Totality and infinity: An essay on exteriority* (A. Lingis, Trans.). Duquesne University Press.

Levinas, E. (1987). *Time and the other and additional essays* (R. A. Cohen, Ed. & Trans.). Duquesne University Press.

Lundy, C. (2004). *Social work and social justice: A structural approach to practice*. Broadview Press.

Mayuzumi, K. (2008). "In-between" Asia and the West: Asian women faculty in the transnational context. *Race Ethnicity and Education, 11*(2), 167–182. https://doi.org/10.1080/13613320802110274

Mullaly, R. (2002). *Challenging oppression: A critical social work approach*. Oxford University Press.

Ong, A. (1999). *Flexible citizenship: The cultural logics of transnationality*. Duke University Press.

Riaño-Alcalá, P., & Lacroix, M. (2008). Introduction: Social work in an interconnected world. *Canadian Social Work Review, 25*(2), 113–116.

Ross, M. (2017). Social work activism within neoliberalism: A big tent approach. In D. Baines (Ed.), *Doing anti-oppressive practice: Social justice social work* (3rd ed., pp. 304–321). Fernwood: Halifax.

Shiva, V. (2004). The custodians. In L. Ricciutelli, A. Miles, & M. H. McFadden (Eds.), *Feminist politics, activism and vision: Local and global challenges*. New York: Zed Books.

Torres, R. (2010). Fanon's pedagogical implications for women's studies in the Philippines. In G. J. S. Dei (Ed.), *Fanon and the counterinsurgency of education* (pp. 133–155). Sense.

Torres, R. (2011). Indigenous spirituality, activism and feminism in the life of my mother. *Canadian Woman Studies, 29*(1–2), 135–140.

Torres, R. (2012). Aeta Women Healers in the Philippines: Lessons and Implications. Toronto: University of Toronto (Unpublished Dissertation).

Torres, R., & Nyaga, D. (2017). Gendered citizenship: A case study of paid Filipino male live-in caregivers in Toronto. *International Journal of Asia Pacific Studies, 13*(1), 51–71. http://dx.doi.org/10.21315/ijaps2017.13.1.3

Wehbi, S. (2011). Anti-oppression community organizing: Lessons from disability rights activism. In D. Baines (Ed.), *Doing anti-oppressive practice: Social justice social work* (2nd ed., pp. 132–145). Fernwood: Halifax.

CHAPTER 19

# Framework for Developing Resilience among Filipino-Canadian Youth during the Covid-19 Pandemic

*Valerie G. Damasco and Rose Ann Torres*

## 1 Introduction

We were invited to deliver a webinar series for developing resilience among Filipino-Canadian youth during the Covid-19 pandemic. This chapter then, showcase what we presented in the webinars. We hope that this chapter will be of used to others who also want to do the same talk/training/workshops on developing resilience. The trainings were delivered during the pandemic, so we used webinars. In this chapter, we include the objectives of the webinars, the anticipated outcomes, methodology and praxis, and delivery method.

## 2 Objectives

Towards the aims of excellence in evaluation and supporting Philippine Centre Canada (PCC) leadership and membership to work with Filipino-Canadian youth, the objectives of the CARE webinar trainings are for participants to: (1) Develop personal competencies to minimize the impacts of the COVID-19 pandemic on their physical, psychological, and emotional wellbeing. (2) Develop self-awareness, positive thinking and resilience, life skills, and in-person entrepreneurship training. (3) Develop individual and community capacity to become resilient for future unexpected events. (4) Develop their capacities to embody equitable, inclusive, and collaborative attitudes and leadership. (5) Develop their capacities to work ethically, effectively, and sensitively in diverse communities. (6) Engage with civility and bystander intervention as a practice in the emphasis of the *Bayanihan* principle. (7) Gain resources that support evaluation theory and practice, which considers their needs and promotes their physical, psychological, and emotional wellbeing. (8) Gain resources that support evaluation theory and practice, which considers the needs and promotes the physical, psychological, and emotional wellbeing of others, and those that have been traditionally underrepresented. And (9), Gain theoretical and practical resources that encourage equity, diversity, and inclusion within communities and organizations.

There is a lack of information regarding the stresses and challenges that Filipino-Canadian youth face during the COVID-19 pandemic. The five-day CARE (Caring for All to be Resilient and Effective) webinar series aims to increase the capacities of Filipino-Canadian youth to adapt to individual and societal changes and risks associated with the COVID-19 pandemic. Moreover, it seeks to foster resilience among the diverse sub-groups of Filipino-Canadian youth in preparation for future unexpected events. The outcomes from the webinar trainings will serve as a preliminary measure to foster encouragement and support from communities and various levels of government in supporting the needs of Filipino-Canadian youth as they acclimate to the uncertainties of the COVID-19 pandemic.

## 3    Anticipated Outcomes

The anticipated outcomes from the proposed program: (1) *Immediate impact for Filipino-Canadian youth:* Development of culturally relevant curriculum and learning process that could be incorporated in intervention projects, and in the design and evaluation of programs for Filipino-Canadian youth. And (2), *Long-term impact for Filipino-Canadian youth:* Outcomes from the webinar trainings will serve as a preliminary measure to foster encouragement and support from communities and various levels of government in fostering the needs of Filipino-Canadian youth as they acclimate to the uncertainties of the COVID-19 pandemic and beyond.

## 4    Methodology and Praxis

During the COVID-19 pandemic, resilience is a fundamental value that Filipino-Canadian youth need to embrace. The youth serve an essential role in planning and executing actions to adapt to individual and societal changes and risks associated with the COVID-19 pandemic. Through collaboration with the youth, we seek to develop sustainable solutions for the issues they may be dealing with and to encourage them to nurture leadership skills in nation-building. The model we emphasize draws upon individual (e.g., individual characteristics and traits) and ecological (e.g., human activities and surroundings) characteristics as critical in building resilience.

FIGURE 19.1 Methodology and praxis approach for developing resilience among Filipino-Canadian youth
SOURCE: DAMASCO & TORRES, 2020

Our role as lead speakers is to capitalize on the assets of youth, to assist them recognize their strengths, and provide them guidance and resources to attain their action and development plans. We motivate participants to think critically and foster a decolonial approach to understanding how changes in society, policies, and systems influences their individual circumstances. Through an approach that fosters equity, diversity, and inclusion, we assist participants develop appropriate activities and programs that involve collaboration with communities. Harnessing this inclusivity leads to innovation and creativity within communities. Importantly, the training is instrumental in providing avenues for emerging youth leaders to implement their proposed program and activities, and to continue to assist generations of youth adapt to future unexpected events (figure 19.1).

## 5 Delivery Method

### 5.1 Webinar 1: Setting the Foundations for Creating a Learning Process for Resilience

This introductory webinar sets the framework for nurturing a learning process for resilience. We will introduce our *Methodology and Praxis Approach for Developing Resilience among Filipino-Canadian Youth* (Damasco & Torres,

2020), and discuss with participants key concepts within the designed framework. The goal is to frame the conversation and build a safe learning environment for the sharing of experiences, observations, ideas, and knowledge exchange. It is also crucial to foster an understanding of how the identities of each member in the online seminar is in relation to axes of difference, power, and privilege. We will engage with concepts related to equity, diversity, inclusion for cultural competence/cultural humility/cultural sensitivity and belonging. During this introductory webinar, we will administer the pre-test questionnaire

### 5.2 Webinar 2: Caring for Oneself

The unprecedented growth of Filipino-Canadian youth in Canada offers an imperative to assist them recognize how they are coping and responding to the challenges of the COVID-19 pandemic. To assist them develop self-awareness of their physical and mental health and how they are coping and responding to stress, it is necessary to examine the relationship between resilience, (acculturative) stress, and the influence of cultural family beliefs or norms in the disclosure of, for example, mental health issues.

Utlizing *Katatagan,* a group-based resilience program that is designed to improve the coping skills of Filipinos (see Hechanova et al., 2016), we will explore, through the use of self-reflection activities, the vulnerabilities and protective factors that Filipino-Canadian youth may exude. Our goal is to develop resources and interventions that ameliorate (acculturative) stress and promote disclosure and help seeking of mental health support. Harnessing Luthar and Cicchetti's (2000) resilience framework, we propose interventions that aim to improve self-efficacy, adaptive coping skills, and wellbeing. An initial application of *Katatagan* will be performed. We expect improvements in the ways in which Filipino-Canadian youth think about adaptive coping behaviours for the purpose of decreasing stress, anxiety, and depressive symptoms.

It is crucial to note that Filipino-Canadian youth who recently arrived in Canada may have a unique acculturation process as a result of the influence of Philippine colonial history, which makes them different from other Asian Canadians. Thus, it is vital to develop nuanced cultural competence skills to promote resilient coping against the stresses associated with acculturation as well as the unprecedented impact brought upon by the COVID-19 pandemic. Exploring situations through which positive physical and psychological outcomes can be fostered among these youth is vital. We will explore the relationship among desirable psychosocial outcomes, including hope, happiness, personal wellbeing, and resilience and to think about creative ways in achieving them.

### 5.3 Webinar 3: Caring for Others

It is important to investigate the individual, family, and community-level factors that promote resilience among Filipino-Canadian youth. It is crucial to note the roles of family-oriented values, community cohesion, and religiosity and spirituality play in buffering the effects of COVID-19 related risks on Filipino-Canadian youth. We advocate greater involvement by communities to inquire about the conditions of others and to be innovative and compassionate in response to the crisis.

An important feature of resilience is that it is a process of overcoming negative effects of risk exposure rather than a static individual trait. Therefore, it is crucial to determine the protective factors that predisposes some people to succeed despite experiencing risk of adversity. Protective factors are resources that safeguard against the negative effects of adverse conditions on an individual's functioning, such as family-level factors including support, cohesion, and quality of communication among members Furthermore, they could be resources outside the family, such as friends, mentors, and other supportive relationships in neighbourhoods and communities. Finally, they may be individual-level factors, such as resourcefulness, intelligence, optimism, self-regulation, and spirituality. Resilience is not just an individual achievement, but a process that is achieved through protective factors that are derived from people and resources in the individual's context.

Developing community knowledge on how to cope with the stresses associated with the COVID-19 pandemic alleviates individual pressure and aims to foster relief and companionship. Community intervention can help manage the growing number of health problems, particularly among youth at home. Other mental health problems arise from, for example, exposure to social media, change in lifestyle, and lack of support and understanding from family.

Resilience speaks to the power of community, rather than society. During this time, youth may also be predisposed to tackle challenges of the COVID-19 crisis together through collective action. Infusing *Bayanihan*, or the collective act of providing unsolicited assistance by members of a community to accomplish a difficult task for the common good, can help each other in creative ways to cope with the current situation. It is also important to check on the mental health and wellbeing of others, such as students and graduates, young workers and entrepreneurs, and those who were laid off. During these difficult times, we need to ensure that they are not only physically healthy and safe, but also mentally and psycho-socially resilient.

## 5.4 Webinar 4: Caring for the Future

It is crucial to address the issues of those who suffer from low education outcomes, high unemployment, and identity conflict issues. These factors may be impacting Filipino-Canadian youth during the COVID-19 pandemic who may lack a voice or agency to participate meaningfully in community life or in making decisions. We seek to support Filipino-Canadian youth think about education, employment, and civic engagement and to assist them on their journey towards economic empowerment.

Including youth economic empowerment in COVID-19 response operations is vital. For example, there needs to be interventions and mentorship for assisting unemployed youth, workers, and entrepreneurs, particularly those who have not benefited from government interventions. We will explore skills that are needed to assist the school-to-work transition of those who are either out of school, unemployed, and who are not receiving any training.

This is the ideal time to maximize e-learning tools and other innovative learning options, such as digital skills and media to generate creative solutions to the challenges faced by Filipino-Canadian youth as a result of the COVID-19 pandemic. Several Filipino-Canadian youths may lack the skills to participate in the labour market, which can be further exacerbated by lockdown restrictions. Therefore, there is a need to support them to establish their own ventures. Filipino-Canadian youth may venture into new opportunities that may call for entrepreneurship instead of regular work. In this webinar, we will introduce the audience to social enterprises, which are businesses driven by a public or community cause (e.g., social, cultural, economic, or environmental). Social enterprises derive most of their income from trade rather than donations or grants and use most profits to work towards their social mission. This form of entrepreneurship attempts to simultaneously tackle conflict, social divides, and economic barriers.

This approach to entrepreneurship is designed to foster civil society participation that supports new forms of work and job creation. Furthermore, it aims to promote inclusive economic development and solutions for the lack of access to employment and possible decreases in education outcomes. Our goal is to nurture active citizenship, advocacy, and enterprise development to build a network of future leaders who can use entrepreneurship to solve social problems. We encourage participants on how to work with various stakeholders, brokering relationships between the Filipino-Canadian community, governments, the business sector, and non-profit organizations.

Youth participation is an instrumental principle that can make the governance process more effective, which consequently can be responsive to the needs of other Filipino-Canadian youth. This may promote a better understanding of the issues related to social exclusion, discrimination, and inequality, and the fundamental need to address social problems. Furthermore, this approach enables youth to reclaim their identity, find a renewed sense of purpose, and promote social cohesion. Social enterprises nurture creativity, resourcefulness, and assist in building resilient and adaptable communities.

## 5.5 *Webinar 5: Reflecting on the Development of a Learning Process for Resilience*

This concluding webinar reflects upon the framework that was applied for nurturing a learning process for resilience and reviewing the objectives and the goals that were achieved during each webinar. The goal is to develop an understanding of how our identities impact our individual and collective work in fostering resilience, in the ways in which we take action and engage in bystander intervention, understanding participatory practices that support inclusive leadership, and setting individual and collective goals moving forward. During this concluding webinar, we will administer the pre-test questionnaire.

## References

Damasco, V., Torres, R. (2020). *Building Resilience among Filipino-Youth Canadian during the Pandemic*. Webinar. Ottawa: Ontario.

Hechanova, M., Waelde, L., & Ramos, P. (2016). Evaluation of a group-based resilience intervention for Typhoon Haiyan survivors. *Journal of Pacific Rim Psychology, 10*, E12. doi:10.1017/prp.2016.9.

Luthar, S., Cicchetti, D. (2000). The construct of resilience: Implications for interventions and social policies. *Development and Psychopathology, 12*(4), 857–885. doi:10.1017/S0954579400004156.

# Index

aboriginal feminism framework 54
Abrams, L.S. 213
Abu-Laban, Y. 36, 130, 211, 213
Accord on the Internationalization of Education (2014) 100, 101, 104, 105, 106
Achinstein, B. 234
Act
   Exclusion 141, 214
   Head tax (1885) 214
   Hospital Insurance and Diagnostic Services 86
   Immigration 90
   Medical Care 86
   Multiculturalism 127, 128, 129, 141, 205, 206, 207, 208, 211, 212, 214
activism
   direct service 230
   feminist 19
   global 239
   in community 245, 246, 248
   indigenous 54, 55
   social justice 221, 222
   structural-level 239
Aeta
   healers 190, 191, 200, 201
   traditions 193, 194
   healing practices 197, 198, 199
   healers and health crisis 201, 202
Aguilar, F.V. 117
Ahmed, S. 11, 13
Ahn, S. 178, 180
Ahok (Basuki Tjahaja Purnama) 135
Alam, S *author of Chapter 5*
Alfred, T. 230, 233
Ali, S.F. *author of Chapter 13*
Allman, D. 159, 160
Altbach, P. 131
ambivalence 26, 50. *See also* Bhabha, H.
Anderson, B. 25, 28
Anderson, B.R. 133
Anderson, K. 40, 85
Anggraeni, D. 131, 132, 133, 134, 135
Angus Reid Institute 208, 209
Anishinaabe 120, 222

anti-Asian racism 130, 143, 208. *See also* systemic racism
anti-racism 207, 212, 226, 227, 233
Antrobus, P. 240
Apayao 193
*aposteriori* theorization of migration 35, 36, 38 *See also* transnational migration
*apriori* theorization of migration 35, 36, 37. *See also* transnational migration
Apu Nahasapeemapetilon (Character from *the Simpsons*) 171, 172
Arab(s) 132, 146, 213
Aranas, M.Q. 35, 87
Arango, J. 34
Ashcroft, B. 212
Asian
   as speaking subject 18
   exclusion of 147
   Other 14. *See also* Other; Othering
Asian Canadians
   exclusion of 90, 141, 143
   in learning and research 12, 13
   presence of 9
   racial trauma of 144, 145
   representation of 49, 50
Asiatic Exclusion League 65
Audre, L. 115
*Ayat* 192, 193

*Badan Pusan Statistik* 130, 132
Bakan, A.B. 86, 87, 91
Bala, S. 110, 16
Bannerji, H. 126, 127, 128, 136, 210
Battiste, M. 225, 227
*Bayanihan* principle 250, 254
Beck, C. 103
Begeny, J.C 99
Beighey, C. 145, 146
Bejar, J. 36, 84
belonging 211, 212, 213, 223
Belshaw, J.D. 12, 14
Bernal, D.D. 230, 233
Bernardes, R.P. 104
Bhabha, H. 26, 27, 30, 48, 50, 51, 52
*Bhinneka Tunggal Ika* 131, 132

bias
  collective  214
  gender  67
  in immigration policy  87. *See also* Policy: Immigration
biographic situations  23
biopolitics  12
Birks, M.  34
Black Lives Matter  117, 208
Black, G.L.  104
Bolger, M.  162
Bonilla-Silva, E.  144
Borjas, G.J.  36
Borocz, J.  34
Boschma, G.  36, 84
Boyd, M.  35, 40, 42, 85, 91
Brata, I.B.  132
Brosseau, L.  125, 126, 127, 128, 129
Brown, L.S.  148, 149
Buenafe, M.C.  36, 39, 87
Building on Success  100, 101, 105, 106
Buscher, T.  154, 163, 165, 167
Bustamante, R.E.  36, 37, 39, 84, 86, 87
Butler, J.  10, 11, 13, 17, 18, 75, 76, 245, 247

Cacho, L.M.  113, 217
Cagayan province  193, 199, 200, 202
Caldoza, W.  *author of Chapter 9*
Calliste, A.  38, 86
Campbell, M.L.  40, 85
Canada National Healthcare system  86
Canadian Charter of Rights and Freedoms (1982)  205, 206, 214
Canadian Points System immigration policy  87
Cantalini-Williams, M.  102
Capitalism  64, 70, 117. *See also* racial capitalism
Caribbean nurses  39, 86, 91 *See also* Filipino nurses
Carr, E.S.  142, 149
Castles, S.  34, 42
Caygill, H.  216
Cena (indigenous healer)  197. *See also* Aeta: healers
Chan, M.  201
Chandra, E.  135
Chang, J.  145, 146

Chapman, Y.  34
Chen, A.B.  36, 39, 84
Child, P.  26, 49, 50, 51, 52
Cho, L.  215
Chui, T.  61, 210
Citizenship  12, 28, 73, 101, 106, 114, 126, 133, 136, 205, 212, 223, 233
Coleman, J.S.  35
Coloma, R.  9, 14, 190
colonial
  identity  50
  mentality  24
  pedagogy  10
colonialism  15, 24, 49, 52, 53, 54, 125, 136, 155, 190; *See also* settler colonialism
colonization  15, 53, 191, 240
color-blindedness  15, 229
Comas-Diaz, L.  145
Constantino, R.  191
Cook, T.  40
Corbett, D.  36, 86
Corbin, J.  34
Corntassel, J.  230, 233
Coulson, R.G.  36
Council of Europe  209
counter stories  215, 225
Covid 19  202, 208, 213, 250
Covid 19 and care  253, 254
Crenshaw, K.W.  119, 155, 161, 164
Critical anti-racist theory (CART)  226, 231, 233, 234
critical consciousness  232, 235
Critical Race Theory  119n, 205, 215, 221
critical reflexivity
  funk strategies of  11
  in teaching and researching  14, 18
  outhabiting in  10, 11, 12 *see also* Disidentification theory
  spirituality in  9, 10
Crosby, A.  196
Cuevas, F.P.  200
cultural capital  69, 94, 117. *See also* social capital
cultural diversity  156
culturally responsive pedagogy  225, 232
currere
  analytical step in  27
  and radical mindfulness  31

definition of  21
progressive step in  25
regressive step in  22
synthetical step in  29
Cusipag, R.J  36, 39, 87

Dacog, M.  194
Dahlhaus, C.  162
Damasco, V.  34, 35, 38;
   author of Chapter 3 and 7
   co-author of Chapter 19
Das Gupta, T.  64, 65
David, E.J.R.  24
Davis, A.  232
Dawis, A.  133, 135
Dawson, R.M.  89, 90
de Hass, H.  34
de La Cruz, J.  196
de Swaaf, A.M.  92, 93
Deaux, K.  40
decolonial future  30, 232
decolonization  10, 13, 29, 30, 54, 193, 232, 233
Dei, G.J.S.  80, 146, 190, 221, 222, 224–230, 232
Delgado  23, 206, 230
democratic racism  15
Dennis, E.  143, 144
Denzin, N.K.  226
dependency theory.  *See* transnational
   migration
Derrida, J.  40, 116
Desai, C.  30
Devoretz, D.J.  36
Dewing, M.  125, 126, 127, 128, 129
Dhalsim (video game character)  173, 174
Dhamoon, R.  130, 211, 213
*Diamond Grill* (Fred Wah)  21
DiAngelo, R.J.  205, 214
diaspora  15, 61, 62, 63, 67, 68, 72, 117
*Die Entführung aus dem Serial*  155, 158, 159, 162
Dinesh Chugtai (character from *The Silicon
   Valley*)  172
discrimination
   Black  164, 165
   gender  66, 68 69, 87, 231, 243 *See also*
      Filipino nurses; South Asian: women
      of Asian teachers of English  181
   of minorities  146, 213, 214
   racial  9, 36, 65, 145

sex  161, 165
structural  87, 92, 146, 148
disempowerment  230, 247
disidentification  12, 14. *See also* critical
   reflexivity
disposable labour  9
diversity.  *See also* multiculturalism; Third
      Space; hybridity
   definition of  156
   dimensions of  156, 157
   discourse  210
   exogenous and endogenous  127
   training  104, 105
   unity in  131, 136
Donnor, J.K.  226, 229
Driedger, L.  128
Dua, E.  228, 230, 233

Earle, S.  195
Ellerby, J.  200, 202
Emont, J.  135
emotional labor  182
empowerment levels  142, 148. *See also*
   Empowerment theory
Empowerment theory  142
endogenous research framework  80
English Language Education
   and NESTs of Asian decent  178
   EPIK program and  176, 177, 178
   JET program and  176, 177, 178
   Native English-Speaking Teachers (NESTs)
      and  176, 177, 178, 179
   native speakerism and  177, 178, 180, 181
   NEST recruitment practices and  179, 180
   NNEST activism and  182
   Non -Native English-Speaking Teachers
      (NNESTs) and  176, 177, 178, 179
   professional legitimacy and 179, 180
   racial hierarchies and  181, 182
epistemic violence  52. *See also* essentialism;
   Orientalism; violence
essentialism  52. *See also* Orientalism;
   strategic essentialism
ethnography  40, 85, 110
Eurocentrism  103, 190, 191, 198, 228, 230
Evitt, R.  145
Exchange Visitor Program (EVP)  85
expansionism  197

Fail, H. 28
Faist, T. 42
Fanon, F. 17, 25, 74, 110, 116, 191
Fawcett, J.T. 35, 42
Felix, Mr. 93, 94
feminism
   indigenous 45, 53, 54, 55. *See also* Peminism
   transnational 243, 244. *See also* indigenous: feminism; Peminism
   White 17, 75, 79
Ferguson, G.M. 145, 146, 147
Fernandez 27, 191, 233
Fierlbeck, K. 86
Filipino-Canadian youths 253
Filipino caregivers
   academics and representation of 74, 76, 77, 79
   and Peminist praxis 79
   and unmapping/denaturalizing spaces 78
   as political bodies 75
   deportability of 73, 77
   double consciousness in representation of 73, 74
   Othering of 73
   Peminist and 76
Filipino nurses
   discrimination of 87, 90
   exception for 91
   mobility of 93, 94
   (racialized) labour migration of 84, 87, 88, 89
Fordham, S. 216
Foster, P. 131
Foucault, M. 50, 77
Francisco Duque III 200
Frank, A.G. 34
Freire, P. 22, 25, 26, 232
Fylkesnes, S. 230

Garlow, G. *author of Chapter 17*
Garvey, M. 222
Gaztambide-Fernandez, R.A. 27, 221, 227, 232, 233
gender based migration 63, 64
gender polarization 54
genocide 133, 196, 230, 233
George, U. 63, 208

Ghaliya, G. 136
Gonzalez, J.L. 198
Gosine, K. 146
Gramsci, A. 216
Green, A.G. 86
Green, D.A. 86
Green, J. 55
Griffiths, G. 212
Guarnizo, L.E. 41
Guy-Sheftall, B. 227

Habtom, S. 117
Hall, L. 145
hampton, r. 113, 120
Hansen, R. 210
Harney, S. 110, 118
Hart, M. 63
Hawkins, F. 36
hegemony 27, 132, 177, 194, 217, 234
Heiser, Victor 189
Henry, F. 15, 206, 208, 209, 214
Hoile, C. 157, 158
Holmes, L. 197
hooks, b. 113, 115, 116, 161, 164, 166, 224, 227, 228
Hsieh, I.H., 147, 181, 182
Hurtado, A. 197
hybridity 24, 26, 31, 51
hyphenated identity 28. *See also* identity formation

identity development 23, 112
identity formation
   fluidity in 23, 113
   hyphenated 28, 112, 113, 234. *See also* Othering
Ifugao 195
Igorot 194, 195, 196. *See also* Aeta; Isneg
Illeto, R. 189, 190
Immigration Points System 1967 36, 37
Immigration Policy (1962) 36, 84, 86, 88, 90
indigenous
   activism 54, 55. *See also* activism
   feminism 53, 54, 55
   feminism and liberation 56
   gender relations 53
   healers 190, 191, 192, 196, 197, 198, 199, 200, 201, 202. *See also* Aeta

healing method   195
knowledge   222, 223
lands and people   127, 130, 131, 132
people of Canada   127, 210
people of Philippines   195, 196, 197, 198
praxis   79. *See also* praxis
reimagination of   213
Indonesia
  Chinese ghettoization in   133
  ethnic groups of   132, 136
  Foreign Orientals of   132
  New Order Regime in   133
  pre-colonial kingdoms of   131
  Pribumi of   132
  Reformation era in   134, 135
Infante, T.   195
Ingketria, E.   132, 133, 135
inhabiting   13 *see also* outhabiting; space creation
Innaurato, A.   161, 165
institutional ethnography   40, 85
interdependent migration systems   39
internalized oppression   24
international
  mentor teachers   103
  practicums (IP)   102, 103, 104, 105
  students in universities   99
internationalization
  definition of   99
  framework of   100
  of teacher education 100, 101
interrogation of oppression   10. *See also* critical reflexivity
intersectionality   70, 119, 155, 160, 164
Isneg   193, 196
Ives, L.   176

Jackson, A.   239, 243
Jamal, A.   65, 66, 67, 68
James, I. M.   146, 224, 229
Japanese-Canadian Internment   129, 212, 213, 215
Japanese-Canadian Redress   129
Jedwab, J.   127, 128
Jeon, M.   176, 180
Jocano, F.L.   190
Johnson, H.M.   215
Joko Widodo (Jokowi)   132, 135, 136
Jones, L.V.   227

K-Pop   145
Kang, P.   116
Kaptainis, A.   160
*Katatagan*   253
Keay, J.   55
Kelley, R.D.G.   217
Kelly, N.   36, 87
Kelly, P.F.   91
Kelly, T.   36, 87, 210
Khan, S.A.   73
King, C.   99
King, N.   196
Knight, J.   99
Kobayashi, A.   216
Komagata Maru   141
Kosnik, C.   103
Kritz, M.M.   35, 42
Kumail Nanjiani (character and writer of *The Big Sick*)   172, 173, 174, 175
*Kuyas*   114

labor market
  gender based roles in   63
  racialized policies of   91, 239. *See also* Filipino nurses:
labor migration
  and nurses   37, 38
  macro-, meso- and micro-level relation in   40, 41, 42
  push factors of   64, 65
  social capital and   42
Ladson-Billings, G.   225, 226, 227, 229, 231
Lam, A. *author of Chapter 12*
Landolt, P.   35
Langford, J.   162
Laquian, E.R.   36, 39, 87
Larsen, M.A.   100, 101, 102, 104, 106
Larsson, P.   130
Lash, S.   35, 36, 38
Lawrence, B.   228, 233
Lembong, E.   133, 134, 135
Lerner, G.   148
Leung, G.   147, 181, 182
Leung, K. *author of Chapter 2 and 8*
Levinas, E.   241
Li, G.   144
Li, P.   209, 210
Li, P.S.   86

Lightstone, A.J. 149, 150, 151
Lim, L.L. 35, 42
Lin, K. 147, 181, 182
Lin, T. 176, 177, 178, 179, 180
Lincoln, Y.S. 226
Lindio-McGovern, L. 73
Lindsey, T. 132, 133, 134, 135
Liodakis N. 9, 12
Liu, H. 161, 162, 164, 165, 224
Locke, R. 155, 156, 160, 162
Lorde, A. 81, 110, 115
Love, B. 205
Lowe, L. 27
Lund, D.E. 208

Mabogunje, A.L. 35
Mahtani, M. 28
Majhanovich, S. 177
Marks, L. 198
Marsh, J. 160
Maynes N. 102
Mayuzumi, K. 243
Mazur, B. 156, 157
McCauley, C. 104, 105
McDermott, M. 232
McKittrick, K. 225
McMahon, B. 229, 234
McPherson, K. 85, 86
McTaggart, N. 144, 146, 148, 150
Medicare (1960) 86. *See also* Canada national healthcare system
Melamed, J. 210, 211
Memmi, A. 17, 191
Miki, R. 25, 234
Mills, C.W. 116, 117
mimicry 51, 113. *See also* Bhabha, H; hybridity
model minority 128, 129, 143, 144, 147, 148. *See also* visible minority
Mohanram, R. 73, 74, 76, 77
Moio, J.A. 213
Moss, B. 119
Moten, F. 110, 118
Mouawad, W. 158, 159, 160, 167
mourning 245
Mozart, W.A. 155, 156, 157, 158, 162
Muffuletto, S.L. 171, 172
multiraciality 27. *See also* hybridity

Munoz, J.E. 11, 12
multiculturalism
  and liberalism 126
  and minorities 210, 211
  definition of 125, 126
  policy of 206, 207
music therapy
  and psychotherapy 143
  associations 143

Nadal, K.L. 24
Nakamura, Mark 93
Narayan, J. 226
National Economic Council 88, 89
negative racialization 25. *See also* racialization
neoliberalism 29, 64, 113, 224, 231
Neville, H.A 145
Nguyen, J. 145, 146, 147; author of Chapter 11
Nielson, E. 145, 146
Noguera, P. 216, 217
Nunan, D. 177
Nunez-Janes, M. 155
Nyaga 15, 17, 73, 215, 244; *co-author of Chapter 1 and 6*

O'Brien, E. 144, 146, 148, 150
Occident 27, 48. *See also* Orientalism
Oikawa, M. 129, 213, 215
Okazaki, S. 24
Okihiro, G. 144
Omi, M. 225, 227, 229
Ong, A. 231, 243
oppression
  internalized 24
  of people of color 63
oral history interviews 85
Orient
  opera and 155, 156, 167
  portrayal of the 163, 164
Orientalism 48, 49, 50, 155, 157, 160, 161, 165, 166
Other 23, 52, 89, 113, 115, 117, 158, 174, 197, 198, 207, 210, 212, 230, 233, 241, 254
Othering 116, 212, 225, 226, 234
outhabiting 12, 13. *See also* inhabiting; space creation

Palfrey, J.G.   225
Paloni, L.   35
*Pancasila*   131, 132
Panesar   A. 173, 174
Panitia Sembilan   132
Papastergiadis, N.   26
Parai, L.   36
Pateman, C.   116
Patterson, C.B.   173, 174
Pausacker, H.   134, 135
Peake, L.   216
Peminism   81, 82
peminist   81, 82. *See also* praxis: Peminist
perpetual foreigner   143, 144, 145, 148
Pham, J.   *author of Chapter 14*
Philippines
   cholera outbreak in   189
   government and healers in   190
   Heiser and cholera treatment in   189
Picot, G.   210
Pinar, W.   21, 22, 23, 27
placenessness   73
Policy
   Assimilation   194
   Canada Immigration   2, 35, 36, 39, 40, 69, 84, 86, 88, 90
   Filipino First   89
   for Student Success   101
   Multicultural.   *See* Act: Multiculturalism
Pollock, D.C.   27
Pon, G.   15, 86, 91, 129, 231
Portelli, J.   225, 229, 232, 234
Portes, A.   34, 35, 42
postcolonial identity   51. *See also* hybridity; multiraciality
postcolonial theory   52. *See also* Bhabha, H.; Spivak, G.C; Said, E
Power, T.P   135
Pratt, G.   215
praxis
   decolonial   17, 26, 228
   disidentification as theory and   12
   dramaturgical   116
   Indigenous   79
   Peminist   79
   reflexive   233
   spiritual vulnerability as   17
   transformative   231

Pribumi   132, 133, 134
Program
   English Exchange   176
   Exchange Visitor   85, 92
   Express Entry   68
   Federal Hospital Grant   85
   Federal Skilled Workers   68
   Hospital Insurance   86
   Live-in Caregiver   87
public health
   and collaboration with healers   201
   and colonies   196
   and WHO   198, 201
Puccini, G.   154, 155, 160, 161, 162
Purdey, J.   133, 134

racial capitalism   117, 226
racialization
   negative   25
   of differences   68
   of minorities   213
   systemic   69
Rahim, A.   61, 66, 67
Rajesh Koothrappali (Character from The Big Bang Theory)   171, 172
Ralph, N.   34, 155
Ramkissoon, S.   63
Rang-ay (indigenous healer)   191, 192, 202
rap and hip-hop
   among Asians   146
   and anti-racist perspectives 147
   and psychotherapy   149
   origin of   145
   political use of   146, 147
rap theory model   149. *See also* rap and hiphop; empowerment theory
Razack, S.H.   74, 75, 78, 213, 225
reflexive practices   76, 80, 232
reflexivity in teacher education   104
Reitz, J.G.   87
representation
   of Asian Canadians   12
   of indigenous healing   196, 199, 200
   of indigenous people in Philippines   190
   of South Asians in movies   170, 171, 172
   of South Asians in video games   173, 174
   of the Orien   164, 165, 166
resilience   252, 253, 254, 256

resistance
  for justice  233
  in schools  224, 225
  of immigrants  214, 215, 216
  of indigenous healers  191
  through music  145, 146, 147
  to social justice education  229, 230, 231
Reyes, G.T.  31, 144
Rhodes  56
Ricklefs, M.C.  132
Rivers, D.J.  178, 181, 184
Rob Buscher  154, 167
Rodrigues, G.  116
Rojas, C.  225
Rolvsjord, R.  142, 149, 150
Ronquillo, C.  36, 84, 86
Root, M.P.P.  23
Rose  9, 17, 48, 72, 76, 77, 189, 239, 250
Roseberry, W.  216
Ross, A.S.  178, 181, 184
Ross, M.  239, 240
Roy, M.  25
Royal Commission on Bilingualism and Biculturalism  128
Ruecker, T.  176, 178, 180, 182
Ryan, L.  35

Said, E.  22, 25, 27, 48, 49, 50, 52, 155, 160, 166, 174, 212
SARA ban  133, 134. See also Indonesia: New Order Regime
Satzewich, V.  12, 15, 36
Schwartz, J.M.  40
Scribe, M.  117
Searle, M.J.  101, 102, 104, 106
self/Other binary.  See Other
Sensoy, O.  205
settler colonialism  29. See also colonialism
Shahjahan, R.  16, 49, 52
Sheftall, B.  227
Shimizu, H.  190
Shiva, V.  242
Shohat, E.  53
silencing  221, 225, 226, 230, 231
Simmons, M.  17
Slagle, M.  173
Smith, D.E.  40, 41, 78, 85

Smith, E.  53
Smith, K.  103
Smith, L.  53
Smith, L.T.  233
Smith, M.P.  41
social capital  35, 35, 40, 69, 177. See also cultural capital
social inclusion  159, 160, 162
Soebagjo, N.  132, 134
Soeharto  133, 134
Soepriatna, V. *author of Chapter 10*
Solorzano, D.G.  217
South Asian Women
  in diaspora  68
  labor power of  69
  patriarchy and  67, 69
  race and gender discrimination of  67, 68, 69
  stereotyping of  67, 69
South Asians
  Canadian culture and  67
  definition of  170
  diaspora  66, 67
  immigration policy on  65, 66
  job market participation of  69
  migration of women and  66
  population of  62
  post-immigrant experience of  64
  push factors of migration and  64, 65
  representation of  See under representation
  under representation of  173
space creation
  and in/outhabiting  12
  colonial pedagogy of  10
  funk as process of  11
  mourning and  11
space of negation  115, 116
spirituality  see also critical reflexivity: spirituality
  and existence  228
  as form of agency and resistance  16, 17
  Asian  10, 16
  imperial and colonial  10
  in teaching and learning  17
  in theorizing Asian Canadians  17, 18
  indigenous  15, 198
Spivak, G.C.  48, 51, 52, 74, 174

Stanton, C.R.   103
Stasiulis, D.   87, 91
Steenbrink, K.   131, 132
strategic essentialism   52
Strauss, A.L.   34
Subaltern   52
Sumi, G.   159
Sunera, T.   233
Suryadinata, L.   132, 133, 134
sustainability   117
Swartz, E.   223, 230, 235
systemic racialization   69. *See also* discrimination; racialization
systemic racism   68, 129, 130, 209, 212, 214, 216, 224

Tabi, E.   146
Tai, C.   146
Tajino, A.   179
Tajino, Y.   179
Takagi, A.   89, 99
Talna (Indigenous healer)   192, 193, 200
Tan, M.   198
Tator, C.   15, 206, 208, 209, 214
Tauli-Corpuz, V.   194
Taylor, D.   30
Thapa, T.R. *author of Chapter 16*
Third Culture Kid (TCK)   27, 28
Third Space   26, 27, 31, 51
Thobani, S.   91, 230
Thomas   M. P. 239, 243
Thompson, J.   40, 85
Tiessen, R.   104, 109
Tiffins, H.   212
Toman, C.   86
Torres, R. A.   15, 53, 54, 73, 76, 191, 215, 240, 242, 244;
*author of Chapter 4, 15 and 18; co-author of Chapter 1, 6 and 19*
Toscanini, A.   154
transculturation   30
transnational labour migration.   *See* labour migration
transnationalism   41, 61, 62, 68
Travis, R.   150
Trebilcock, M.J.   36
Truong, T.D.   63
Tuck, E.   29, 221, 223, 228, 230, 200

Tunggal   131, 132
Turandot   154, 155, 160, 161, 162, 164, 165
transnational migration   34
  *a posteriori* theorization and   35, 36
  *a priori* theorization and   35, 36

Ulvik ,M.   103, 109
Undang-Undang Dasar, 1945   131
Unnithan, N.   145, 146

Van Reken, R.E.   27
Vanderplaat, M.   63
Villalpando, O.   230, 233
violence
  against women and minorities 16, 75, 145, 247
  and morality   76
  as reparative practices   11
  cultural   191
  epistemic   52
  negotiation of   12, 14, 73
  police   209
  sexual   77
  state-sanctioned   14, 75, 77, 78, 80, 117, 130, 134, 136, 213
visible minority   126, 127, 128, 129, 130. *See also* model minority
vulnerability   13, 17, 64, 68, 75, 247

Wah, F.   21, 25, 28, 234
Wajdi Mouawad   158, 167
Walker, G.   28
Walker, J.W.S.G.   214
Wane, N.   10, 13, 15, 16
Wang, L.   144, 176, 177, 178, 179
Warren, A.   145
Wartha, I.B.   132
Washington, A.R.   149, 151
Wehbi, S.   81, 246
Weinman, J.   158
Western feminism   *See also* Indigenous feminism; South Asian Feminism
Western gaze   191, 225, 231
White supremacy   30, 65, 144, 224, 227, 228, 230, 239
Wickramasekara, P.   64, 65
Wila (indigenous healer)   198
Williams, D.   173, 174

Williams, P.   26, 49, 50, 51, 52
Willis, K.   63
Winant, H.   225, 227, 229
Wood, C.H.   34
Worcester, Dean   189
World systems theory.   *see* transnational migration
Wu, M.H.   147, 181, 182

Xiong, Z.B.   145

Yang, J.H.   147, 181, 182
Yang, K. W.   29, 223, 228, 230
Yellowface   165, 166
Yemini, M.   99
Yeoh, B.   63
Yetka Kara   157, 158
Young, R.   52

Zimmerman, M.A.   142
Zlotnik, H.   35, 42

www.ingramcontent.com/pod-product-compliance
Lightning Source LLC
Chambersburg PA
CBHW070914030426
42336CB00014BA/2410